THE COGNITIVE BASES
OF INTERPERSONAL
COMMUNICATION

LEA's COMMUNICATION SERIES
Jennings Bryant/Dolf Zillmann, General Editors

Selected titles in Interpersonal/Intercultural Communication (W. Barnett Pearce, Advisory Editor) include:

Cupach/Spitzberg • The Dark Side of Interpersonal Communication

Daly/Wiemann • Strategic Interpersonal Communication

Frey • Group Communication in Context: Studies of Natural Groups

Kalbfleisch • Interpersonal Communication: Evolving Interpersonal Relationships

Leeds-Hurwitz • Semiotics and Communication: Signs, Codes, Cultures

For a complete list of other titles in LEA's Communication Series, please contact Lawrence Erlbaum Associates, Publishers.

THE COGNITIVE BASES OF INTERPERSONAL COMMUNICATION

Edited by
DEAN E. HEWES
University of Minnesota

LAWRENCE ERLBAUM ASSOCIATES, PUBLISHERS
1995   Hillsdale, New Jersey   Hove, UK

Lawrence Erlbaum Associates, Inc., Publishers
365 Broadway
Hillsdale, New Jersey 07642

Library of Congress Cataloging-in-Publication Data
The cognitive bases of interpersonal communication / edited by Dean E.
  Hewes.
      p. cm.
    Includes bibliographical references (p.) and index.
    ISBN 0-8058-0469-2 (alk. paper)
    1. Social perception.   2. Interpersonal communication.   I. Hewes,
  Dean E.
  HM132.C545 1995
  302'.12—dc20   94-37841
                                                               CIP

Printed in the United States of America
10 9 8 7 6 5 4 3 2 1

This volume is dedicated to my colleagues and, especially,
to my students at the University of Wisconsin, Madison,
and the University of Illinois, Urbana-Champaign,
who shaped my interests in the cognitive approach
to interpersonal communication.
You know who you are.
Thank you.

Contents

Introduction

Dean E. Hewes
University of Minnesota

How we see our world determines, in part, what we will think, how we will feel, and how we will act. How we see our world is not necessarily a straightforward reflection of how the world "is." Our mental descriptions of previous experiences and current events, and the very mental processes by which those descriptions are formed and retained, influence our perceptions and interpretations. We may see ourselves as "healthy," or "intelligent," or "independent" and, by that, become so. On the other hand, who and what we are is, in part, a function of how others see the world and what the world really is. To be completely without illusions would be as tragic and unnatural as to be completely governed by them.

Our interpretations of the world in which we live, and the people and institutions that comprise it, are acquired through complex interactions among what we believe to be true, what the world is, and/or what others think it is. Understanding those complex interactions is one of the most important goals of the social sciences. Of the many disciplines that have contributed to that understanding, two take center stage in this volume, one well known (psychology), and one less so (communication).

The impact of cognitive psychology and artificial intelligence (the cognitive sciences)[1] on the social sciences is no secret. To say that it has been monumental is no exaggeration. But that impact has not been uniform across disciplines. In some cases, it has been to transform the foci of specific disciplines. In other

---

[1] I do not mean to suggest that the program of the late 1970s and early 1980s to create a field called "cognitive science" was successful. In fact, artificial intelligence and cognitive psychology have never been satisfied lovers, although the infatuation is as sporadic as it is natural.

1

cases, like seeds scattered across partially isolated environments, the original DNA has mutated.

As an example of the former, the impact of the cognitive psychology on social psychology has been to "psychologize" it, which is, to place more emphasis on the representation and processing of stimuli concerning social action and less on the social action per se (Fiske & Taylor, 1991; Wyer & Gruenfeld, (chapter 1, this volume)).[2] This impact has been salutary for the most part since the understanding of social interaction generally must be anchored in a detailed understanding of the mind.[3] Nevertheless, the interrelationship between cognitive processes and social behavior remains understudied.

About the time that social psychologists Robert Nisbett and Lee Ross' published their seminal work (1980) connecting cognitive and social psychology, researchers in the field of communication began exploring cognitive connections to what they called "interpersonal communication" (cf. Planalp & Hewes, 1982; Roloff & Berger, 1982). In essence, the study of interpersonal communication centers on the antecedents and consequences of: (a) communicative behavior, (b) patterns of behavior, (c) communicative strategies, (d) patterns of strategies, and (e) interpretation of both behavior and strategy.

With social interaction at its center, interpersonal communication researchers have reacted both similarly and differently than their social psychological counterparts to the cognitive revolution. Some communication researchers reacted similarly by concentrating on cognitive representations and processes, with special emphasis on cognitive efficiency and capacity limitations. Others have reacted quite differently than their counterparts because communication researchers share a historic commitment to studying concrete, contextualized social phenomena such as (a) personal relationships, (b) message strategies, and (c) social behavior. In addition, the discipline of interpersonal communication has been affected by artificial intelligence (AI) to a greater extent than has social psychology. AI's interest in natural language processing has led directly to communication research on metaphors, scripts, plans, interpretation, and the like.

The purpose of this volume is to reconnect the partially isolated environments of social psychology and communication. Because I am a member of the latter discipline, I chose to build the bridge from my side. To that end, this volume contains four building blocks: (a) the cognitive foundations of interpersonal communication as it might be studied from a social psychological perspective (section 1, chapter 1 by Wyer & Gruenfeld), (b) insiders' views of interpersonal communication from a cognitive psychological standpoint (section 2, chapters 2–4 by Greene, Smith, and Hewes respectively), (c) insiders' approaches to

---

[2]Happily, this trend is moderating according to Fiske and Taylor (1991) as indicated by the growing prominence of the *motivated tactician* metaphor in preference to the *cognitive miser* metaphor.

[3]This is because it must be anchored equally in an understanding of society.

interpersonal communication from an AI perspective (section 3, chapters 5 and 6 by Berger and Kellermann respectively), and (d) reflecting the strong philosophical grounding of communication, a critique of the cognitive enterprise (section 4, chapter 7 by McPhee).

Each of these chapters represents a current description of "serial processing" cognitive theories and research[4] that have made a real contribution to the cognitive approach to interpersonal communication. Each of these chapters is long by conventional standards. I have tried to ensure that each chapter is long enough to guarantee (a) attention to the fundamental assumptions of each theory, (b) a description of each theory including its empirical status, and (c) its implications for everyday life.

In chapter 1, Wyer and Gruenfeld recognize that most cognitively oriented social psychological research has been performed in situations largely divorced from everyday life. This reflects the "psychologizing" of social psychology. Yet, they claim that this research does have implications for the more contextualized problem of concern to interpersonal communication. They discuss a general model of cognitive processing applicable to both social and nonsocial stimuli, pioneered by Wyer, and trace its implications for interpersonal communication. In this regard, their work, though different in content, is in the same genre as that of Planalp and Hewes (1982; Hewes & Planalp, 1982) and Greene (1984a; 1984b; chapter 2, this volume).

Chapter 2 by Greene introduces a philosophical orientation to the study of communication, generative realism, and a specific theory of interpersonal communication, action assembly theory, which has a powerful influence on cognitive thinking in my field. Greene's theoretical work bears the strong stamp of a general cognitive theory, although it clearly has important implications for understanding the production of interpersonal messages.

Smith's contribution (chapter 3) focuses on a narrower range of cognitive processes than do the first two chapters, emphasizing attributional processes, and connects them to the interpretation of nonverbal communication. In a similar vein, I (chapter 4) concentrate on one aspect of cognition; the processing of messages with multiple interpretations. Both these chapters balance off the breadth of the first two chapters nicely with depth substituted for breadth.

The next two chapters display the creative applications of thinking in AI to the study interpersonal communication and suggest that more be done. Chapter 5 by Berger highlights the implications of the "planning" to the study of interpersonal messages. This chapter is an excellent summary and extension of his burgeoning research program in this area. Kellermann's chapter 6 on memory organization

---

[4]Parallel distributed processing models of the type championed by Rummelhart and McClelland (1986) have as yet had little impact on the study of interpersonal communication. I expect that they will shortly. My own efforts are bent in that direction.

packets (MOPs) applies them to the mental representation of everyday conversations.

In the concluding chapter, McPhee offers up a spicy stew of criticism of the cognitive revolution extracted from interpretative and critical theoreticians and philosophers. McPhee's chapter reminds us that, as successful as the cognitive sciences have been to date, those successes have bought at the expense of some fidelity to the phenomena to which they have been applied. We must keep in mind McPhee's criticisms as we evaluate the future of cognitive research.

Overall, these chapters typify some of the most interesting cognitive work done in the study of interpersonal communication. My hope is that they promote productive dialogue across disciplinary boundaries and that they stimulate further work within the field of interpersonal communication research.

REFERENCES

Fiske, S. T., & Taylor, S. E. (1991). *Social cognition*. New York: McGraw-Hill.

Greene, J. O. (1984a). Evaluating cognitive explanations of communicative phenomena. *Quarterly Journal of Speech, 70,* 241–254.

Greene, J. O. (1984b). A cognitive approach to human communication: An action assembly theory. *Communication Monographs, 51,* 289–306.

Hewes, D. E., & Planalp, S. (1982). There is nothing as useful as a good theory. . . . The influence of social knowledge on interpersonal communication. In M. E. Roloff & C. R. Berger (Eds.), *Social cognition and communication* (pp. 107–150). Newbury Park, CA: Sage.

Nisbett, R. E., & Ross, L. (1980). *Human inference: Strategies and shortcomings of social judgment*. Englewood Cliffs, NJ: Prentice-Hall.

Planalp, S., & Hewes, D. E. (1982). A cognitive approach to communication theory: *Cogito ergo dico?* In M. Burgoon (Ed.), *Communication yearbook 5* (pp. 49–77). New Brunswick, NJ: Transaction Press.

Roloff, M. E., & Berger, C. R. (Eds.) (1982). *Social cognition and communication*. Newbury Park, CA: Sage.

Rummelhart, D., & McClelland, J. (Eds.). (1986). *Parallel distributed processing: Explorations in the microstructure of cognition* (vol. 1). Cambridge, MA: MIT Press.

Shank, R. C. (1982). *Dynamic memory: A theory of reminding and learning in computers and people*. Cambridge, England: Cambridge University Press.

INTERPERSONAL COMMUNICATION: COGNITIVE SOCIAL PSYCHOLOGISTS' PERSPECTIVE

1 Information Processing in Interpersonal Communication

Robert S. Wyer, Jr.
Deborah H Gruenfeld
University of Illinois at Urbana-Champaign

Interpersonal communication is fundamentally a process of information transmission (Berger, 1987: Berger & Bredac, 1982). One participant in a social interaction receives a verbal or nonverbal communication from another, interprets its meaning, construes its implications, and then decides how, if at all, to respond to it. Both the original message and the recipient's response are usually guided by certain goals or objectives: (a) to be informative, (b) to persuade the recipient to adopt one's point of view, (c) to create a good impression, or (d) simply to understand the issues being discussed. A complete conceptualization of interpersonal communication obviously requires: (a) an understanding of the processes of information acquisition, (b) the interpretation of information in terms of concepts and knowledge that are retrieved from memory and brought to bear on it, (c) a construal of the implications of this information, and (d) the generation of an overt response that will attain one's immediate or long-range objectives.

It might seem reasonable to suppose that sociopsychological theory and research would help us to gain this understanding. Group performance, decision making, and conflict resolution, which obviously involve interpersonal communication, have been investigated extensively (Blumberg, Hare, Kent, & Davies, 1983; McGrath, 1984). Moreover, information processing has been the focus of substantial research and theory in social cognition for over a decade (cf. Higgins, Herman, & Zanna, 1981; Sorrentino & Higgins, 1986; Wyer & Srull, 1984, 1989). Unfortunately, the implications of this work for an understanding of information processing in interpersonal situations are more limited than one might expect. In fact, little if any research on group dynamics has attempted to understand the cognitive processes that underlie the communications that mediate individual behavior in group settings (cf. Altman, 1989; for notable exceptions, see Gouran, 1986; Hastie, Penrod, & Pennington, 1983; Hewes, 1986). Social-cognition research is more directly concerned with information processing. With few exceptions, however (cf. Snyder, Tanke, & Berscheid, 1977), it has typically been performed under conditions in which the information is presented out of its social context. Consequently, several factors that are fundamental to the exchange of information in social interactions have not been taken into account.

Research and theory on social-information processing is not without value, however. The general questions on which this research is focused are clearly relevant to an understanding of information processing in social-interaction situations, despite the failure to investigate these situations directly. An analysis of interpersonal communication in terms of fundamental components of information processing helps to identify phenomena for which our present knowledge of social cognition is likely to have implications. It also pinpoints areas in which additional research and conceptualizing are imperative. The objective of this chapter is to provide such an analysis.

For purposes of our discussion, a *communication* is broadly defined as any information that is directly or indirectly transmitted by one person to another. This definition (for alternatives, see Dance & Larson, 1976) ignores several important differences between communications, including: (a) whether the information transmitted is verbal or nonverbal, (b) whether it consists of a single word or sentence or is an entire monologue, (c) whether the message is generated in the presence or absence of the receiver, and (d) whether the transmission of the information to the receiver is intentional. Thus, according to this definition, a husband's coming home at 2 a.m. after promising to be home at 10 p.m. constitutes a communication, as well as does a statement he makes to his wife at dinner. We focus our discussion in this chapter on communications that are transmitted in the course of a conversation or other direct interaction between the persons involved. However, much of this discussion is equally applicable to communication as more broadly conceived.

The recipient of a communication from another may perform several cognitive steps in the course of generating a response:

1. *Semantic encoding.* Components of the message are interpreted in terms of semantic concepts that have been acquired and stored as part of general semantic knowledge. Thus, giving someone an answer during an exam may be encoded into memory as "helping someone out" or as "kind." As this examples implies, a given piece of information can often be interpreted in terms of several quite different concepts, the implications of which may correspondingly differ.

2. *Organization.* A configuration of several pieces of information may be organized into a mental representation of the person, object, or event to

which the information is relevant. This is often done with reference to a previously formed representation of either a particular or prototypic object whose features match those described in the information. When some features of the information are novel, or are particularly relevant to one's processing goals, they may be thought about in relation either to one another or to other concepts and knowledge about the person or object to which the information refers. Such cognitive activity establishes associations among the features of the representation. Furthermore, it can lead to the addition of features that were not mentioned in the information. For example, the representation that is formed from a conversation is likely to include not only encodings of the specific statements that were made, but also thoughts or reactions that one had while listening to the conversation or trying to understand it.

3. *Storage.* The cognitive representations that result from processing at the first two stages described are theoretically stored in long-term memory at a location that refers to the person or object being represented.

4. *Retrieval and inference.* When the recipient later requires knowledge about a person, object, or event to which the information is relevant, he or she may retrieve the representation that has been formed on the basis of the information (perhaps along with other previously acquired knowledge about its referent) and may compute its implications for the response.

5. *Response generation.* Suppose one is called on to respond to the information one has received or to the object to which the information refers. Once the goal of such a response has been determined, one must decide on the verbal or nonverbal "language" to use in communicating the thoughts or feelings that one wishes to convey. Such decisions are often guided by both the nature of the information to be communicated and the expectations for how the other will react to alternative means of conveying it.

These five phases of processing are involved in almost all situations in which information is exchanged. That is, they occur in an experiment when subjects receive information about a person and report their liking for the person along a numbered response scale. They are also likely to underlie a husband's response to his wife's statement that she wants to take the children to visit her mother, or a person's decision to hire someone on the basis of a colleague's recommendation. However, at least two additional considerations arise in conceptualizing the nature of these processes in conversations.

First, a person often communicates at two levels of meaning (Watzlawick, Beavin, & Jackson, 1967). At a descriptive or *content* level, one's statements to another may convey information about the person or object to which they refer. At a second, *relationship* level, the statements may convey information about one's feelings toward the recipient, toward oneself, or toward one's relationship with the other. Thus, a man who tells a woman that he can repair her automobile may, on the one hand, be imparting descriptive information about his ability. On the other hand, at the relationship level, he may be conveying that he is superior to her in skills and abilities or, alternatively, that he likes her and wants to be helpful. More generally, the statements that a communicator makes about someone else, or about the topic under discussion, constitute communicative acts that often convey information about the speaker as well. This consideration does not usually arise in the conditions that have typically been investigated in social-cognition research.

Second, the way information is processed at virtually every stage depends, to a large extent, on the objective of the processor (cf. Srull & Wyer, 1986). Although this contingency is widely recognized, our research has nevertheless been restricted to only a few task-objective conditions. In the most common situation we have investigated, subjects receive verbal information about a person for the purpose of forming an impression of this person. Although impression formation is certainly an objective of many persons who engage in interpersonal communication, it is not the only one. A person in the course of a conversation may describe a story he or she has read, may express an opinion about a social issue, or may propose a good place to go to dinner. The recipients of such information may sometimes simply try to understand it. At other times, however, they may be motivated to elaborate it or refute its implications. Other communication objectives can also play a role. For example, parties to a conversation sometimes wish to communicate their personal feelings toward one another, or to convey their competence or expertise in the area being discussed. They may also wish to be polite, informative, or to respond in a manner that others consider socially desirable. The pursuit of these various goals can affect both the communications that one generates in the conversation and the interpretation of the communications that one receives from others.

Because the effects of these factors have rarely been explored empirically, we are often unable to provide definite statements about the type of information processing that occurs in the course of information conversations or in social-interaction situations more generally. Nevertheless, a conceptualization of interpersonal communication, in terms of the mechanisms that potentially operate at each stage of processing, helps to identify several issues that need to be explored research on communication processes. This becomes clear in the pages to follow.

THE INTERPRETATION OF SOCIAL COMMUNICATIONS

The comprehension of information that is conveyed in a social context is likely to occur in two stages. First, the literal meaning of the information is understood in terms of semantic concepts that are descriptively applicable and easily accessible in memory. These processes often occur automatically and independently of the social context in which the information is presented (Bargh, 1984, 1994; Wyer & Srull, 1989). However, once this is done, the communication may often be evaluated with reference to prior knowledge about the persons and events to which the information refers and features of the social context in which it is transmitted. In combination, these factors may lead the recipient to question why the information was communicated. These pragmatic considerations may lead the recipient to make inferences about the intended meaning of the message that are not reflected by its semantic implications. Each of these stages of comprehension is worth discussing in some detail.

Semantic Encoding Processes

General Principles

To understand information, people must initially interpret it in terms of previously acquired concepts that the features of this information exemplify. The applicability of a concept is determined by the number of features it has in common with those of the information to be interpreted. More than one concept is often applicable for interpreting the same subset of information. In such instances, the concept that comes to mind most quickly and easily is typically used, and other, less easily accessible concepts are ignored. The importance of this phenomenon arises from the fact that, once information is encoded into memory in terms of one set of concepts, these concepts, which may not capture all of the implications of the original information, are later used as the basis for judgments and decisions about the persons or objects to which the information refers. Moreover, the impact of these encodings increases over time in relation to that of the original information. The research and theory bearing on these phenomena are extensive (for reviews, see Bargh, 1984; Higgins & King, 1981; Wyer & Srull, 1989), and are not elaborated on here. Rather, we simply summarize briefly several empirically supported conclusions that have been drawn and that have implications for interpersonal communication:

1. The use of a concept to interpret a piece of information is a function of both the frequency and the recency with which the concept has been used in the past (Higgins, Bargh, & Lombardi, 1985; Srull & Wyer, 1979).
2. The accessibility of a concept in memory is unlikely to affect the interpretation of information unless its descriptive features can be instantiated in terms of the information (Higgins, Rholes, & Jones, 1977). For example, activating the trait concept "kind" may lead one's giving a person an answer to an examination to be interpreted as "kind" (a favorable attribute) rather than "dishonest" (an unfavorable one) because descriptive features of the behavior are contained in the definition of this concept. However,

activating the concept "adventurous" (which may be equally favorable) will not affect the interpretation of the behavior because the behavior has no features in common with the concept.

3. Once a piece of information has been interpreted in terms of a general concept, this concept may be used later as a basis for inferring attributes and behaviors that are implied by the concept but not by the original information. Thus, once "kind" has been used to interpret "giving an answer on an exam," and, consequently, the actor is inferred to have the attribute, this attribute may be used as a basis for inferring other traits of the actor that are believed to be typical of kind persons, but are not at all implied by the original behavior and may sometimes even be inconsistent with it (cf. Carlston, 1980; Srull & Wyer, 1979, 1980).[1]

4. Once information has been encoded into memory in terms of one set of concepts, it is rarely retrieved and reinterpreted in terms of other concepts that are accessible later (Massad, Hubbard, & Newtson, 1979; Srull & Wyer, 1980). Consequently, concepts that are activated at the time the information is first received have a major impact on its interpretation and, therefore, on judgments and decisions that are based on it. In contrast, concepts that are activated subsequently, at the time the judgments and decisions are actually made, do not have much influence.

It is easy to imagine the potential implications of these principles for the impact of information conveyed in informal conversations. Suppose a man has had a heated argument with his wife before arriving at work. The concepts that were activated in the course of this conversation may later lead him to encode a student's comment to him as hostile. Consequently, when he is later asked by a colleague whether he would recommend the student for a teaching position, the man may retrieve and use this encoding of the student's behavior as a basis for his judgment, without considering alternative interpretations. This may be true even though concepts and knowledge that suggest alternative interpretations of the student's past behavior are accessible to the man at the time he reports his recommendation. Note also that the effect of this initial encoding on judgments of the student is likely to increase with the time interval between the man's encounter with the student and the judgment he reports.

---

[1]These effects are worth noting in the context of the first principle noted previously. That is, the activating "adventurous" at the time one learns that a person "gave someone an answer during an examination" will not affect the inference that the person who performed this act is "kind" because the primed concept is descriptively inapplicable for encoding the behavior. On the other hand, activating "kind" may affect inferences that the actor is "adventurous" as a result of (a) the interpretation of the behavior as "kind," and (b) the inference that persons with this attribute are likely to have other favorable attributes.

Determinants of Concept Accessibility

The factors that potentially influence the accessibility of a concept in memory are manifold. A few general factors of particular relevance to the issues of concern in this chapter are worth noting briefly.

1. Expectations.   The concepts that are most accessible in memory at the time information is received may be activated by one's expectations concerning either the implications of this information or characteristics of its course. Therefore, people who expect a person to have a certain attribute are likely to interpret statements about this person in terms of concepts that pertain to the attribute. For similar reasons, people who expect the communicator to believe that someone has a particular attribute may interpret the communicator's comments about the person in terms of concepts that are activated by this expectation. Therefore, for both reasons, people often encode the information into memory in ways that confirm their expectations for its implications.

2. Communication Objectives.   Concepts that are relevant to the purpose for which one intends to use information at the time it is received may influence the interpretation of this information. A particularly interesting situation of this sort arises in interpersonal communication. A person often attempts to communicate information in a way that will not antagonize the recipient. Therefore, if the interpretation of this information is somewhat ambiguous, the communicator is apt to convey it in terms of concepts that will be minimally offensive. If these concepts are then stored in memory, they are likely to be retrieved later and used as a basis for the communicator's own responses to the object to which the information pertains. Thus, the process of communicating information to another can bias the communicator's own judgments and decisions about the person or object he or she has described.

This phenomenon was empirically demonstrated by Higgins and Rholes (1978). Subjects received information about a target person with instructions to write a paragraph about the person to someone who either liked or disliked this person. The information they received contained descriptions of behaviors (e.g., "wants to go skydiving," "was well aware of his ability to do things well," etc.) that could be interpreted in terms of either favorable attributes ("adventurous," "self-confident") or unfavorable ones ("foolhardy," "conceited," etc.). Not surprisingly, subjects tailored the favorableness of their own descriptions of the target to the ostensible attitude of the recipient. More important, their later estimates of how well they personally liked the target, and their memory for the original information, were evaluatively biased in the direction of the descriptions they had generated. These biases were not evident when subjects anticipated writing a communication but did not actually do so. Therefore, these findings support the hypothesis that subjects who generate a communication may later recall and use their cognitive representations of the communication to infer the implications of the original information on which the communication was based without actually consulting their memory for this information.

3. Fortuitous Experiences.   Experiences that have occurred a short time before information is received can activate concepts that are fortuitously applicable for interpreting this information and, therefore, can affect judgments and decisions that are based on it. This may be true even though the experiences that activated these concepts are totally unrelated to the particular person, object, or issue to which the information refers (cf. Higgins & King, 1981; Wyer & Srull, 1986, 1989). The activation of the concepts may occur with little, if any, conscious awareness (cf. Bargh & Pietromonaco, 1982).

Although the effects of fortuitously activated concepts on the interpretation of information conveyed in social-interaction situations have not been empirically demonstrated, these effects seem likely to occur. An early study by Berkowitz and Lepage (1967) is suggestive. Subjects were exposed to a learning situation in which they ostensibly evaluated one another's performance by administering shocks. However, in anticipation of this situation, subjects were asked to wait in a room that either contained a gun and ROTC equipment or had no distinguishing features. In the learning situation, one subject (a confederate) first administered shocks to the real subject at a level that indicated that his performance left something to be desired. The real subject then had an opportunity to evaluate the other. Subjects who had waited in the "gun" room administered more shocks to the confederate than did control subjects. One interpretation of this is that concepts activated by the gun led subjects to interpret the confederate's shocks as aggressive and, therefore, stimulated them to respond in kind. (For a more recent indication that activating aggression-related concepts affects behavior in similar situations, see Carver, Ganellen, Froming, & Chambers, 1983).

Analogous situations clearly exist in everyday life. Suppose a wife mentions to her husband that she wishes he would pick up his clothes. If the husband has had a bad day at the office, or has just been watching a Clint Eastwood movie on television, he may have hostility-related concepts easily accessible in memory. Consequently, he may be more inclined to interpret his wife's comment as hostile or aggressive and, therefore, to respond accordingly. Moreover, his encoding of his wife's comment may be stored in memory. Therefore, it may be later retrieved and used as a basis for judgments or behavioral decisions to which it is potentially relevant.

4. Individual Differences.   General individual differences in the chronic accessibility of concepts can affect the likelihood of using these concepts to interpret the information received in a variety of situations. These differences can result, in part, from life goals, values, or interests that predispose people to call on a selective subset of concepts very frequently for use in a number of situational contexts (Bruner, 1957, Klinger, 1975; for reviews, see Srull & Wyer, 1986; Wyer & Srull, 1989). The effects of such general individual differences in concept accessibility are not overridden by situationally induced differences. Rather, individual difference and situational factors may combine additively to affect the likelihood of applying a given concept to the interpretation of information (Bargh, Bond, Lombardi, & Tota, 1986). In conceptualizing the determinants in persons' interpretation of the information they exchange in informal conversations, and their responses to this information, the effects of these more pervasive differences in concept accessibility must therefore be taken into account.

A Qualification

The effects of recently activated semantic concepts on the interpretation of information can often occur without awareness (Bargh, 1984). In some cases, however, people are aware that the concept that comes to mind at the time they receive information might be the result of recent events that have nothing to do with the information. In such a case, they might actively avoid use of the concept and, as a result, might be less likely to apply it than they would had the concept not been recently activated.

Research supports this possibility. For example, when subjects' concepts have been primed by requiring subjects to use them in an ostensibly irrelevant experimental task, they have a less positive influence on the interpretation of later information when subjects can recall the priming stimuli than when they are unable to do so (and, therefore, are presumably unaware that the concepts have come to mind as a result of exposure to these stimuli; Lombardi, Higgins, & Bargh, 1987). In the former case, the priming stimuli often have a contrast effect on the interpretation of information. (Thus, for example, subjects are more likely to interpret one's desire to cross the Atlantic ocean in a sailboat as adventurous when *adventurous* has been primed than when *reckless* has been primed.) These contrast effects only occur, of course, when subjects are both able and motivated to search for an alternative concept to avoid being biased. When this is not the case, priming is likely to have a positive effect even when subjects are aware of its possible influence (Martin, 1986; Martin, Seta, & Crelia, 1990).

The implications of these findings for the interpretation of information in a social context is not completely clear. In many conversations, and in cases when information is transmitted orally (as on television), the information is conveyed very quickly, and subjects do not have the time to search for alternative concepts to use in interpreting the information. Under these conditions, previously activated concepts might be used to interpret the information even when subjects are aware of the possible bias produced by using them. When information is conveyed in writing, and people can process it at their own pace, they might be more inclined to seek alternative concepts and to avoid the biasing influence of recent irrelevant experiences. The possibility that the interpretation of communications is more likely to be influenced by irrelevant experiences when the communications are conveyed orally (e.g., on television) than when they are conveyed in writing (e.g., in a newspaper) remains to be investigated.

Pragmatic Influences on the Interpretation of Information

The Role of Communication Norms

The preceding discussion focused on factors that affect perceptions of a communication's semantic meaning. However, when information is conveyed in a social context, its interpretation may be guided, in part, by recipients' perceptions of why the information is being transmitted as well as its literal meaning. This possibility has long been recognized by psycholinguists (Clark, 1985; Green, 1989; Grice, 1975; Sperber & Wilson, 1986), and is of considerable importance in understanding social communication (Higgins, 1981; Wyer & Carlston, 1994). The question is how the indirect, pragmatic meaning of a message is actually identified by the recipient and when it is taken into account. One answer may lie in the communication axioms identified by Grice (1975) and others (Green, 1989; Higgins, 1981; Sperber & Wilson, 1986). These principles presumably guide both the generation of messages by the communicator and the interpretation of these messages by the recipient. Three principles are of particular importance in the present context.

Informativeness.   Communicators presumably try to convey information to another that the other does not already have. Moreover, the recipient generally assumes that this is the communicator's intent. Consequently, the recipient actively attempts to interpret messages in a way that makes them informative. (For a detailed discussion of these processes, see Clark, 1985.) A common example occurs in the interpretation of assertions that would normally go without saying. Suppose a person hears someone comment that a particular U.S. senator is not a child molester. This would normally go without saying; most public figures are not in the habit of molesting children. Therefore, to make this statement informative, the receiver may infer that there must be some reason to believe that this particular senator *was* a child molester, thus making it necessary to deny this accusation. This inference may plant a seed of doubt as to the senator's morality and, therefore, may change the receiver's belief in a direction opposite to that implied by the assertion's literal meaning.

The influence of the informativeness principle on the interpretation of information conveyed in the public media was demonstrated in a study by Gruenfeld and Wyer (1992). Subjects read a series of statements that they believed were from either a newspaper (a source whose primary objective is presumably to convey new information) or an encyclopedia (a source whose primary goal is to record archival knowledge accurately). In certain conditions, some of the statements asserted the validity of propositions that college students were likely on a priori grounds to consider untrue (e.g., "Lyndon Johnson was responsible for the assassination of John F. Kennedy," "The CIA is involved in illegal drug trafficking," etc.). In other conditions, the statements denied the validity of these propositions ("The CIA is not involved in illegal drug trafficking," etc.). In each case, after reading the statements, subjects estimated the importance of the information and then indicated their personal belief in the proposition in question. They also reported beliefs in related propositions (e.g., "The CIA is involved in illegal activities other than drug trafficking").

We expected that positive assertions of the validity of the propositions (affirmations) would constitute new information, and would have a positive influence on subjects' personal beliefs in them. However, denials were expected to be redundant with subjects' prior knowledge, and thus to violate the informativeness principle. These violations should lead subjects to consider why the information was being transmitted and, therefore, to speculate that there might be some reason to suppose that the propositions were true. As a consequence of planting this seed of doubt, denials might also increase subjects' beliefs that the propositions were in fact valid. Moreover, this should be true to a greater extent when the source is a newspaper, whose objective is to be informative, than when it is an encyclopedia.

Results support this assumption. Table 1.1 shows the increase in beliefs in both the target proposition and related propositions (relative to control conditions in which no statements concerning the propositions were conveyed) as a function of source and assertion type. When the source was an encyclopedia, affirmations

TABLE 1.1
Effects of Affirmations and Denials of Uninformative Assertions on Assertion-Relevant Beliefs

	Assertion Type	
Variable	Affirmation	Denial
Effect on beliefs in target proposition		
Newspaper source	1.16*	1.06*
Encyclopedia source	1.81*	.48
Effect on beliefs in related propositions		
Newspaper source	1.15*	1.20*
Encyclopedia source	1.62*	.91*

Based on data from Gruenfeld and Wyer (1992).
Note. Cell entries indicate differences between beliefs reported in experimental conditions and context-free beliefs reported in the absence of exposure to assertions.
*Differences are significantly greater than 0, $p < .05$.

had more influence than denials. However, when the source was a newspaper, both affirmations and denials increased beliefs in the propositions. In other words, denials of the propositions' validity, which appeared to violate the informativeness principle, had "boomerang" effects on beliefs that the propositions were true. Moreover, these effects were just as great as the effects of assertions that the propositions were valid.

Politeness and Accuracy.   The "accuracy" principle states that communications should convey accurate information. The "politeness" principle states that communications should not offend the listener. The implications of these principles may often conflict. For example, there are many times when a communicator who wishes to avoid offending the recipient will construct a message that he or she feels is not entirely accurate. Thus, a colleague will say that another's talk is "interesting" rather than a bunch of drivel, and a man will describe a woman's new hairstyle as "imaginative" rather than conveying his true feelings. Thus, the communicator is often forced to choose between accuracy and politeness.

The accuracy and politeness principles are presumably also applied by the recipient in interpreting a communicator's message. When the literal meaning of a message has favorable implications for the recipient, the recipient is likely to interpret it as both polite and accurate without much detailed consideration. However, when the message has unfavorable implications, an interpretation of it as both polite and accurate is more difficult. It if is accurate, it is unlikely to be very polite. On the other hand, it is polite only if the statement is made in jest and, therefore, is intended to be seen as inaccurate. Thus, all things being equal, it seems intuitively likely that recipients of an unfavorable communication are more inclined to interpret it in the second way than in the first.

The role of accuracy and politeness in informal communication was recognized by Wyer and Collins (1992) in a conceptualization of humor elicitation in informal conversation. Much of this humor is conveyed through sarcasm and irony (i.e., statements whose literal meanings are not their intended meanings). For example, "Central Illinois is certainly a great place to spend one's summer vacation" is clearly not to be taken literally; its intended meaning is to disparage central Illinois and not to praise it. However, to recognize this fact, one must be aware that the literal meaning is false and, therefore, in violation of a communication norm to be accurate.

Politeness and accuracy norms can sometimes combine to affect the identification of disparaging statements toward someone as teasing rather than genuine expressions of hostility. Thus, a statement that a colleague is so dumb that he can't find his car in the parking lot is less likely to be interpreted as an expression of hostility if it is conveyed in the colleague's presence (and therefore violates a politeness principle) than if it is conveyed in his absence. Moreover, it is more likely to be interpreted as a tease if the colleague is known to be exceptionally brilliant (and thus is clearly inaccurate) than if he is generally known to be dull.

(For a more detailed explication of the conditions in which humor is actually elicited by such statements, see Wyer & Collins, 1992.)

The Identification of Emotional Meaning

The application of communication norms in interpreting communications conveyed in a social context becomes particularly important to consider in understanding the transmission of emotional meaning. Identification of the pragmatic meaning of a communication often requires not only knowledge that the communication violates a conversational norm, but also knowledge that the communicator is aware of this violation. In our previous example, a very bright psychologist may believe that a colleague's description of him as too dumb to find his car in the parking lot violates the accuracy principle. However, he may not interpret the statement as a tease unless he believes that the colleague considers it to be inaccurate as well. If he has reason to believe that the colleague is unaware of his intellectual brilliance, he may not appreciate the comment at all. Thus, perceptions of the emotional meaning of the communication depend on awareness of the communicator's knowledge as well as one's own beliefs in the validity of the statement.

The shared knowledge that surrounds a communication can often lead emotional meaning to be transmitted to a recipient of which other recipients are unaware. For example, a husband's statement to his wife that "it's cold in here" might be interpreted by naive listeners as simply a statement of opinion. To the wife, however, it might be interpreted as an expression of anger at her persistence in keeping the thermostat too low. The husband's intention to convey this anger may be based on his assumption that she already knows he feels chilly and her awareness of his sensitivity to cold. Of course, if the wife were unaware of these matters, she might not identify the feelings of anger that the husband attempted to communicate.

This example implies a general principle. That is, communications whose semantic features do not have emotional implications are nevertheless likely to be attributed emotional meaning when (a) their literal meanings are redundant with what the listener already knows, and (b) the listener believes that the communicator is aware of this redundancy. This principle suggests how miscommunications can arise in conversations concerning the implications of one another's messages. Suppose a communicator attempts to convey emotional meaning through an indirect speech act. However, if the literal meaning of the message is actually informative, the recipient may not interpret it as such and, therefore, may miss the implications that the communicator wanted to convey. On the other hand, suppose a communicator intends to convey new information, but the recipient considers the message to be redundant with his or her prior knowledge. The recipient may incorrectly interpret it as an indirect speech act, and may assign meaning and emotional content to it that the communicator did not intend to transmit.

Situation-Specific Influences on Pragmatic Meaning

The communication norms described in the preceding sections are likely to affect the interpretation of communications transmitted in a wide variety of situations, in which the objectives of the conversing parties are simply to exchange information or, perhaps, to be entertaining. However, the effects of these norms can be overridden by situation-specific expectations that interacting parties have for one another by virtue of the role relationship between them, or other factors that give rise to more specific interaction objectives. These expectancies, which may be quite conscious, can also increase sensitivity to the pragmatic meaning of messages. If a male professor with a reputation for making sexual advances to his subordinates asks a female graduate student out for a beer, the student is likely to interpret this as an expression of sexual interest, and perhaps as sexual harassment, rather than as simply a desire to discuss professional matters in an informal atmosphere. More general role-defined expectations can also play a role, leading to possible misconstruals and misinterpretations.

Such misinterpretations are particularly evident in emotional communications, which are inherently ambiguous. A study by Gaelick, Bodenhausen, and Wyer (1985) provides an example. In this study, married couples engaged in a discussion about a problem they were having in their relationship. Later, the partners viewed a videotape of the conversation and identified specific statements that they considered important. Finally, partners rated the statements along dimensions pertaining to the love and hostility that they conveyed. Speakers' estimates of the emotions they intended to communicate were then compared to recipients' judgments of the emotions they perceived. When men responded in a way they considered to be affectively neutral, their female partners interpreted it as an expression of love, whereas when women responded in a way that they considered to be neutral, men interpreted it as an expression of hostility. These misinterpretations make sense in the context of general gender role-defined expectations for men to respond in a dominant, aggressive manner and women to be relatively warm and supportive. That is, women who expected their male partners to be generally aggressive interpreted their absence of hostility as an indication of love, whereas men, who expected their female partners to be warm and nurturant, interpreted the absence of these characteristics as an expression of hostility.

Summary

Our application of communication norms to the interpretation of social communications is obviously somewhat superficial. Nevertheless, it suffices to point out that the consistency of conversations with these norm-based expectations can have an important influence on the interpretation of interpersonal communications. This influence occurs over and above the effects of concept accessibility on perceptions of the semantic meaning of these messages. Indeed, recipients' construal of the pragmatic meaning of a communication may often be a far more important consideration than their perception of its literal meaning in understanding their responses to these messages.

REPRESENTATIONAL PROCESSES

The statements made in the course of an informal conversation are typically part of a sequence of communicative acts involving one or more of the conversing parties. In combination, these acts may compose a conversational episode (e.g., "Peter's discussion with Fred about graduate training," "last night's argument with my wife about having another child"). These configurations of interrelated actions may be stored in memory, and later retrieved as units, and their features may then be used as bases for judgments and decisions. The structure of such configurations, and the associations among their features, can affect the amount and type of information that is later extracted from them. Consequently, it is necessary to understand what the configurations "look like."

There is no single answer to this question. One's cognitive representation of a conversation is likely to depend on the content and structure of the conversation, as well as one's goals at the time the conversation takes place and whether one is personally a participant in it. Research in social cognition has only recently begun to confront these matters. However, two bodies of literature are worth noting. One concerns the mental representation of temporally ordered event sequences that one forms in the course of trying to understand what went on in a given situation. The second concerns the representations that are formed from conversations in which subjects are not participants, but listen to for the purpose of forming an impression of the participants or the person being discussed. Neither body of research bears directly on the sort of representations that are formed of a conversation by participants. Nevertheless, several aspects of the results we have obtained in this research help to identify issues that must be confronted in conceptualizing the nature of such representations.

The Representation of Event Sequences

If a conversation is viewed as a temporally organized sequence of communicative acts, it may be represented in memory in much the same way as other types of event sequences that we observe or otherwise learn about. There has been substantial research and theorizing on the representation of both situation-specific sequences that one observes (Allen & Ebbesen, 1981; Newtson, 1976), reads about (Trafimow & Wyer, 1993; Wyer & Bodenhausen, 1985; Wyer, Shoben, Fuhrman, & Bodenhausen, 1985) or personally experiences (Fuhrman & Wyer, 1988), and the prototypic event sequences that are often used to interpret them (Bower, Black, & Turner, 1979; Graesser, 1981; Schank & Abelson, 1977). We focus here on situation-specific sequences. In doing so, we do not consider in detail the specific research that has been conducted (for a review and theoretical integration, see Wyer & Srull, 1989). Rather, we summarize the conclusions that seem justified on the basis of this research.

General Considerations

The events that we encounter in everyday life can be encoded in terms of concepts at many different levels of specificity. The events that occur during a visit to a Chinese restaurant may be encoded at levels that are very abstract (e.g., "went to a restaurant"), moderately abstract ("ate chop suey"), or very specific ("picked up his chop suey with chopsticks and placed it in his mouth"). Normally, people do not encode events into memory at all of these levels simultaneously. Rather, they are likely to break an event sequence into conceptual units, each of which instantiates a different previously formed event concept. The number and size of the units depend on the purpose for which subjects believe they will later use the information and the detail they will have to remember it (Cohen & Ebbesen, 1979; Newtson, 1976).

For example, consider a television show about a woman, Willa. She is awakened one morning by a telephone call from her brother informing her that her father is dying. She gets up, makes plane reservations, packs, and hurries to the airport. She gets on the plane, has three martinis to calm herself, and feels dizzy by the time the plane lands in San Francisco. She takes a cab into the city, but finds that she has forgotten the name of the hospital where her father is staying. She breaks down and cries on the streets of San Francisco.

A person who watches this sequences of events on television may note many details of Willa's behavior and the events surrounding it. However, it seems unlikely that the person will spontaneously perform the cognitive activity that is required to encode an ongoing event sequence into memory in terms of concepts at a level of specificity that captures all of these details. Wyer, Shoben, Fuhrman, and Bodenhausen (1985) postulated that people who learn about a sequence of events typically encode them at only two levels. First, they break them into conceptual units, each corresponding to a previously formed event concept at a level of abstractness that is sufficient to attain their processing objectives at the time. They then assign temporal codes to these concepts that correspond to their temporal order. The individual actions comprising the units are then encoded in terms of instantiated features of the event concepts that are used to define these units. However, these actions are not assigned temporal codes because their order is usually dictated by the concepts that are used to encode them, or else they can be computed on the basis of general knowledge about their causal relatedness. Therefore, a representation of the story about Willa might have the form shown in Fig. 1.1.

Three implications of this formulation are not reflected in the previous example. First, if events are encoded at a more abstract level than they are conveyed in the original information, certain implications of these events may not be captured by the representation that is formed from them. Second, events in the sequence that are not relevant to the concepts that are used to interpret them may also not be included in the representation. Third, features that were not mentioned, but

a. The telephone rings
b. Willa gets out of bed
c. Willa learns her father is dying
d. Willa gets on the plane
e. Willa has three drinks
f. Willa feels dizzy
g. The plane lands in San Francisco
h. Willa can't find the hospital
i. Willa breaks into tears

FIG. 1.1.   Representation of event sequence composed of actions surrounding Willa's trip to California. Each square in the diagram denotes an action unit formed from the set of actions indicated.

are part of the event sequence represented by the concept, may be spontaneously inferred in the course of comprehending it. These "intrusions" may become part of the representation that is formed of the events. Consequently, they may be reported later as actually having been observed if the person is called on to reconstruct what occurred (cf. Spiro, 1977). In short, the recall and reconstruction of the original event sequence from the representation that is formed of it is likely to omit some features that were described in the original information and to include others that were actually not mentioned.

Implications for Interpersonal Communication

To the extent that a conversation is represented as a series of communicative acts, a mental representation of it might be constructed in the manner described earlier. Several considerations limit the generalizability of such a conclusion, however. For one thing, the implications of statements contained in a conversation may often be thought about in ways that do not reflect the order in which they were mentioned. This may, in fact, be more the rule than the exception. For example, if our story about Willa were conveyed in a conversation, it might actually begin with the punch line and progress backward in time (e.g., "Did you hear about Willa? She got lost looking for the hospital her father was in, and broke down and cried in the street. I guess she'd had too many drinks on the plane and got confused. She'd only just learned that her father was dying that morning . . . "). Moreover, the description of these events might often be interrupted by questions or comments by the other persons involved, and by digressions to other, unrelated topics. A person who listens to the story with the objective of understanding what happened may attempt to construct a representation of the events that reflects the order in which they actually occurred, rather than the order in which they were mentioned, and may store a representation of them in memory in this revised order (cf. Wyer & Bodenhausen, 1985). In short, although the structure of the conversation is a continuous sequence of temporally related communicative acts, the structure of the mental representations that are formed from it may not always reflect this sequence.

In some instances, of course, the statements made in a conversation are represented in approximately the order they were uttered, and can later be reported in this order. Whether this is done may depend on one's processing objectives at the time the conversation takes place. Suppose a man listens to two people discuss the morality of having an abortion. If the listener's objective is to obtain information about the issue being discussed and to form his or her own opinion about it, he or she may organize the statements made during the conversation in terms of theme-related concepts that will help him or her attain this objective independently of the order they were mentioned or who mentioned them. In contrast, suppose the listener's objective is to understand the two persons' feelings about one another. To gain this understanding, the temporal sequence of the protagonists' comments and their responses to one another may be quite important. Consequently, the order of these communications is more likely to be preserved in the representation that is formed.

Considerations similar to those noted previously arise when conceptualizing the representations that are formed of a conversation by the protagonists. Yet another factor is important to consider under these conditions. That is, the actual participants in a conversation are particularly likely to have thoughts and emotional reactions that are not overtly expressed. These thoughts and reactions constitute subjective events that may be encoded into the event representation in much the same way as the overt statements and behavior that occur. As suggested earlier, inferences that are made in the course of thinking about a sequence of events may be included in the representation that is formed, and these inferences may not be distinguishable from the events that were actually described (cf. Spiro, 1977). In the present context, this suggests that thoughts or feelings that one experiences during the course of a conversation may later be recalled as having been overtly expressed. This provides yet another example of how, as the result of a conversation, misconstruals and misperceptions can arise that are difficult, if not impossible, for the parties involved to resolve.

The Role of Narratives and Stories in the Representation of Personal Experiences

Because conversations are sequences of communicative acts, research and theory on the representation of event sequences may help to understand the way in which conversations are organized in memory. However, a conceptualization of the structure of event representations, and the processes that underlie their formation, are important for another reason as well. That is, descriptions of sequences of events are an integral part of the content of a conversation. Indeed, a large portion of informal conversation is likely to be devoted to the exchange of stories or narratives about oneself and others.

Schank (1990) argued that stories are, in fact, the fundamental basis for comprehending information that is conveyed in a social context. That is, we typically respond to descriptions of another's personal experience by recounting an experience of our own that has similar features, and use this story to understand the experience the other has had. In doing so, two related processes may occur. First, as suggested by Spiro's (1977) study, we may fill in gaps in the other's story with components of our own, thus permitting us to construe the reasons for the events that occurred, the emotional reactions to these events by the parties involved, and the possible consequences of the events. In similar ways, we may also fill in gaps in our own story with aspects of the experience the other describes. That is, we use the other's story to infer reasons for our own behavior and the events that have occurred to us, and to predict outcomes of our own actions. In short, not only do the narratives we have constructed of our own experiences affect our representations of others' experiences, but descriptions of others' experiences can affect the content and structure of stories we tell about ourselves.

Although these processes are intuitively self-evident, and have been conceptualized fairly rigorously by Schank and others (McAdams, 1993; Ross, 1989), an empirical examination of them is obviously difficult. This is because the stories that people construct are often idiosyncratic. Means of coding narratives in ways that permit them to be meaningfully compared must ultimately be developed. The difficulty of this task is increased by the fact that, as Schank pointed out, the interpretation of a narrative can depend heavily on the context in which it is conveyed, and cannot be extracted from the content of the story considered in isolation. Nevertheless, several promising procedures have been suggested (Demorest & Alexander, 1992; Ross, 1989; Schank, 1990). In fact, by coding personal stories in the form of a script (Schank & Abelson, 1977), Demorest and Alexander (1992) were able to demonstrate that subjects' stories about themselves had a significant impact on their interpretations of stories they read about others several weeks later. Although this study was not conducted in a conversational context, it seems likely that comparable processes occur in the latter situations as well. In any event, future research and theory on interpersonal communication is likely to take cognizance of the important role of stories and narratives in the exchange of social information, and, in so doing, will make important advances in our understanding of the content and use of event representations in these exchanges.

Impression Formation in Informal Conversation

Not all of the information conveyed in conversations is likely to be organized in the form of an event sequence. This is particularly true when participants in the conversations have a particular objective in mind to which the information pertains. In this case, people may extract particular aspects of the conversation that are relevant to this objective. Moreover, they may think about the information in relation to one another in a way that helps them attain their goals. This cognitive activity may lead a mental representation to be formed from the information that is stored in memory as a unit. This representation may then be retrieved and later used as a basis for judgments and decisions.

A particularly common objective that pervades informal communication is that of impression formation. That is, people in a conversation typically exchange information about themselves and others, describing behaviors that they have performed and experiences they have had. Listeners are likely to form impressions of what the individuals described are like on the basis of this information. In addition, they often form impressions of the speakers on the basis of what they have said. The cognitive representations that underlie these impressions have only recently begun to be investigated (Wyer, Budesheim, & Lambert, 1990; Wyer, Budesheim, Lambert, & Swan, 1993). Nevertheless, the approach we have taken, and several aspects of our results that have more general implications, are worth describing briefly.

In our research, subjects listen to a conversation between two other individuals, rather than participating in the discussion. Moreover, their objective at the time they hear the conversation is to form an impression of either the person who is discussed by the speakers or, alternatively, the speakers. As might be expected, the representations that are formed in such conditions do not at all reflect the temporally related sequence of conversational acts that actually occurred. On the other hand, the representations also differ from those that are usually formed from similar information that is acquired out of any conversational context. These differences appear to result largely from a factor that we alluded to earlier. That is, subjects who listen to a conversation interpret the statements that are made in it not only as descriptive information about the person whom they describe, but also as communicative acts of the speakers. Because of this, subjects spontaneously form concepts of the speakers and organize the information around these concepts, rather than a concept of the person whom the speakers are discussing.

To understand more precisely the representations that are formed and the processes that underlie their construction, it is useful to consider them with reference to the representations and processes that occur when people form impressions of a person on the basis of similar information that is conveyed out of its conversational context. In much of the research on person-impression formation (for a review and theoretical integration, see Srull & Wyer, 1989; Wyer & Srull, 1989), subjects are first given a set of favorable or unfavorable trait-adjective descriptions of a person. These descriptions are followed by a series of behaviors that the person has performed. Some of these behaviors are evaluatively consistent with the initial trait descriptions, and others are evaluatively inconsistent with these descriptions. Under these conditions, subjects with an impression-formation objective appear to form a general evaluative concept of the person on the basis of the first (trait-adjective) information. (This is evidenced by the fact that subjects' liking for the person is primarily influenced by this information independently of the implications of the behaviors that follow it.) Once the concept is formed, subjects think about the individual behaviors with reference to this concept. Moreover, when subjects encounter a behavior that is evaluatively inconsistent with the concept, they think about it more extensively in relation to other behaviors that the person has performed in order to reconcile its occurrence. This increased cognitive activity typically establishes associations between the inconsistent behavior and others, making the behavior more accessible in memory and giving it a recall advantage later. The representations that result from this cognitive activity can be represented metaphorically as an associative network of the form shown in Fig. 1.2, where the associations formed between concepts and behaviors as a result of the cognitive activity performed in the course of thinking about the information are denoted by pathways connecting them. (For a further elaboration of the theory on which these conclusions are based and empirical evidence for its validity, see Srull & Wyer, 1989; Wyer & Srull, 1989.)

However, quite different processes appear to occur when comparable information is presented in the course of a conversation. In the research we have conducted so far, we have considered two general conditions. In one, subjects listen to two persons describe a third. In the second, the conversation concerns one of the speakers rather than a third party. Each set of studies raises a different set of factors that must be considered in conceptualizing the representation of conversations in general.

The Representation of Conversations About a Third Party

In one study reported by Wyer et al. (1990), subjects listened to a male speaker and a female speaker exchange anecdotal descriptions of the behavior of a male target person. Before hearing the conversation, subjects were given trait-

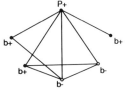

FIG. 1.2. Hypothetical representation of a person described by favorable personality-trait adjectives followed by behaviors that are either favorable (b+) or unfavorable (b−) and are presented in the sequence b+b+b−b−b+. Each unfavorable (evaluatively inconsistent) behavior is assumed to be thought about with reference to the two behaviors that immediately precede it in the sequence, thus forming associations with these behaviors. P+ is the central person concept around which the behaviors are organized.

adjective descriptions that each speaker had provided. The speakers' trait descriptions (which were either similar or different in their evaluative implications) and the behaviors that each speaker mentioned were the same as those presented in previous studies of person-impression formation under the conditions described earlier (cf. Wyer & Martin, 1986). However, in this case, several differences occurred in subjects' responses to this information, the nature of which depended on the task objectives that subjects were given.

These differences can best be understood by first considering conditions in which subjects were explicitly told to form impressions of the two speakers. In this case, subjects' liking for each speaker increased with the favorableness of the speakers' trait descriptions of the target. However, these trait descriptions had a slight contrast effect on subjects' liking of the target; that is, subjects liked the target less when speakers' trait descriptions were favorable than when they were unfavorable. This pattern of results suggests that subjects used the speakers' trait characterizations of the target in particular as an indication of how the speakers were likely to respond to people in general and, therefore, of the speakers' general likableness. Having formed these concepts, subjects used them as comparative standards when they were later asked to evaluate the target.

The recall data were particularly provocative. That is, subjects recalled behaviors better if they were evaluatively inconsistent with the trait description provided by the speaker who did not mention them, independently of their consistency with the description provided by the speaker who actually reported them. One interpretation of this finding is that subjects were uncertain about the validity of their assumption that the speakers' trait descriptions of the target reflected general dispositions to evaluate others favorably or unfavorably (and, therefore, the speakers' likableness), rather than characteristics of the target that the adjectives ostensibly described. Consequently, they thought more extensively about information that confirmed their assumption. Behaviors that a speaker mentioned that were evaluatively inconsistent with the other speaker's trait description of the target suggested that this trait description might not, in fact, be accurate and, therefore, provided confirmation of subjects' assumption that the description reflected the general likableness of the speaker. Consequently, subjects may have thought more extensively about these behaviors with reference to their concept of this speaker, producing associations that led the behaviors to be more easily recalled later. If this is so, the representation of the conversation that resulted from this activity might resemble that shown in Fig. 1.3a under conditions in which the two speakers' trait descriptions differ in favorableness.

Now consider conditions in which subjects were told to form an impression of the target person. The speakers' trait descriptions of the target affected judgments in the same manner as in the first study. That is, they had a positive influence on subjects' liking for the speakers, but a negative, contrast effect on their liking for the target. This suggests that, despite instructions to form impressions of the target, subjects spontaneously formed concepts of the speakers instead and used these concepts as standards of comparison in evaluating the target when they were later asked to do so.

Although the judgment data in this study were similar to those we obtained when subjects were explicitly told to form impressions of the speakers, the recall data were not. Specifically, the recall of behaviors in this study was a function of their inconsistency with the trait description provided by the female speaker, regardless of which speaker had mentioned them. Apparently when subjects were not explicitly told to form impressions of both speakers, they did not take a disinterested perspective. Rather, they thought about the implications of the behaviors that were mentioned only with reference to their concept of the female. Behaviors mentioned by the male that were inconsistent with the female's description of the target confirmed their assumption that this description reflected the female's own likableness rather than attributes of the target. These behaviors may have been processed more extensively for this reason. On the other hand, behaviors that the female mentioned that were inconsistent with her trait description of the target disconfirmed the concept they had formed of her as likable or dislikable. These behaviors were apparently thought about more extensively in relation to other behaviors she mentioned in an effort to reconcile their occurrence (i.e., to understand why a likable person would mention an unfavorable action of the target, or why a dislikable person would mention something favorable). This latter cognitive activity should produce associations between the

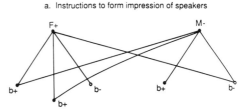

a. Instructions to form impression of speakers

FIG. 1.3. Hypothetical representations formed when subjects are told to form (a) impressions of speakers and (b) the target. In each case, F+ and M− denote concepts formed of the female speaker (based on favorable trait descriptions of the target) and the male speaker (based on unfavorable trait descriptions of the target). Two favorable and one unfavorable behavior is mentioned by the female, in the order b+b+b−. One favorable and one unfavorable behavior are mentioned by the male, in the order b+b−.

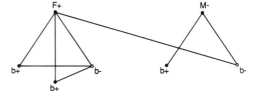

b. Instructions to form impression of target

inconsistent behavior and others. Therefore, the representation implied by these processes would resemble that shown in Fig. 1.3b.

The Representation of Conversations About One of the Speakers

The processes described previously come into play when two persons describe someone who is not personally a participant in the conversation. When the person being discussed is actively or passively involved, additional factors must be taken into account. These considerations arise from the fact that the communications that are transmitted in a conversation convey descriptive information about the person to whom they refer, as well as serve as communicative acts that convey information about the speakers. These acts may often be viewed as either socially desirable or socially undesirable. For example, it may generally be considered in bad taste to point out undesirable behaviors a person has performed in this person's presence.[2] (Put another way, it may violate a conversational norm to be polite, or to convey information that will not offend the recipient.) Note that this consideration generally applies only to things that another speaker mentions about the person being described. Mildly unfavorable things that a person mentions about him or herself are not counternormative. Rather, the mention of these things may be taken as an indication of modesty, and, therefore, may be considered socially desirable.

Two other studies we performed (Wyer et al., 1993) bear on these possibilities. The studies were conceptually similar to the others we have described. However, in this case, two persons, P and O, exchanged anecdotal behavioral descriptions of P. Thus, O mentioned favorable and unfavorable behaviors that P had performed, and P mentioned favorable and unfavorable things that he personally had done. Before hearing the conversation, subjects read trait-adjective descriptions of P that were ostensibly provided both by O and by P. Subjects received the information with instructions to form an impression of either P or O.

The results of this study were fairly similar regardless of the instructions that subjects were given. Specifically, subjects' liking for O increased with the favorableness of O's description of P, whereas their liking for P was unaffected by P's self-description. Moreover, behaviors that O mentioned were recalled better if

---

[2]In the first two studies described, where the two speakers exchanged information about an acquaintance in this person's absence, the mention of specific things the person did may not have been considered either favorable or unfavorable. Because people are expected to behave in ways that they and others will regard favorably, the mention of these actions in a conversation about these people may be regarded as uninformative and uninteresting. On the other hand, moderately undesirable behaviors, by virtue of their novelty, more often may be the subject of conversation, and, therefore, may not be considered counternormative.

they were unfavorable, and, therefore, were in violation of conversational norms to say things that would not offend or embarrass P than if they were favorable. This was true regardless of the favorableness of O's trait description of P. In contrast, the recall of behaviors that P mentioned was not a function of their favorableness.

The conclusion that people have better memory for statements in a conversation that violate conversational norms is probably not too surprising to most readers of this book. This finding is important from the perspective of research on person impression formation, however, because it reinforces our conclusion that the information conveyed in conversations is processed quite differently from comparable information that is presented out of its conversational context. For one thing, it is thought about with reference to concepts that are specific to the persons to whom the information refers, or the conversation participants. In addition, it is thought about with reference to more general, normative considerations that pertain to conversations in general. A conceptualization of the way that information in conversations is represented in memory, and how these representations are later used to make judgments and decisions, must take these factors into account.

The studies described herein found no evidence that the information conveyed in conversations was represented as a temporal sequence of communicative acts. Indeed, the correlation of the order in which behaviors were mentioned in the conversations and the order in which they were recalled was negligible (Wyer et al., 1990). In evaluating the generalizability of the conclusion, however, two related factors need to be reiterated.

First, the way in which the information conveyed in conversations is represented in memory depends, to a considerable extent, on the goals of the persons who receive and process the information at the time the conversations take place. In the studies we have described, subjects appeared to form impressions of the speaker spontaneously, even when they were told to focus on the person whom the conversation was about. This suggests that, in many instances, people who listen to a conversation automatically form concepts of the participants regardless of any other considerations. This may be due, in part, to the need to evaluate communicators in order to assess the implications of their messages for the topic under discussion. As we pointed out earlier, however, people may sometimes have the objective of forming an impression of the conversation, or of inferring the two participants' feelings about one another. Or the content of the conversation may be particularly conducive to being represented as a temporally or causally related sequence of communicative acts. In such instances, the representations that are formed may be quite different from those that are implied by our research to date.

Second, perhaps the most serious limitation to the generalizability of the research described previously is that subjects were not involved in the conversations, but rather were passive observers. Participants in a conversation not only generate the statements made in the conversation, but elicit responses that are relevant to these statements, thereby playing an active role in the sequence of communicative acts that unfolds. The representations that are formed in these circumstances seems much more likely to have the structure of a temporally related event sequence of the sort postulated to exist in research on event memory (cf. Wyer & Srull, 1989; Wyer, Shoben, Fuhrman, & Bodenhausen 1985). We are just beginning to investigate these matters.

STORAGE AND RETRIEVAL

Most conversations are multifaceted. That is, a given conversation may pertain to several different topics. Moreover, both the participants in a conversation and the people who listen to it may have objectives that change over the course of the discussion. That is, their goals at some points may be simply to understand the issue being discussed or to form an opinion about it. At other times, their objectives may be to form an impression of one of the participants or to understand this participant's impression of them. Therefore, it seems likely that people do not form a single representation of a conversation. Rather, they form several different representations pertaining to different objectives. These representations may be stored separately in memory at locations that pertain to these objectives. To this extent, the likelihood of later retrieving any given one of the representations to use as a basis for a judgment or decision may depend, in part, on where it is stored.

In the latter regard, people acquire a large amount of information about several different persons, objects, and issues, and they obviously do not bring all of this knowledge to bear on judgments and decisions to which it is relevant. Much of this knowledge does not even come to mind at the time the response is made. The knowledge that is potentially relevant to a given decision may be distributed throughout the memory system. For example, my knowledge of a student may include a conversation I had with him or her in my office, in which he or she made several extremely insightful comments about some research I was doing. When I am asked to evaluate this student's intellectual ability, however, I may not retrieve this information, which was thought about with reference to the issue being discussed rather than the student. Consequently, I may judge the student to be rather dull and conceptually unsophisticated, based on my discussion with the student concerning his or her grades during the past semester. (This latter discussion might have even taken place in the same conversation as the first.)

Therefore, to understand both the determinants and the effects of interpersonal messages, one must develop a conceptualization of where the information that is acquired in conversations is stored in memory, and what determines which aspects of this information are later retrieved and used at any given time. One conceptualization that is both useful and convenient for our present purposes was proposed by Wyer and Srull (1986, 1989). Although this conceptualization is complex in detail, it has several features that are of particular relevance to the issues raised here.

Storage Assumptions

Long-term memory is conceptualized metaphorically as being composed of a set of content-addressable storage bins. These bins are used to store information that is relevant to one's information-processing objectives at the time the information is received. Thus, each bin typically pertains to the referent (person, object, event, or issue) on which these objectives focus. Each bin is denoted by a "header" that specifies its referent and contains other features that are strongly associated with the referent, or that otherwise circumscribe the bin contents. Thus, suppose a person listens to a politician's speech about abortion with a goal of forming an opinion about the morality of this act. In this case, the information is theoretically be stored in an "abortion" bin. However, if the person's objective is to evaluate the politician, he or she may store the information in a bin pertaining to the politician. Several different units of knowledge, acquired at different times but concerning the same referent, may be deposited in the same bin. On the other hand, much of our knowledge about a particular referent may be stored in different bins, depending on the processing objectives that exist at the time the knowledge is acquired.

Bins can pertain to referents at different levels of generality. One could have a "Mary" bin that contains general information, and also a "Mary as a graduate assistant" bin that pertains to her in this particular role. Whether a piece of information is stored in one bin or the other (or neither) depends on whether the information at the time it is received is thought about with respect to Mary in general or with respect to her in her assistantship role.

In the present context, these assumptions imply that not all aspects of a given conversation are likely to be stored in the same place. If a listener's goals change during the conversation, different segments of the conversation may be stored at different locations. Moreover, the bin in which these segments are stored may contain other information about the referent as well.

Retrieval Assumptions

According to the Wyer and Srull model, an individual who requires knowledge about a particular referent compiles a set of "probe cues" or features that are relevant to the attainment of this objective. These features typically include a specification of the referent and, in some cases, the type of information to be sought. A bin whose header contains these features is then identified, and the contents of the bin is searched for information that will be useful in attaining the objective at hand. This latter search is top–down.

A further assumption of the model is that not all of the information that is relevant to a judgment or decision is typically retrieved from the bin in which it is contained. That is, only a subset of this information is considered that is deemed sufficient to attain one's goal at the time. Therefore, if several knowledge representations with different implications are stored in the bin, the first one that is identified is most likely to be used. As noted earlier, this representation is usually the one that has been deposited in the bin most recently and, therefore, is closest to the top.

These assumptions, in combination with the storage assumptions outlined earlier, help to conceptualize the conditions under which the information one acquires in a conversation is likely to have an impact on later judgments or communication decisions. Imagine that at a dinner party, John and Mary engage in a heated discussion about antiabortion laws. During the course of the argument, John expresses the view that abortion is equivalent to murder, and Mary calls John a sexist pig. Suppose John's objective in the conversation is to clarify his personal attitude toward abortion, whereas Mary's objective is to form an impression of John and to infer John's opinion of her. Thus, John theoretically stores the information in an "abortion" bin, whereas Mary stores it in a "John" bin. Some time later, the two individuals may be asked to report their impressions of one another and to infer how they are likely to get along. Both parties should search for judgment-relevant information in a bin pertaining to the other. Therefore, although the discussion is equally relevant to both individuals' inferences, Mary is more likely than John to retrieve and use its implications as a basis for the inference.

To continue our example, suppose a third party has listened to the conversation between John and Mary with the objective of forming an impression of both individuals. This person would presumably store a representation of the discussion in both a "John" bin and a "Mary" bin. However, suppose the listener subsequently acquires additional information about John, but no further information about Mary. The representation of the discussion should be buried under the more recently acquired information in the "John" bin, but should remain on top of the "Mary" bin. This means that a representation of the conversation is more likely to be retrieved later if the listener has occasion to think about Mary than if he has reason to think about John. This may be true even if the time interval between the conversation and the situation in which information is sought is the same in both cases, and even if the total amount of knowledge the listener has about each individual is similar.

This example is obviously oversimplified. Nevertheless, it suffices to make several points. First, the information that one acquires in a conversation is unlikely to be retrieved and used as a basis for later judgments and decisions unless one's objective at the time of judgment pertains to the same referent as that to which one's goals were relevant at the time the information was first received and stored. Second, information that concerns a particular topic is more likely to be retrieved and used as a basis for later judgments and decisions if it is among the most recent knowledge one has acquired about this topic. However, information and knowledge that have not been thought about for some time could also be retrieved and used if no other information pertaining to the topic has been acquired in the interim and thought about with reference to this topic (i.e., if no new information has been deposited on top of it in the bin in which it is stored).

More generally, conversations typically have implications for the matter being discussed as well as the participants. Therefore, the information they provide could potentially guide subsequent communications about the issue being discussed, as well as judgments and behaviors toward the other participants in the conversation, and even participants' perceptions of themselves. However, whether the discussion is actually used as a basis for a given judgment or decision depends, in large part, on how the discussion was originally thought about by the participants.

A possible example of this contingency is provided by the study (Gaelick et al., 1985) described earlier. To reiterate, married couples engaged in a videotaped discussion of a problem they were having in their relationship. Later, they judged selected events that occurred during the conversation in terms of the love and hostility they personally experienced and the emotions their partners conveyed to them. Finally, partners reported their satisfaction with their relationship. Wives' satisfaction was related negatively to both the hostility they personally perceived to characterize the conversation and the hostility that their husbands believed was exchanged. In contrast, husbands' relationship satisfaction was unrelated to either their own or their wives' perceptions of the hostility that was communicated. It is interesting to speculate that although both partners formed similar representations of the discussion, males thought about it with reference to the problem being discussed and, therefore, stored a representation of it in a bin pertaining to the problem per se. In contrast, females thought about the discussion in terms of its implications for their relationship and, therefore, stored it in a "relationship" bin. Consequently, only females retrieved and used the implications of the conversation when later asked to report their relationship satisfaction. Although there are undoubtedly other interpretations of these findings, the results are nonetheless consistent with the conceptualization we have proposed.

INFERENCE PROCESSES

Responses to communications that occur in the course of a conversation are guided, in part, by inferences one makes about their implications and the consequences of alternative ways of responding. These implications may pertain to the issue being discussed, to attributes and motives of the communicator, or to the communicator's beliefs and feelings about the recipient. Perceptions of these implications are presumably influenced by many of the factors we have discussed in previous sections. Such perceptions presumably mediate inferences of the consequences of alternative responses that might be made to it and, therefore, affect decisions as to which response to generate.

The implications of a communication, and of the consequences of alternative responses to it, may often be inferred by applying event representations of the sort we postulated to exist in our discussion of organizational processes. To reiterate, an event representation presumably consists of a sequence of temporally and causally related acts. These sequences may pertain to particular situations that occurred in the past, or to more general, prototypic situations. In either case, the use of such representations to construe the implications of a given communication is theoretically straightforward (for a more formal statement of these processes, see Abelson, 1976, 1981; Schank & Abelson, 1977). That is, once the communication has been encoded on the basis of processes described earlier, the receiver retrieves an event representation from permanent memory, a frame of which contains features of the communication and its situational context. Once the features of this frame have been instantiated in terms of the new communication situation's features, frames that precede it in the representation can be used to infer antecedents (causes) of the communication, and frames that follow it can be used to infer its implications (consequences). In many instances, a particular communicative act may exemplify a frame of more than one previously formed event representation. In such cases, inferences of the motivation underlying the communication, and perceptions of its consequences, may depend on which of the event representations happens to come to mind.

As a simplified example, suppose a man has previously formed the following two event sequences pertaining to his wife's behavior: (a) X has a bad day at the office; X criticizes me; I get angry; X apologizes and tells me about her problem. (b) X is angry whenever I invite my parents to come for a visit; X criticizes me; I get angry; X stalks out of the house and goes to sleep at her sister's. Suppose the wife makes a statement at dinner that her spouse interprets as a criticism. Depending on which of the previous event sequences he happens to identify, the husband may infer that the criticism was either an indirect result of his spouse's troubles at work or a displacement of her resentment about his parents' impending visit. Moreover, he may anticipate different consequences of responding to this remark with anger, and these expectations may affect his actual response.

Although these observations are self-evident at the general level, they are important in the context of considerations raised earlier. That is, people are typically unlikely to consider all possible interpretations of a communication or its alternative implications. Rather, they use only the concepts and knowledge that come to mind quickly and easily. Which knowledge this happens to be is presumably governed, in part, by the considerations raised in earlier sections of this chapter.

The brief analysis provided does not, of course, address many other factors that must be taken into account in developing a general formulation of how people construe the implications of information they receive. For one thing, it is undoubtedly an oversimplification to assume that these inferences are based on a single event representation. In many cases, several different representations, with different implications, might be considered. This could be done through the use of an algebraic combinatorial process (cf. Anderson, 1981) or a heuristic process (for a review, see Sherman & Corty, 1984). Although our discussion of the role of these processes and when they come into play is beyond the scope of this chapter, this matter must ultimately be addressed.

RESPONSE GENERATION

The response to a communication is presumably influenced by all of the cognitive processes we have described in previous sections. That is, it may be affected by (a) the encoding of individual features of the conversation in terms of previously formed concepts; (b) the consistency of the information with conversational norms to be polite, accurate, and informative; and (c) the particular knowledge that happens to be retrieved and used as a basis for construing the consequences of alternative responses to it. Of course, overriding considerations are the communicator's objectives, and the strategy that he or she believes is most effective in attaining these objectives. This strategy may be determined, in part, by previously acquired event representations that permit the communicator to infer the likely consequences of alternative courses of action and of alternative ways of conveying the information to be communicated. The specific factors that underlie the selection of one alternative strategy over another are important to identify. Presumably, their effects can be understood in terms of the processes outlined in the earlier sections of this chapter.

Three considerations that have not been mentioned previously must be taken into account, however. The first places qualifications on the generalizability of the assumption that the generation of responses is mediated by a conscious construal of alternative strategies for attaining a given communication objective. The other related considerations surround the role of (a) affect and emotion and (b) self-focused attention in interpersonal communication.

Automatic Responding

Our analysis of interpersonal communication implicitly assumes that people's communications are based on a deliberate, conscious construal of the meaning of the previous messages they have received and an evaluation of the possible consequences of the messages they generate in response. This is obviously not always the case. Many communications are little more than spontaneous "knee-jerk" responses to another's statements or behavior, and are minimally mediated by conscious cognitive processing (cf. Langer, 1978; Langer & Abelson, 1972).

A formal conceptualization of this possibility was suggested by Smith (1984, 1990). Expanding on Anderson's (1983) ACT* model, Smith postulated the existence of "IF . . . THEN . . . " production rules. These rules, which are acquired through learning, determine responses to different configurations of stimulus conditions. These productions are theoretically applied automatically when the conditions that activate them exist. Suppose a communicator's message is encoded in terms that fulfill the "IF . . . " conditions of a production. This production may then be activated and may generate the response specified in its "THEN . . . " component. This may occur without any of the cognitive processing that we have postulated to guide inferences based on a previously formed event representation.

As a simplified example, suppose people have acquired a production of the form "IF someone communicates emotion X to me, THEN communicate X to this person." The use of this production would lead someone who has interpreted a speaker's message as hostile to reciprocate this hostility without considering either of the antecedents of the communicator's response or its implications. More generally, when the features of a communication and its situational context satisfy the conditions of a production, experiences that affect the accessibility of alternative concepts for use in interpreting the implications of the communication and alternative means of responding to it will have little impact on the response that is actually generated. (For further discussion of these possibilities, see Roloff & Berger, 1982).

Productions undoubtedly govern communications in a wide range of social-interaction situations in which the patterns of interaction have become routine. Thus, they are particularly likely to guide communications that take place between persons who know one another very well (e.g., close friends, or partners in close relationships). The conditions in which communications are mediated by productions, rather than a more deliberative construal of the implications of a communicator's message, warrant further consideration.

The Role of Affect in Response Generation

Communications often elicit emotional reactions. These reactions may be mediated by perceptions of the communicator's intentions to convey affect and emotion. Or they may simply result from statements that one interprets as having favorable or unfavorable implications for oneself or for things that one likes or despises. When these reactions occur, they may guide the content of the recipient's response.

One principle that appears to govern affective response to communications is *reciprocity*. That is, individuals appear to reciprocate the affect or emotion that they perceive a communicator has conveyed to them. As suggested in our discussion of production rules, the application of this principle may sometimes reflect an automatic response to perceptions of the other's communication of the sort we have postulated to be governed by "productions."

Evidence that a reciprocity principle governs emotional communication was reported by Gaelick et al. (1985) in the study noted earlier. To reiterate, marriage partners first discussed a conflict they were having. Their later ratings of individual events that occurred indicated that they responded to one another's statements in ways that reciprocated the emotion (love or hostility) that they perceived their partners had conveyed to them. Thus, they responded with love if they perceived their partners had conveyed love, and with hostility if they perceived their partners to have been hostile.

Of course, this does not mean that subjects actually reciprocated the emotions that their partner conveyed. Whether this occurred depended on whether their perceptions of their partner's emotions were accurate. In fact, Gaelick et al. found that partners were only accurate in perceiving hostility. The accuracy with which they perceived the love their partners intended to communicate was very low. Consequently, hostility was actually reciprocated over the course of the interaction, whereas love was not. One implication of this is that expressions of hostility tended to escalate over the course of the discussion, whereas expressions of love did not. Some caution should be taken in generalizing these conclusions to other types of communication situations. That is, people may be more attentive to expressions of hostility, and they may perceive these expressions more accurately, if they are discussing a conflict they are having than if they are discussing a more pleasant topic. Nonetheless, the study points out the importance of considering the roles of affective *and* descriptive factors in response generation.

THE ROLE OF PROCESSING OBJECTIVES IN COMMUNICATION AND RECEPTION

In discussing the cognitive processes that underlie the transmission and reception of information in a social context, we have tended to ignore an obvious and important contingency in the nature of this processing. That is, people who exchange information in a social context typically do so with certain objectives in mind. In many informal conversations, people may simply try to be interesting and entertaining. In other cases, they may attempt to provide new information or, alternatively, to persuade others of a particular point of view.

Research performed in the domain of social cognition has focused primarily on the objectives of the recipient. Far less attention has been given to the way the goals of the communicator affect the transmission of information and, ultimately, the impact of the information on the listener. One recent attempt to examine these effects (Gruenfeld & Wyer, 1993) identified some considerations that were not touched on in the research and theory described thus far in this chapter.

In this research, we were particularly concerned with how a communicator's perceptions of the source of the information to be transmitted would affect the communicator's own reactions to the information, and how these reactions would, in turn, affect the communicator's transmission of the information to someone else. We expected that these effects would depend on both the ostensible purpose for which the information was originally conveyed and the communicator's own goals in passing in on to the other. The objectives we chose to consider typically underlie the dissemination of information in the public media—to be interesting and accurate. Although these objectives are related, they seemed likely to have different effects on both the reception of the information and the transmission of it. To be interesting, information must be both novel and important. In contrast, being accurate may simply entail conveying information in a factual manner without embellishment. It seemed reasonable to suppose that a communicator's expectations concerning the purpose for which the information was originally conveyed would affect the content and organization of the mental representation the recipient formed from it. Moreover, the communicator's own goals were expected to influence the way he or she used this representation to communicate the implications of the information to a naive recipient and, therefore, the impact of the information on the recipient's beliefs.

This was investigated in two studies. In Experiment 1, subjects read a communication about a little-known disease that was ostensibly taken from either a newspaper (a source whose primary objective was to be interesting) or an encyclopedia (a source whose primary objective was to be accurate). They received the information with the expectation that they would later have to communicate it from memory in a way that was either as interesting as possible or as accurate as possible. Instead of doing so, however, they were asked to recall the information that they had read.

Analyses of subjects' recall protocols indicated that the purpose for which the original information was generated and subjects' own communication goals had similar effects. Specifically, subjects recalled fewer items of information, but intruded more unmentioned material into their recall protocol, when the passage had ostensibly come from a newspaper than when it had come from an encyclopedia. Analogously, subjects who expected to have to be interesting also recalled less information, and distorted the implications of what they did recall to a greater extent than subjects who anticipated having to be accurate. These parallel effects could reflect a common assumption that people make about the context and structure of a communication that is supposed to be interesting. That is, people might believe that such a communication should be relatively undetailed, but should contain expressions of opinion and statements with extreme implications. These expectations could influence not only the attention that subjects pay to aspects of information they believe is supposed to be interesting, but also the type of information they convey to others when their own goal is to stimulate interest.

Experiment 2 was similar to the first study except that communicators actually transmitted messages to naive recipients. The recipients were simply told to listen to the communication without being given information about either its source or the communicators' objective. After hearing the communication, recipients reported their opinions concerning the general importance of the issue conveyed in the message (e.g., the severity of the disease and the need for treatment), as well as their beliefs in specific factual details that were mentioned in the original passage. Recipients' reactions were influenced primarily by the consistency of the communicators' objective in transmitting the information with the purpose for which the information had originally been conveyed (as implied by its source). Specifically, communicators' messages had less impact when their goals were inconsistent with that of the original information source (i.e., when they tried to convey information from a newspaper accurately or to convey interesting from an encyclopedia in a way that was interesting) than when their goals were consistent with that of the source. Content analyses of communicators' messages revealed that this was due primarily to the way the communicators delivered their speeches, rather than to the content of these speeches per se. That is, speeches by communicators whose goals were consistent with that of the original information source were characterized by poorer speech style (i.e., more "mms" and "ers," a greater number of pauses, etc.) than those by communicators whose goals were consistent with the original source. Apparently, subjects who perceived their objective to differ from those of the information source believed they should modify the manner in which the information was conveyed, but they were not sure how to do it. This uncertainty was conveyed in their speech style, thus making their communication less effective.

Interestingly, despite the effects of the source and communication objectives on communicators' representation of the information content and also on the impact of the communication on recipients' beliefs, communicators' own beliefs were not influenced by either of these factors. Apparently, communicators formed their own beliefs and opinions on line, as they read the original message, and these reactions were not reflected in either the representation of the information that they stored in memory or the content of the communication that they delivered subsequently. This does not mean that communicators' beliefs were not conveyed to recipients through their messages. In many instances, the two sets of beliefs were positively correlated. However, these effects were independent of the speakers' communication objectives.

Although this research is quite preliminary, it makes salient a number of considerations that were not addressed earlier in this chapter. In particular, it focuses attention on the goals of the communicator of a message, as well as the communicator's perception of the source of the information that he or she wishes to transmit. Moreover, it points out the need to understand the effects of *how* a communication is transmitted on its interpretation and impact. Finally, it focuses attention on the cognitive processes that underlie the transmission of information by the communicator, as well as those that underlie the recipient's interpretation of the information. These factors warrant attention in future research.

CONCLUDING REMARKS

We have attempted to (a) identify several phases of information processing that underlie interpersonal communication, and (b) to describe briefly (and at times superficially) the cognitive activities that occur at each stage. An obvious and important additional consideration is the way in which the various stages of processing interface, and how they operate to influence the perception of communications and responses to them. For one thing, many situational and individual difference factors may influence processing at more than one stage, and the nature of their influence on responses that are ultimately generated may often depend on which stage is involved. For another, certain stages of processing may not always come into play. For example, the activation and use of a "production" could occur at any stage of processing, and could lead to the generation of a message without being mediated by other stages of processing.

A general conceptualization of social-information processing that attempts to specify the interaction of different cognitive processes and the influence of memory on these processes has been proposed by Wyer and Srull (1989). Although an explication of this formulation and application to the issues of concern in this volume is beyond the scope of our present discussion, a simplified flow diagram that captures many of the processes we outlined in this chapter and their interrelations is provided in Fig. 1.4. In this diagram, an executive unit is postulated that directs the transmission of stimulus input and previously acquired knowledge to and from various, more specific "processing units."

Each of these latter units corresponds to a different cognitive function (e.g., encoding, organizing, etc.). The directed pathways that connect various components of the diagram indicate the directions through which information can flow through the system. Thus, the executive unit typically controls the transfer of the output of one processing unit to a second, and governs the transfer of previously acquired knowledge and newly encoded and organized information to and from permanent memory. However, the output of several stages of processing can have a direct influence on the generation of an overt response through the use of a production rule, rather than being mediated by executive-monitored activities.

Figure 1.4 does not constitute a complete model of information processing either in the domain of interpersonal communication or more generally. However, it summarizes many of the considerations we have raised in this chapter, and conveys the scope and complexity of the conceptualization that must ultimately be developed. An enormous amount of work at both the theoretical and empirical levels is necessary to fill all of the gaps in our knowledge, which is necessary to develop a viable conceptualization of communication phenomena and the cognitive processes that mediate them. The remaining chapters in this volume are valuable starts toward the attainment of this goal. As becomes clear, the issues addressed in these chapters, and empirical work bearing on them, can be conceptualized as bearing on one or more of the processes we have outlined

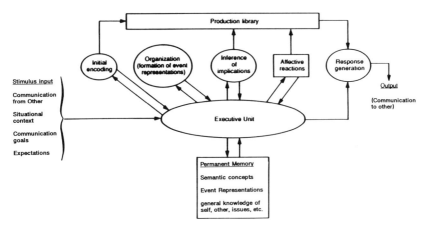

FIG. 1.4. Incomplete flow diagram of information processing hypothesized to mediate the effects of a communication from another on an
overt response to the other. Arrows denote pathways through which
information flows between memory and processing units and from
one processing unit to the other. Circles and ovals denote processing
units, and squares and rectangles denote memory or temporary storage units.

here. As work progresses, a viable conceptualization of information processing
in interpersonal communication may become a reality.

ACKNOWLEDGMENTS

The writing of this chapter and much of the research described was supported by
grant MH 3-8585 from the National Institute of Mental Health. Many of the ideas
conveyed, and the empirical work bearing on them, were developed in collabora-
tion with Robert Fuhrman, Lee Budesheim, and Alan Lambert. Appreciation is
extended to the University of Illinois Social Cognition Group for stimulation and
criticisms of many of the ideas expressed.

REFERENCES

Abelson, R. P. (1976). Script processing in attitude formation and decision-making. In J. S. Carroll &
    J. W. Payne (Eds.), *Cognition and social behavior.* Hillsdale, NJ: Lawrence Erlbaum Associates.
Abelson, R. P. (1981). The psychological status of the script concept. *American Psychologist, 36,*
    715–729.
Allen, R. B., & Ebbesen, E. B. (1981). Cognitive processes in person perception: Retrieval of
    personality trait and behavioral information. *Journal of Experimental Social Psychology, 17,*
    119–141.

Altman, I. (1989). The reemergence of small group research. *Contemporary Psychology, 34,* 253–254.

Anderson, J. R. (1983). *The architecture of cognition.* Cambridge, MA: Harvard University Press.

Anderson, N. H. (1981). *Foundations of information integration theory.* New York: Academic Press.

Bargh, J. A. (1984). Automatic and conscious processing of social information. In R. S. Wyer & T. K. Srull (Eds.), *Handbook of social cognition* (Vol. 3, pp. 1–43). Hillsdale, NJ: Lawrence Erlbaum Associates.

Bargh, J. A. (1994). The four horsemen of automaticity: Awareness intention, efficiency, and control in social cognition. In R. S. Wyer & T. K. Srull (Eds.), *Handbook of social cognition* (2nd ed., vol. 1, pp. 1–40). Hillsdale, NJ: Lawrence Erlbaum Associates.

Bargh, J. A., Bond, R. N., Lombardi, W., & Tota, M. E. (1986). The additive nature of chronic and temporary sources of construct accessibility. *Journal of Personality and Social Psychology, 50,* 869–878.

Bargh, J. A., & Pietromonaco, P. (1982). Automatic information processing and social perception: The influence of trait information presented outside of conscious awareness on impression formation. *Journal of Personality and Social Psychology, 43,* 437–449.

Berger, C. R. (1987). Communication under uncertainty. In M. E. Roloff & G. R. Miller (Eds.), *Interpersonal processes* (pp. 39–62). Newbury Park, CA: Sage.

Berger, C. R., & Bredac, J. J. (1982). *Language and social knowledge.* London: Edward Arnold.

Berkowitz, L., & Lepage, A. (1967). Weapons as aggression-eliciting stimuli. *Journal of Personality and Social Psychology, 7,* 202–207.

Blumberg, H. H., Hare, P., Kent, V., & Davies, M. (Eds.). (1983). *Small groups and social interaction* (Vol. 1). New York: Wiley.

Bower, G. H., Black, J. B., & Turner, T. J. (1979). Scripts in memory for test. *Cognitive Psychology, 11,* 117–220.

Bruner, J. S. (1957). On perceptual readiness. *Psychological Review, 64,* 123–152.

Carlston, D. E. (1980). Events, inferences and impression formation. In R. Hastie, T. Ostrom, E. Ebbesen, R. Wyer, D. Hamilton, & D. Carlston (Eds.), *Person memory: The cognitive basis of social perception* (pp. 89–120). Hillsdale, NJ: Lawrence Erlbaum Associates.

Carver, C. S., Ganellen, R. J., Froming, W. J., & Chambers, W. (1983). Modelling: An analysis in terms of category accessibility. *Journal of Experimental Social Psychology, 16,* 779–804.

Clark, H. (1985). Language use and languages users. In G. Lindzey & E. Aronson (Eds.), *Handbook of social psychology* (3rd ed., Vol. 2, pp. 179–232). Reading, MA: Addison-Wesley.

Cohen, C. E., & Ebbesen, E. B. (1979). Observational goals and schema activation: A theoretical framework for behavior perception. *Journal of Experimental Social Psychology, 15,* 305–339.

Dance, F. E. X., & Larson, C. E. (1976). *The functions of human communication.* New York: Holt, Rinehart & Winston.

Demorest, A. P., & Alexander, I. E. (1992). Affective scripts as organizers of personal experience. *Journal of Personality, 60,* 646–661.

Fuhrman, R. W., & Wyer, R. S. (1988). Event memory: temporal-order judgments of personal life experiences. *Journal of Personality and Social Psychology, 54,* 365–384.

Gaelick, L., Bodenhausen, G. V., & Wyer, R. S. (1985). Emotional communication in close relationships. *Journal of Personality and Social Psychology, 49,* 1246–1265.

Gouran, D. S. (1986). Inferential errors, interaction, and group decision making. In R. Y. Hirokawa & M. S. Pool (Eds.), *Communication and group decision making* (pp. 93–112). Newbury Park, CA: Sage.

Graesser, A. C. (1981). *Prose comprehension beyond the word.* New York: Springer-Verlag.

Green, G. M. (1989). *Pragmatics and natural language understanding.* Hillsdale, NJ: Lawrence Erlbaum Associates.

Grice, H. (1975). Logic and conversation. In P. Cold & J. Morgan (Eds.), *Syntax and semantics: Vol. 3. Speech acts* (pp. 68–134). New York: Academic Press.

Gruenfeld, D. H., & Wyer, R. S. (1992). The semantics and pragmatics of social influence: How affirmations and denials affect beliefs in referent propositions. *Journal of Personality and Social Psychology, 62,* 38–49.

Gruenfeld, D. H. & Wyer, R. S. (1993). *Media effects in social communication: The influence of information source and communication objectives on memory, communication content, and recipients' beliefs.* Unpublished manuscript, University of Illinois, Champaign, IL.

Hastie, R., Penrod, S., & Pennington, N. (1983). *Inside the jury.* Cambridge, MA: Harvard University Press.

Hewes, D. (1986). A socio-ego-centric model of group decision-making. In R. Y. Hirokawa & M. S. Poole, (Eds.), *Communication and group decision making* (pp. 265–291). Beverly Hills, CA: Sage.

Higgins, E. T. (1981). The "communication game": Implications for social cognition and persuasion. In E. T. Higgins, C. P. Herman, & M. P. Zanna (Eds.), *Social cognition: The Ontario Symposium* (Vol. 1, pp. 343–392). Hillsdale, NJ: Lawrence Erlbaum Associates.

Higgins, E. T., Bargh, J. A., & Lombardi, W. (1985). The nature of priming effects on categorization. *Journal of Experimental Psychology: Learning, Memory and Cognition, 11,* 59–69.

Higgins, E. T., Herman, P. C., & Zanna, M. P. (Eds.) (1981). *Social cognition: The Ontario Symposium* (Vol. 1). Hillsdale, NJ: Lawrence Erlbaum Association.

Higgins, E. T., & King, G. (1981). Accessibility of social constructs: Information processing consequences of individual and contextual variability. In N. Cantor & J. F. Kihlstrom (Eds.), *Personality, cognition and social interaction.* Hillsdale, NJ: Lawrence Erlbaum Associates.

Higgins, E. T., Rholes, W. S. (1987). "Saying is believing": Effects of message modification on memory and liking for the person described. *Journal of Experimental Social Psychology, 14,* 363–378.

Higgins, E. T., Rholes, W. S., & Jones, C. R. (1977). Category accessibility and impression formation. *Journal of Experimental Social Psychology, 13,* 141–154.

Klinger, E. (1975). Consequences of commitment to and disengagement from incentives. *Psychological Review, 82,* 1–25.

Langer, E. J. (1978). Rethinking the role of thought in social interaction. In J. Harvey, W. Ickes, & R. Kidd (Eds.) *New directions in attribution research* (Vol. 2). Hillsdale, NJ: Lawrence Erlbaum Associates.

Langer, E. J., & Abelson, R. P. (1972). The semantics of asking a favor: How to succeed in getting help without really dying. *Journal of Personality and Social Psychology, 24,* 26–32.

Lombardi, W. J., Higgins, E. T., & Bargh, J. A. (1987). The role of consciousness in priming effects on categorization. *Personality and Social Psychology Bulletin, 13,* 411–429.

Martin, L. L. (1986). Set/reset: The use and disuse of concepts in impression formation. *Journal of Personality and Social Psychology, 51,* 493–504.

Martin, L. L., Seta, J. J., & Crelia, R. A. (1990). Assimilation and contrast as a function of people's willingness and ability to expend effort in forming an impression. *Journal of Personality and Social Psychology, 59,* 27–37.

Massad, C. M., Hubbard, M., & Newtson, D. (1979). Perceptual selectivity: Contributing process and possible cure for impression perseverance. *Journal of Experimental Social Psychology, 15,* 513–532.

McAdams, D. P. (1993). *The stories we live by: Personal myths and the making of the self.* New York: Morrow.

McGrath, J. E. (1984). *Groups: Interaction and performance.* Englewood Cliffs, NJ: Prentice-Hall.

Newtson, D. A. (1976). Foundations of attribution: The perception of ongoing behavior. In J. Harvey, W. Ickes, & R. Kidd (Eds.), *New directions in attribution research* (Vol. 1, pp. 223–247). Hillsdale, NJ: Lawrence Erlbaum Associates.

Roloff, M. E., & Berger, C. R. (Eds.). (1982). *Social cognition and communication.* Beverly Hills, CA: Sage.

Ross, M. (1989). Relation of implicit theories to the construction of personal histories. *Psychological Review, 96,* 341–357.

Schank, R. C. (1990). *Tell me a story.* New York: Charles Scribner's & Sons.

Schank, R. C., & Abelson, R. P. (1977). *Scripts, plans, goals and understanding.* Hillsdale, NJ: Lawrence Erlbaum Associates.

Sherman, S. J., & Corty, E. (1984). Cognitive heuristics. In R. S. Wyer & T. K. Srull (Eds.), *Handbook of social cognition* (Vol. 1.). Hillsdale, NJ: Lawrence Erlbaum Associates.

Smith, E. R. (1984). Models of social inference processes. *Psychological Review, 91,* 392–413.

Smith, R. R. (1990). Content and process specificity in the effects of prior experiences. In T. K. Srull & R. S. Wyer (Eds.), *Advances in social cognition* (Vol. 3). Hillsdale, NJ: Lawrence Erlbaum Associates.

Snyder, M., Tanke, E. D., & Berscheid, E. (1977). Social perception and interpersonal behavior: On the self-fulfilling nature of social stereotypes. *Journal of Personality and Social Psychology, 35,* 656–666.

Sorrentino, R., & Higgins, E. T. (Eds.). (1986). *Handbook of motivation and cognition.* New York: Guilford.

Sperber, D., & Wilson, D. (1986). *Relevance: Communication and cognition.* Oxford: Basil Blackwell.

Spiro, R. J. (1977). Remembering information from text: The "state of schema" approach. In R. C. Anderson, R. J. Spiro, & W. E. Montague (Eds.), *Schooling and the acquisition of knowledge.* Hillsdale, NJ: Lawrence Erlbaum Associates.

Srull, T. K., & Wyer, R. S. (1979). The role of category accessibility in the interpretation of information about persons: Some determinants and implications. *Journal of Personality and Social Psychology, 37,* 1660–1672.

Srull, T. K., & Wyer, R. S. (1980). Category accessibility and social perception: Some implications for the study of person memory and interpersonal judgment. *Journal of Personality and Social Psychology, 38,* 841–856.

Srull, T. K., & Wyer, R. S. (1986). The role of chronic and temporary goals in social information processing. In R. M. Sorrentino & E. T. Higgins (Eds.), *Handbook of motivation and cognition.* New York: Guilford.

Srull, T. K., & Wyer, R. S. (1989). Person memory and judgment. *Psychological Review, 96,* 58–83.

Trafimow, D., & Wyer, R. S. (1993). Cognitive representation of mundane social events. *Journal of Personality and Social Psychology, 64,* 365–376.

Watzlawick, P., Beavin, J. H., & Jackson, D. D. (1967). *Pragmatics of human communication.* New York: Norton.

Wyer, R. S., & Bodenhausen, G. V. (1985). Event memory: The effects of processing objectives and time delay on memory for action sequences. *Journal of Personality and Social Psychology, 49,* 304–316.

Wyer, R. S., Budesheim, T. L., & Lambert, A J. (1990). The cognitive representation of conversations about persons. *Journal of Personality and Social Psychology, 58,* 218–238.

Wyer, R. S., Budesheim, T. L., Lambert, A. J., & Swan, S. (1993). *Person memory and judgment: Pragmatic influences on impressions formed in a social context.* Unpublished manuscript, University of Illinois, Champaign, IL.

Wyer, R. S., & Carlston, D. E. (1994). The cognitive representation of persons and events. In R. S. Wyer & T. K. Srull (Eds.), *Handbook of social cognition* (2nd ed., vol. 1, pp. 41–98). Hillsdale, NJ: Lawrence Erlbaum Associates.

Wyer, R. S., & Collins, J. E. (1992). A theory of humor elicitation. *Psychological Review, 99,* 663–688.

Wyer, R. S., & Martin, L. L. (1986). Person memory: The role of traits, group stereotypes and specific behaviors in the cognitive representation of persons. *Journal of Personality and Social Psychology, 50,* 661–675.

Wyer, R. S., Shoben, E. J., Fuhrman, R. W., & Bodenhausen, G. V. (1985). Event memory: the cognitive representation of social action sequences. *Journal of Personality and Social Psychology, 49,* 857–877.

Wyer, R. S., & Srull, T. K. (1984). *The handbook of social cognition.* Hillsdale, NJ: Lawrence Erlbaum Associates.

Wyer, R. S., & Srull, T. K. (1986). Human cognition in its social context. *Psychological Review, 93,* 322–359.

Wyer, R. S., & Srull, T. K. (1989). *Memory and cognition in its social context.* Hillsdale, NJ: Lawrence Erlbaum Associates.

II

THE COGNITIVE PSYCHOLOGICAL PERSPECTIVE INSIDE INTERPERSONAL COMMUNICATION THEORY

2

An Action-Assembly Perspective on Verbal and Nonverbal Message Production: A Dancer's Message Unveiled

John O. Greene
Purdue University

> Sometimes I smile and act like I'm in a good mood even if things don't feel right. 'Cause . . . I'm . . . some of the girls . . . that's what I get complimented the most, besides what I look like, is my attitude, because I try never to be crappy towards a man. Sometimes they have money and sometimes they don't, and its my, my job is to party. You know, to act like I'm having a good time, even if I'm not. Most of the time its genuine; most of the time I don't mind. But its like with any other job, sometimes you just prefer not to be there.
> —"Sully," 28-year-old bar dancer and narcotics addict

If called on to analyze or describe the previous message, the readers of this volume would doubtless produce widely divergent reports. We commonly recognize that communicative behavior lends itself to multiple, only partially overlapping conceptual schemes, each of which serves to illuminate a portion of the properties of a given message (and then only to the satisfaction of some). Hence, each conceptual scheme provides a perspective that emphasizes some details while leaving us blind to others. My aim here is to capitalize on this fact in explicating action-assembly theory by describing the way this passage "looks" from that vantage point. Such a treatment involves two interrelated issues: (a) How are we to conceive of social action (i.e., what are its essential properties as seen from this perspective)? and (b) How is social action so constituted to be explained?

In pursuit of these issues, the action-assembly perspective has developed along three distinct, but mutually coherent lines of inquiry. It is these three levels of analysis that I wish to examine here. The first of these focuses on meta-theoretical concerns, the second on theoretical specification of the behavioral output system, and the last on empirical investigations of message production. Each of these hierarchical levels serves to highlight certain facets of social action in general, and the sample message in particular, that are central to the action-assembly perspective.

METATHEORETICAL FOUNDATIONS: GENERATIVE REALISM

The focus of action-assembly theory is the production of *human action,* where that term is given a broad interpretation and taken to encompass the range of verbal and nonverbal, planful and automatic, abstract and concrete behavioral features produced by individual actors.[1] Thus, this conception of *action* incorporates both components of the familiar "action-movement" distinction (Harré & Secord, 1973; Stigen, 1970). Although not restricted to the realm of communicative behaviors, it includes activities such as self-disclosure, compliance-gaining message production, deception, facial expressions of emotion, and so on. Explicitly not included in the domain of human action is the activity of collectives (e.g., riots), as contrasted with the behaviors of individuals (e.g., throwing rocks; see Greene, 1990a). Further, human action is usefully distinguished from elements of social structure such as regulative rules, language, and so forth, which are seen to be the relatively enduring products and media of human action.

The metatheoretical foundation of the action-assembly approach to the various problems of human action is that of *generative realism* (Greene, 1990a). This philosophical stance incorporates a realist conception of scientific explanation (see Bhaskar, 1978; Manicas & Secord, 1983), in that human action is seen to be the result of the complex interplay of numerous causal mechanisms; explanation is held to be given by specifying the nature of the causal structures and processes that give rise to the phenomena of interest.

Beyond this commitment to a realist stance, the primary thrust of generative realism centers around the claim that human action is the product of an integrated system composed of social, physiological, and psychological components. To be more precise, these three elements are held to play a mutually causally interactive role in the production of behavior. The point, then, is not simply that social scientists should acknowledge the role of social, physiological, and psychological factors in producing human action, or that views that emphasize one element of this tripartite system to the exclusion of the others are incomplete. Instead, the issue is how to conceive of these factors and of the nature of the causal mechanisms governing their functional interaction in behavioral production.

---

[1]The focus of action-assembly theory does not extend to input processes such as pattern recognition, language comprehension, attribution, inference making, and the like, although they are held to be inextricably linked to behavioral production.

There is a striking parallel between this position and the development of person-by-situation interactionism (see Ekehammar, 1974; Magnusson & Endler, 1977; Pervin, 1978). In the case of interactionism, there was merit in acknowledging that both person and situation factors were necessary for explaining behavior and in recognizing the limitations of approaches that focus on only one of these components. However, the true value of interactionism lies in specifying the nature of person and situation factors and the processes of their interaction (see Endler, 1983; Greene, 1989; Mischel, 1983; Mischel & Peake, 1982). In much the same way, generative realism poses the task of specifying the nature of social, physiological, and psychological factors relevant to human action and the causal mechanisms that govern their interaction.

Generative Realism as an Alternative to Prevailing Metatheoretical Perspectives

The claims of generative realism concerning the nature of the terms appropriate for theories of human action are markedly divergent from those reflected in various other metatheoretical stances. Therefore, it is instructive to consider some of the points of contrast with prevailing approaches that are represented by generative realism. Particularly relevant in this context are generative realism's approach to the locus of explanation problem and the problem of explanatory stance.

The Locus of Explanation Problem.   A key implication of identifying human action as the focus of inquiry is to locate the relevant explanatory mechanisms squarely within the individual social actor. There is simply no source of the behavioral specifications that constitute human action other than the output system of the individual. Extraindividual factors (e.g., social prescriptions for behavior) impact upon a person's actions only when they are represented in some way within that individual (Greene, 1984a). This is not to suggest that social factors are not important. However, with respect to the production of human action, the issue becomes one of how social factors are possessed and used by the individual.

Although the identification of the individual as the locus of explanatory mechanisms follows rather directly from a focus on human action, there is a significant tradition of argument against such a view (see Gergen, 1985; Harré, 1981; Lannamann, 1991; Sampson, 1981; 1983). The thrust of these arguments is to reject the individual as the locus of generative mechanisms in favor of an emphasis on social structures and routines. From the perspective of generative realism, there is value in emphasizing the role of the social in human action, but acceptance of the interpenetration of the individual and society in no way necessitates rejection of the individual as the locus of explanatory mechanisms for human action. Further, approaches that focus solely on the social are fundamentally incomplete as accounts of human action, and, as a result, are rendered rather impoverished tools for predicting and explaining the complex fabric of behavior. Thus, in contrast to such socially based approaches, generative realism attempts to accord a place for social factors and, more importantly, to focus on the intraindividual causal mechanisms by which social factors interact with psychological and physiological factors in the production of action.

The Problem of Explanatory Stance.   Identifying the individual as the locus of causal mechanisms for human action is an important conceptual move, but there remains the question of what sort of terms are appropriate for characterizing these intraindividual mechanisms. On this point, generative realism stands in contrast to approaches that seek to eliminate the social and psychological by recourse to physiological reduction (see Churchland, 1984). Although it seems reasonable to assume that there must be some physiological instantiation for all the social and psychological factors that play a role in behavior, one can accept this premise of fundamental materialism without accepting the desirability of eliminative materialism or physiological reduction. It is commonly observed that the autonomy of higher level (i.e., nonreduced) constructs is preserved because the terms of physiological theories may not be particularly useful in the explanation and/or prediction of various features of human action (e.g., Bhaskar, 1978; Fodor, 1975; Putnam, 1973). In essence, physiological mechanisms may be too far removed from many of the phenomena characteristic of human action to be of much use in illuminating those phenomena. As a result, although there are clearly aspects of human behavior that are profitably approached from a physiological stance that excludes social and psychological constructs, generative realism, owing to its focus on the broad fabric of human action, seeks to accord a place for social and psychological terms as well.

If we accept the need for nonreduced terms in theories of human action, the problem remains of what sort of characterizations of intraindividual factors are appropriate for addressing the problems of human action. Among communication scholars, the most prominent approach to this problem has been to pursue accounts of intentional stance (Dennett, 1971), where explanation is given by recourse to the actor's goals (intentions, desires) and knowledge (beliefs, abilities; e.g., Fishbein & Ajzen, 1975; Harré & Secord, 1973). Although the intentional stance has advanced the conception of people as active agents, it, too, is limited as an approach to theorizing about human action. The frequency of performance failures in behavioral production makes clear that people may possess requisite knowledge and/or ability and be sufficiently motivated, and yet still fail to perform adequately (see Greene & Geddes, 1993).

This fact has far-reaching implications for the intentional stance as an approach to human action. Dennett (1971) showed that, as an approach to explanation and prediction, the intentional stance is predicated on an assumption of rationality and optimal design. That is, a theoretical account based on goals and relevant knowledge will yield accurate predictions only when the system in question behaves in accordance with its goals and the information at its disposal. Thus, the various performance failures characteristic of human action give testimony to the imperfect rationality of the social actor and, by extension, to the limitations of the intentional stance as an approach to explanation and prediction of behavior.

A new twist on the problem of explanatory stance is thus suggested: If intentional accounts of human action are not wholly adequate, what sort of characterization of intraindividual constructs is needed? Dennett argued that, when systems are characterized by imperfect rationality, it becomes necessary to pursue functional accounts of those systems' behavior (i.e., explanations that involve specification of the functional architecture of the system in question). Such functional specifications afford the potential for explaining the failure of the system to perform in an optimal fashion. From the functional perspective, theoretical constructs (e.g., mental structures and processes) are inferred from observed input–output regularities and are distinct from neurophysiological structures and processes in the sense that they are elements of noncorporeal "mind" rather than brain.

With respect to the problem of explanatory stance, then, generative realism accords a place for nonreduced, intraindividual terms. Although recognizing the value of intentional-stance constructs (i.e., goals, intentions, beliefs, etc.), generative realism opts for a hybrid approach that incorporates functional terms as well. In taking such a position on the problem of explanatory stance, generative realism is generally in keeping with the mainstream of cognitive science (see Churchland, 1984; Flanagan, 1984; Gardner, 1987). However, there are points on which generative realism diverges from cognitivism or, more accurately, from the metatheoretical foundations of cognitivism specified in computational functionalism (see Fodor, 1975; Pylyshyn, 1984). As Gardner (1987) noted, cognitivism deemphasizes the social and physiological, and instead pursues "a level of analysis wholly separate from the biological or neurological, on one hand, and the sociological or cultural, on the other" (p. 6). Hence, generative realism represents a departure from cognitivism on both of these points.

As noted earlier, the essence of the functional approaches reflected in cognitivism is to pursue explanation by positing mental structures and processes responsible for input–output regularities. In contrast to such an approach, generative realism holds that there are aspects of the action-production system that are more appropriately viewed in physiological, rather than functional, terms.[2] Thus, from the perspective of generative realism, there is a need to avoid physiological reduction and to maintain the autonomy of functional accounts. How-

---

[2]The position reflected in generative realism is not that it is impossible to model physiological factors in terms of representational and computational properties, but rather that there may be more useful and appropriate ways of characterizing such factors.

ever, at the same time, it is necessary to preserve a place for physiological terms as well (see Churchland, 1981, 1984; Rey, 1980; Searle, 1980, 1984). In short, neither a strictly materialist nor a strictly functional approach is seen as adequate to address the problems of human action. With respect to social terms, generative realism's departure from the mainstream of cognitive science is primarily one of emphasis. That is, rather than eschew the social in favor of other foci, generative realism emphasizes the role of the social in the production of human action.

Summary

As a metatheoretical perspective, generative realism focuses on the sort of terms appropriate for theories of human action. According to generative realism, human action is most appropriately viewed as the result of a tripartite system of physiological, psychological, and social influences. For this reason, the essential theoretical task is seen to be one of developing accounts that accord a place for all three components of the tripartite system, and that specify the causal mechanisms that govern the mutual interaction of these components in the production of behavior.

In its emphasis on the role of the tripartite system and in its treatment of the locus of explanation problem and the problem of explanatory stance, generative realism stands in marked contrast to other current metatheoretical approaches to human action. For example, in contrast to social-constructionist and historically situated approaches, which attempt to locate the mechanisms of human action in social structures and practices, generative realism locates the mechanisms that give rise to action within the individual. Although generative realism acknowledges the essential interpenetration of the individual and social structure, it places emphasis on explicating *how* elements of social structure play a role in the behavior of the individual. At the other extreme, generative realism stands in contrast to reductive and materialist approaches, which attempt to eliminate the social and psychological by recourse to physiological reduction. Moreover, although recognizing the need for theoretical constructs relevant to the actor's goals and beliefs, generative realism departs from the intentional stance by arguing for functional mechanisms as well. Finally, generative realism is contrasted with the sort of functional approach on which mainstream cognitive science rests; it accords a role for physiological terms and gives emphasis to the role of social factors in the production of action.

Message Behavior From the Perspective of Generative Realism

At the outset of this chapter, I posed two questions that might be used to guide explication of the action-assembly perspective. The first of these focused on how we are to conceive of human action, and the second focused on how action so constituted is to be explained. To summarize, I now consider the approach taken toward these issues in generative realism—the metatheoretical level of the action-assembly perspective. With respect to the first of these questions, human action is held to be the result of the causal interaction of social, physiological, and psychological factors. Thus, Sully's message given at the beginning of this chapter is not seen as the product of a social being, a physiological being, or a psychological being, but instead is held to be the result of a tripartite system reflecting all of these elements. On the second question, explanation of message behavior is held to be given by specifying the structures and mechanisms that give rise to such actions.

ACTION-ASSEMBLY THEORY

Distinct from the metatheoretical claims that constitute generative realism is a second level of inquiry; this focuses on theoretical specification of the mechanisms that compose the output system (Greene, 1984b, 1989). As currently stated, action-assembly theory could hardly be said to realize the ultimate goals of generative realism in the sense that it fully specifies the nature of physiological, social, and psychological factors and the mechanisms by which they interact in behavioral production.[3] However, the terms of the theory are generally consistent with the prescriptions of generative realism, and the theory does suggest one approach for incorporating each of the elements of the tripartite system in a coherent framework.

As was noted previously, it does not take us very far simply to note that social, physiological, and psychological factors play a role in the production of behavior. The task set in generative realism is to move beyond this observation toward specification of the generative mechanisms of action (with the additional requirement that those mechanisms be capable of accommodating social, physiological, and psychological factors and their interactions). Action-assembly theory is an attempt to do this by specifying the mental structures and processes underlying the production of behavior.

The specific form and content of action-assembly theory grew out of a set of observations concerning the nature of human action (Greene, 1983). The first of these is that behavior is at once novel and creative, yet patterned and repetitive (see Bregman, 1977; Greene, 1984b, 1989). Clearly this is true with respect to verbal messages, where any utterance is almost certain to be novel, and yet also to reflect an established repertoire of words, syntactic frames, phrases, themes, and so on. More generally, however, it appears that even the simplest and most repetitive actions are characterized by variation in movement parameters from

---

[3]The treatment given here focuses on first-generation action-assembly theory (Greene, 1984b, 1989) and incorporates only relatively minor conceptual extensions of the original version.

trial to trial (see Marteniuk & Romanow, 1983). From a theoretical perspective, the concurrent creative and repetitive aspects of human action raise the questions of (a) how such repetitive features of action are to be conceptualized and (b) the nature of the processes capable of giving rise to creative action (see Greene & Cody, 1985).

A second observation involves the relation of thought and action. Human action requires the coordination of a large number of degrees of freedom related to efferent control (see Reed, 1982; Saltzman & Kelso, 1983, 1987; Stelmach & Diggles, 1982). However, despite the requirements for specification of efferent commands, our phenomenal experience of human action is considerably more abstract than this (see Greene, 1990b; Greene & Cody, 1985). That is, our conception of our behavior consists of rather abstractly specified acts such as "speaking," "driving," "throwing," and so forth (see Vallacher & Wegner, 1987). It seems clear that these abstract conceptions must permit control of our behavior, but at the same time they do not fully specify our actions. This observation raises questions concerning the nature of the system by which such higher level control is effected and the relation between our phenomenal experience of action and the lower level activity by which that action is executed.

A third point concerns the relation of input processing and behavioral production. There may be no more common observation in the social sciences than that people act on the basis of the meanings they attach to the behavior of others, situations, and other stimulus inputs (e.g., Ekehammar, 1974; Harré & Secord, 1973; Lewin, 1936; Mischel, 1973; Pervin, 1978). This fact raises the question of how it is possible for interpretations to influence behavior, and suggests the theoretical task of specifying the processes linking meanings to action.

Finally, a fourth observation is that, although our behavior is often deliberate and planful, in other cases it is possible to act automatically, with little demand on processing resources (Schneider & Shiffrin, 1977; Shiffrin & Schneider, 1977, 1984). Further, even in those cases where certain features of action are deliberately controlled, other features may proceed quite automatically (see Bock, 1982; Greene, O'Hair, Cody, & Yen, 1985; Reason, 1979). Thus, although a person may carefully plan and monitor his or her verbal production, various nonverbal behaviors (e.g., gestures, facial expression) accompanying those utterances may be executed automatically. These automatic features of behavior are commonly held to emerge through repeated performance (see Logan, 1979; Shiffrin & Schneider, 1977). Again, these points suggest the theoretical tasks of (a) explaining how it is possible to produce behavior automatically and (b) specifying the nature of the mechanisms underlying automatic and controlled actions. Further, any such account would presumably include an explication of the link between repeated performance and the development of automaticity.

As noted, from the perspective of generative realism, the task of developing theories of human action involves describing the generative mechanisms that give rise to behavior. Therefore, the generative mechanisms of the output system would include those elements of the system that (a) preserve repetitive features of behavior, (b) govern the production of novel acts, (c) link abstract conceptions of behavior to motor responses, (d) permit meanings and interpretations to impact on behavior, and (e) underlie deliberate and automatic actions. In keeping with the mainstream of cognitive science (see Anderson, 1976; Greene, 1984a), action-assembly theory seeks to explicate the generative mechanisms of the output system by recourse to conceptions of: (a) representational structures and (b) the processes that operate over those structures. In simplest terms, the theory posits a long-term memory store of modular elements that each represents a feature or property of behavior, where behavior is conceived as a collocation of a large number of constituent features. These features are represented in various symbolic codes reflecting a number of abstraction levels. Behavioral production involves the selective retrieval and subsequent integration of some subset of these behavioral features to form a coherent output representation.

Representation

At the heart of action-assembly theory, there is a conception of a long-term memory system that preserves the information used in behavioral production (see Greene, 1989). Description of such a representational system involves consideration of two fundamental properties of that system. The first of these involves the code or symbol system in which the information is represented, and the second concerns the structural organization of that information. Thus, code and structure are distinct from symbolic content in that, taken together, they specify *how* information is represented, but not *what* specific information is held in the representational system.

With respect to issues of symbolic code, action-assembly theory holds that, rather than a single code, the information used in behavioral production is represented in a number of distinct codes. A portion of the information used in behavioral production consists of abstract specifications that roughly correspond to our phenomenal experience of behavioral control. At the same time, other long-term memory information is used to control (a) effector-unit configurations, (b) trajectories, and (c) velocities in order to implement abstractly defined acts. Thus, action-assembly theory suggests that there are a number of representational codes ranging from abstract propositional and lexical formats to low-level sensorimotor codes.[4]

Distinct from issues of symbolic code are issues of representational structure. The basic structural assumptions of action-assembly theory are common to a number of network models of memory representation (e.g., Anderson, 1983;

---

[4]The thrust of this claim is not that there are levels of abstraction within a single code system, but instead that there are distinct code systems that vary in levels of abstraction (see Greene, 1990a).

Collins & Loftus, 1975; McClelland & Rumelhart, 1985). Such network structures are typically held to be composed of nodes and associative links where each
node represents some symbolically coded feature. Associative relations develop
between nodes when the individual processes some causal or temporal relationship between those nodes (see Bradley & Glenberg, 1983; Fisk & Schneider,
1984; Kellogg, 1980; McClelland & Rumelhart, 1985; Raaijmakers & Shiffrin,
1981; Smith, 1979).

Building on these common conceptions of nodes and associative relations, the
"procedural record" is proposed as the basic unit of procedural memory. Each
procedural record is a modular entity composed of nodes and associative links
where the nodes of the record are of three basic types: (a) a symbolic representation of action, (b) a representation of an outcome associated with that action, and
(c) situational and intrasystemic features that have proven relevant to the action–
outcome relationship represented in the record. In essence, a procedural record
preserves an action–outcome–in situation relationship. More specifically, the
symbolic representation of action is held to reflect some property or feature of
behavior where the entire complex of action at any moment is seen to be a
collocation of many such features. Similarly, the outcome component is a symbolic representation of some result associated with that feature.

Consistent with the notion of multiple-code systems, the symbolic representation of features of actions, outcomes, and situations contained in procedural
records may reflect any of a variety of levels of abstraction. Thus, an action
feature may specify some efferent parameter, or it may be represented as some
abstract property of action such as "act friendly." In much the same way, features
of outcomes and situations are also held to be represented in multiple codes.
Thus, in some procedural records, situational features may correspond to the
configuration of a person's limbs, or to physiological factors such as arousal
level, whereas in others the situation node concerns the power and status of our
interlocutor.

In addition to level of abstraction, a second essential property of procedural
records is that the associative relations comprising each record are characterized
by a "strength" parameter, where strength is held to be a function of the recency
and frequency of activation of the link (see Anderson, 1983; Collins & Loftus,
1975; McClelland & Rumelhart, 1985). As a result, the strength of associative
relations tends to decay over time if the record is not used or if the relationships
between features of actions, outcomes, and situations represented in the record
do not continue to hold.

Because of the properties of the processes governing the development and
decay of associative links, there is a tendency for procedural records to be
structurally independent of other records. Although it certainly would be possible
to store procedural information in more complex structures (e.g., scripts), there
are many advantages to a modular representational system of the sort proposed in
action-assembly theory. As I have noted elsewhere (Greene, 1984b, 1989), a

modular system of elemental units permits the production of novel behaviors without the need to decompose complex structures into more fundamental units appropriate to the current situation (see also the discussion of the "novelty problem" in Schmidt, 1976). Further, a representational system involving complex action sequences would not be very parsimonious or economical (see Schmidt, 1976). Finally, Allport (1979) noted that a memory system composed of many modular units would facilitate acquisition of new procedures because no major restructuring would be required to incorporate the new information.

Having said this, it is important to note that the same processes that lead to structural independence of procedural records also permit retention of more complex combinations of behavioral features in long-term memory. In other words, associative links may develop between behavioral features in two different records. These "unitized assemblies" arise when a particular set of procedural records is repeatedly activated and combined (see the following discussion of the assembly process). Such unitized assemblies may then be retrieved and processed as a single unit.

In addition to procedural records and unitized assemblies, there is one other structure specified in action-assembly theory. The view advanced thus far is of a procedural memory system composed of a large number of modular units, each specifying some single feature of behavior where behavior is conceived as an integration of many constituent features. The final structure specified in action-assembly theory is the "output representation." This structure specifies (a) the behavioral features that comprise action, (b) their sequential order, and (c) timing. The behavioral features comprising this structure at any moment are organized hierarchically according to the level of abstraction of the symbolic code in which they are represented. Thus, upper levels of the output representation are composed of the most abstract specifications for action, and lower levels are constituted by increasingly concrete symbolic codes terminating at the level of efferent commands (see, also, Fowler & Turvey, 1978; Greene, 1982; MacKay, 1982, 1983; Marteniuk & MacKenzie, 1980; Rosenbaum, 1984; Saltzman, 1979).

Processes of the Output System

These conceptions of procedural records and the output representation suggest two distinct processes underlying behavioral production. First, there must exist some process by which appropriate procedural records are selected for use from long-term memory; second, once a particular set of procedural records has been selected, there must be some process by which the action specifications contained in those records are integrated to form the output representation.

Selection of procedural records involves the activation level of the record. That is, at any moment, each record is characterized by some level of activation, where activation is held to be a continuous quantity. As the level of activation of a record increases, so, too, does the probability that the action feature represented in the record will play a role in behavioral production. This activation process is held to occur in parallel such that a large number of procedural records may be activated at any particular time.

The activating conditions for any procedural record are defined by two types of occurrences, and the level of activation for each record is contingent on the degree to which these conditions are met. As a result, once a record has been activated and conditions change, the record will rapidly decay back toward resting levels. The first of these activating conditions is the occurrence of a goal or functional requirement that matches the outcome represented in the record. Without this fundamental property, procedural memory would be of little value because behaviors would have little relation to our current goals. Beyond this, the activating conditions for a procedural record include the occurrence of any situational or intrasystemic features that match those represented in the record. As a result, procedures tend to be activated when they are relevant to some goal, as well as when they are appropriate to features of the situation. Thus, the most highly activated records tend to be those whose outcome representation matches current goals and whose situational features match current situational conditions.

A final property of the activation process concerns the time course of increase in activation level once appropriate activating conditions occur. Speed of activation is held to be a function of the strength of the record. That is, records characterized by strong associative links due to recent and/or frequent activation are more quickly retrieved than records activated less often. As a result, practice with stimulus–response associations leads to faster reaction times for a variety of tasks (see Anderson, 1984; Kahneman, 1973; Keele, 1973; Klein, 1976; Logan, 1979).

The nature of the activation process is such that a number of procedural records relevant to a variety of goals and functional requirements, and reflecting several levels of abstraction in their symbolic specifications of action features, are activated at any particular moment. For example, in pursuit of some compliance-gaining goal, an individual may also need to (a) formulate the ideational content of his or her message, (b) regulate turn taking, (c) specify lexical items and syntactic order, (d) maintain physiological homeostasis, and so on. For this reason, we should expect that procedural records relevant to many ends and goals will be brought into play. The role of the assembly process is to integrate activated behavioral features to form a coherent output representation. The assembly process proceeds by incorporating into each hierarchical level of the output representation those action specifications appropriate to that level of abstraction. In contrast to the activation process that occurs in parallel, assembly is serial: Within each level of the output representation, behavioral features are incorporated serially in order of their activation level.

Assembly is characterized by a downward, abstract-to-concrete influence in which higher level, abstract action specifications constrain the permissible features specified at lower levels of abstraction. However, within the constraints imposed by higher levels, lower levels remain relatively autonomous in their execution of higher order commands. The specific content of lower levels of the output representation is the result of assembly of activated behavioral features appropriate to those levels of abstraction. Thus, lower levels of the output representation reflect the influence of both higher order specifications and situational and intrasystemic conditions relevant to those lower levels.

One final property of the assembly process of note here is that it makes considerable demand on processing resources. As a result, assembly is reflected in the speed and latency of behavioral production. However, there are two conditions under which the processing-capacity demands of assembly can be alleviated. The first of these involves those situations in which people are able to make use of unitized assemblies in behavioral production. To the extent that components of our behavior are represented in appropriate unitized assemblies, the need for assembly of those features, and the attendant demand on time and processing capacity, can be avoided. Thus, we should expect that routinized behaviors can be executed with minimal time and processing-capacity demands. There is a large body of evidence in support of this point for a variety of tasks (see Kahneman, 1973; Logan 1979; Navon & Gopher, 1979; Newell & Rosenbloom, 1981; Norman & Bobrow, 1975).

Facilitation of behavioral production should also be expected where the output representation or, more accurately, portions of the output representation have been assembled in advance of actual production. In support of this point, advance preparation has been shown to reduce reaction times in cognitive and motor tasks (e.g., Dixon & Just, 1986; Doll, 1969; Goodman & Kelso, 1980; Hayes & Marteniuk, 1976; Rosenbaum, 1980). Similarly, advance planning of message content, meaning, or structure improves the speed and fluency of speech (e.g., Greene, 1984c; Lindsley, 1975; MacKay, 1981).

Summary

Action-assembly theory posits a long-term memory store of procedural records that include symbolic specifications of features of actions, outcomes, and situations. These features are represented in codes that reflect a number of levels of abstraction. Procedural records are selectively retrieved and brought to bear on behavioral production by the occurrence of goals and situational features that match those stored in the record. Once activated, the action specifications contained in each record are assembled to form a hierarchical output representation of behavior. The higher levels of this output representation constrain the contents of lower levels by defining properties of behavior that the lower levels must satisfy.

To bring this discussion full circle, consider how action-assembly theory addresses the four properties of behavior outlined at the beginning of this section.

With respect to the simultaneous, repetitive, and creative character of behavior, action-assembly theory holds that the patterned aspect of behavior is the result of a vast repertoire of procedural records stored in long-term memory. Thus, the creative character of behavior arises from the selective activation and subsequent assembly of procedural information. That is, creativity arises from the formation of novel configurations of behavioral features. As I have noted elsewhere (Greene, 1990a), "Much as in the case of a musical score, where a finite number of notes can be selected and organized to produce novel arrangements, elements of procedural memory are combined to produce creative behavior (although on a much more complex scale due to the multiple levels of abstraction and number of features involved)" (p. 27). The second observation advanced previously involved the relationship of our abstract, phenomenal experience of action, and the lower level activity by which behavior is executed. From the perspective of action-assembly theory, it is the downward, constraint-setting property of the assembly process that permits the control of behavior via specification of abstract behavioral plans. From this view, lower level operators refine and concretize behavioral features given at higher levels. Thus, the abstract behavioral specification calling for a wave to a friend is sufficient to control the general features of my actions, which are then implemented via a series of muscle commands specified at lower levels of the output representation. The third observation suggested the question of how it is possible for meanings assigned to inputs to impact subsequent behavior. According to the action-assembly perspective, meanings define the activating conditions for procedural records (Greene, 1989). Therefore, the proposal is that meanings impact on behavior through the selective activation of procedural records. As a result, as the meanings assigned to some feature of the environment change, so, too, will the behaviors exhibited in that situation. Finally, I raised the question of how it is possible to produce behavior automatically, with little demand on processing capacity, and further, why automaticity tends to develop over repeated performance. According to action-assembly theory, automaticity is the result of the formation of unitized assemblies of procedural records that allow us to circumvent the assembly process. As we have seen, these unitized assemblies develop when a particular subset of procedural records is activated and assembled on repeated occasions. Hence, action-assembly theory provides a means of addressing a number of fundamental properties of behavior. Perhaps more importantly, it does this by recourse to conceptions of just two basic structures (i.e., procedural records and the output representation) and two processes (i.e., activation and assembly).

Given this brief summary of the theory, we are now in a position to consider the two questions about our sample message posed at the beginning of this chapter: (a) How are we to conceive of human action? and (b) How is action, so conceived, to be explained? With respect to the first of these questions, action-assembly theory suggests a conception of behavior that is in marked contrast to our common-sense view of a sequence of abstractly defined acts, such as "talking to a customer," "asking for a tip," and so on (see Greene, 1990a, 1990b). Rather than a sequence of abstract act types, behavior is seen as a dynamic and complex organization of interlocking features or properties, where each feature represents some limited aspect of the whole. Thus, Sully's message is composed of: (a) features corresponding to ideational content, (b) a plan for structuring the sequence of ideas, (c) lexical items, (d) syntactic order, (e) pauses to aid in listener comprehension, and (f) a rich array of other properties. Beyond this conception of interlocking features, the theory emphasizes that behavior is fundamentally (a) hierarchical, (b) multifunctional, and (c) creative (Greene, 1990a). With respect to the second question, that of how behavior is to be explained, action-assembly theory seeks to provide explanations by recourse to the properties of procedural records and the activation and assembly processes.

Taken together, these views on the nature of behavior and explanation suggest one final point worthy of mention. Elsewhere (Greene, 1990b) I have noted that one course in building cognitive theories of message production is to identify abstract act types and to assume that these act descriptions correspond to cognitive structures that give rise to them. Thus, if we observe that someone uses a compliance-gaining tactic such as "bargain" in order to secure assistance from another, then it is tempting to conclude that the person possesses some long-term memory representation corresponding to "bargain" and to ascribe explanatory status to that structure. Such a move assumes an isomorphism between the realm of long-term memory representation and overt behavior. However, consider that, in contrast to such isomorphism, the link between abstract cognitive representations and actual behavior is characterized by indeterminacy; the hierarchical nature of the output system permits an abstract action specification to be manifested in a number of distinct ways. Further, paralleling this "behavioral indeterminacy" in moving from abstract cognitive representations to behavior, there is a "structural indeterminacy" such that identification of a particular structure on the basis of an act description is unwarranted. That is, a person may employ a compliance-gaining tactic such as "promise" without possessing a cognitive structure corresponding to that act type. Further, even if the individual does possess a cognitive representation of that act type, that structure may not play a role in the production of a specific message reflecting that property. Thus, the complex and hierarchical nature of human behavior suggests principles of behavioral and structural indeterminacy and prompts a move away from simplistic accounts predicated on an assumption of isomorphism between the representational and behavioral domains.

Extensions of the Theory

Although the focus of action-assembly theory is on the production of behavior, and specifically on verbal and nonverbal message behavior, elements of the theory have been applied in addressing a number of diverse phenomena. One of these extensions has involved bringing action-assembly theory to bear on the cross-situational consistency controversy and processes of person-by-situation interactionism (Greene, 1989). At the heart of this treatment is the assumption that stability and discriminativeness are properties of behavior; for this reason, they are likely to be understood only by recourse to models of the behavioral production system that gives rise to such properties. The primary aims of this effort were to: (a) specify the nature of behavioral dispositions and the causal mechanisms by which a general disposition is manifested in specific behavior, (b) provide a theoretical account for when such a disposition will come into play, (c) specify the nature of situational factors and the mechanisms by which such factors influence behavior, and (d) approach these issues within the context of a unified theoretical framework. In essence, this extension of action-assembly theory can be seen as an effort to develop a model of dynamic, rather than mechanistic, interaction (Magnusson & Endler, 1977). At the risk of oversimplification, this approach identifies the content of procedural records as the locus of behavioral dispositions. Such dispositions are selectively called into play via the activation process and then exert influence on specific behaviors as a result of the constraint-setting property of the assembly process. Situations impact behavior because situational features have come to be represented in procedural records, which are then activated in circumstances where those features arise. Thus, rather than view any particular behavior as the result of either person or situational factors, the action-assembly approach to this issue holds that behavior is more correctly seen as the result of a continuous interaction of these components.

A second area of application for elements of action-assembly theory has been to explicate the nature of the self and its role in guiding behavior (Greene & Geddes, 1988). This model attempts to address a number of self-relevant phenomena, including: (a) the fact that the self does not always influence our behavior, (b) only a portion of our self-relevant perceptions come into play at any particular time, (c) there may exist inconsistencies in various self-relevant perceptions, and (d) self-concept is subject to short-term changes under a variety of experimental conditions. At the root of this model is the assumption that self-relevant information is held in action-relevant modular units that guide and regulate cognition and behavior. Conceptions of activation and assembly are then invoked to explain how these self-relevant conceptions are brought to bear in particular circumstances. From this view, self-concept consists of the subset of currently activated self-relevant information; for this reason, self-concept is subject to relatively rapid shifts as information decays and new conceptions are activated.

One final extension of action-assembly theory has been to the domain of social skill and competence (Greene & Geddes, 1993). Although theorizing in this area has traditionally emphasized intentional-stance constructs such as motivation, knowledge, and ability, people often possess appropriate knowledge and motivation and yet still fail to perform in an appropriate or effective fashion. Thus, our behavior is characterized by numerous performance failures, including: (a) omission of requisite behavioral features or failure to implement knowledge at our disposal, (b) intrusion of inappropriate actions, (c) errors in behavioral sequencing and transposition errors, and (d) production of actions that are hesitant or nonfluent (see Fromkin, 1980; Harley, 1984; Motley, Baars, & Camden, 1983; Norman, 1981; Reason, 1979; Singley & Anderson, 1989).

Greene and Geddes' (1993) approach to social skill emphasizes the processes of behavioral production relevant to skilled performance (Trower, 1982; Wiemann & Bradac, 1988), and their focus is on the functional mechanisms that give rise to performance failures. More specifically, the structural properties of memory and the properties of the activation and assembly processes are invoked to account for various types of errors and deviations from optimality and to specify conditions under which such performance failures are likely to occur.

Generative Realism Revisited

From the perspective of generative realism, the task of explaining human action involves developing a theoretical account sufficiently powerful to: (a) incorporate social, physiological, and psychological factors; and (b) specify the mechanisms governing their mutual causal interaction. In simplest terms, the approach to these problems suggested by action-assembly theory is to treat the activation and assembly processes as the generative mechanisms of action, and to assume that it is through these processes that the various elements of the tripartite system exert their influence on behavioral production. Beyond this general orientation, the action-assembly approach to the tripartite system rests on a distinction between two different sorts of processual attributes: (a) those dependent on representational properties and content, and (b) various operational characteristics that are independent of specific content (see Greene, 1990a). With respect to content-based aspects of the output system, action-assembly theory makes explicit that features of actions, outcomes, and situations in procedural records are represented in a number of distinct code systems. This conception suggests a system capable of representing features relevant to each component of the tripartite system.[5] Thus, in some procedural records, features of actions, outcomes, and situations may correspond to various physiological states and effector-unit configurations; other procedural records will preserve features of social ends and contexts. From this perspective, elements of social structure are treated as cogni-

---

[5]The claim here is that the codes of the output system are capable of representing social, psychological, and physiological information, rather than that there is a social code (or codes), physiological code, and so on.

tive content that is brought to bear on behavior via the activation and assembly processes.[6] Beyond such representationally based properties, the action-assembly characterization of the tripartite system identifies a second avenue by which psychological and physiological factors may come to impact on behavioral production. Certain aspects of the psychological and physiological domain play a role in behavior not because they are represented as memory content, but because they influence the acquisition of memory content or because they impact the operating characteristics of the activation and assembly processes that operate over that content (see Greene, 1990a). As examples, various physiological states and physiologically based individual differences may affect the speed with which cognitive processes are executed (see Brebner, 1980; Campbell & Noldy-Cullum, 1985; Vernon, 1987; Welford, 1980).

EMPIRICAL APPLICATIONS: STUDIES OF MESSAGE DESIGN AND IMPLEMENTATION

The third hierarchical level in the action-assembly program consists of the application of various aspects of the theory in empirical research. Elements of action-assembly theory have played a role in experimental investigations of a range of phenomena (e.g., Booth-Butterfield, 1987; Greene & Geddes, 1988; Greene & Sparks, 1983a, 1983b; Sparks, 1986), but the primary domain of application has been in the area of message production. These studies have typically examined hesitation phenomena as indicants of the time course of the activation and assembly processes. That is, because activation and assembly take time (and, in the case of assembly, makes demands on processing resources), these temporal characteristics of message production provide a means of examining underlying cognitive processes (see Greene, 1988).

Of course, there is a long tradition of using hesitation phenomena as a means of illuminating message-production processes (see Appel, Dechert, & Raupach, 1980; Butterworth, 1980a; Dechert & Raupach, 1980; Siegman & Feldstein, 1979). With respect to the time and processing-capacity demands of cognitive (as opposed to articulatory) processes, these variables are typically of three major types: (a) silent-pause variables (including response latency, speaker-turn latency, pause-phonation ratio, speech rate, and so on), (b) filled-pause variables (based on the frequency of "er," "um," and "ah" vocalizations), and (c) speech disruptions (including sentence incompletions, slips of the tongue, and incoherent sounds; see Greene, 1988). It is significant, too, that such hesitation phenomena are related to perceptions of competence and social attractiveness (Brown, Strong, & Rencher, 1973; Lay & Burron, 1986; Street & Brady, 1982). Thus,

---

[6]See Greene (1990a) for a detailed treatment of the acquisition of socially given procedural content.

from the perspective of communication researchers, these message properties are particularly important because they have significance for both cognitive and social levels of analysis.

Studies of Message Preparation and Advance Planning

We have seen that a central claim of action-assembly theory is that the assembly process takes time and makes considerable demands on processing resources. However, as noted, these time and processing-capacity requirements can be lessened by preparing portions of the output representation in advance of actual production. Therefore, we should expect that, given the opportunity to plan messages, or features of messages, in advance, people will exhibit more rapid or fluent message production; there is considerable experimental evidence in support of this point (e.g., Lindsley, 1975; Miller, deTurck, & Kalbfleisch, 1983; O'Hair, Cody, & McLaughlin, 1981; Tannenbaum & Williams, 1968). Similarly, successive repetition of one's own message content has been shown to be associated with more fluent production (Goldman-Eisler, 1961; MacKay, 1981).[7]

A pair of early studies (Greene, 1984c) suggested by action-assembly theory sought to extend research in this area by examining the effects of preparing the organizational structure of a message in advance. Rather than focus on planning of the entire message, these studies attempted to restrict advance assembly to the general organizational scheme to be used in structuring the information in a message. The rationale was that subjects provided with such an abstract plan would not have to assemble those components of the output representation; as a result, they would enjoy an advantage over their counterparts who had to assemble an organizational scheme for guiding their talk.

In the first of these studies (Greene, 1984c, Experiment 1), participants were assigned to one of three experimental conditions. First, those in the "problem–solution" condition were provided with an abstract, four-step sequence that could be used to structure discussion on a variety of topics: (a) statement of the problem, (b) explanation of the problem, (c) statement of the solution, and (d) explanation of the solution. Second, participants in the "solution–problem" condition received a similar four-step plan. Finally, those in the control group were provided with a four-step sequence that was irrelevant to their subsequent speaking task. The participants were then trained in the use of the appropriate sequence. Subjects were told that they would be given a topic to discuss, and that they should be as persuasive as possible in arguing for that proposal. No participant knew in advance the topic he would be required to discuss, thus no preassembly of message content was possible. The dependent variable of primary

---

[7]In some cases, this repetition effect may not apply to reproducing the messages of others (see Sabin, Clemmer, O'Connell, & Kowal, 1979).

interest in this study was defined as the ratio of total duration of silent pausing after the onset of speech to the total duration of the monologue.[8] This sound–silence ratio revealed that both the problem–solution group and the solution–problem group were more fluent than control-group participants, but that this difference reached significance only for the problem–solution condition.

The failures in this study to find a significant difference in speech fluency between the solution–problem group and the control group may have arisen from the participants' relative unfamiliarity with the solution–problem sequence. That is, in contrast to the problem–solution sequence, the solution–problem sequence simply may not have been familiar to the participants. Recall from the summary of the theory given previously that familiar sequences of behavioral features afford an advantage in assembly relative to less-practiced sequences.

This line of reasoning lead to a second study (Greene, 1984c, Experiment 2) designed to determine whether increased practice with the solution–problem sequence would lead to more fluent message production. To test this hypothesis, subjects were again assigned to one of three conditions. First, participants in the "one-trial" group received the same solution–problem sequence employed in the first experiment; like people in that experiment, they received one practice trial where they employed that organizational scheme. Second, participants in the "two-trials" condition were given the solution–problem sequence and two practice trials where they employed that organizational plan in discussing two different topics. Finally, as in the first study, there was also a control group. In the test phase of the investigation, all subjects spoke on the same topic, which, again, was not known in advance. Two different temporal variables were examined in this study. The first of these, speech-onset latency, revealed a significant linear trend over experimental conditions, such that control-group participants were slower to respond than people in the one-trial group, who, in turn, were slower than those given two practice trials. An analysis of sound–silence ratios in this experiment revealed means in the expected direction, but again this difference was not significant. Despite this, taken together, these studies indicate that, quite apart from planning message content in advance, it is possible to increase the speed and fluency of speech production by preparing the general plan for a message in advance. This conclusion is consistent with the conception of the assembly process and the output representation specified in the theory.

As a follow-up to these experiments, a second pair of studies (Greene & Cappella, 1986) brought action-assembly theory to bear in addressing a controversy over the presence of temporal rhythms in spontaneous speech. Goldman-Eisler and her associates (e.g., Beattie, 1980; Butterworth, 1980b; Butterworth & Goldman-Eisler, 1979; Goldman-Eisler, 1967) argued that speech production is executed in two stages: a semantic planning phase and an execution phase.

---

[8]As in many of the studies reported here, filled-pause ratio was also examined; not unexpectedly (see Greene, 1988), it produced no significant differences across experimental conditions.

Further, they suggested that speech is characterized by alternating periods of hesitation and fluency that reflect these stages of speech production. In support of this claim, these researchers reported several studies that indicate the presence of speech rhythms on the order of 5–30 seconds in duration (e.g., Beattie, 1979; Butterworth, 1975; Henderson, Goldman-Eisler, & Skarbek, 1966). In each of these studies, the cycles of fluency were detected by plotting cumulative speech time versus cumulative pause time, and then visually fitting straight lines to these graphic arrays to reveal alternating periods of steep and shallow slopes. This method of detecting cycles has been criticized by a number of authors (e.g., Jaffe, Breskin, & Gerstman, 1972; Rochester, 1973; Schwartz & Jaffe, 1968), and it has been shown that similar patterns of fluency can be found in random data (Jaffe et al., 1972; Schwartz & Jaffe, 1968). Moreover, other studies have failed to find evidence of temporal rhythms on the order of those suggested by Goldman-Eisler and her colleagues (see Jaffe & Feldstein, 1970; Power, 1983; Warner, 1979). Thus, the research in this area has been characterized by considerable controversy over both appropriate methods and findings.

Action-assembly theory is relevant to the question of temporal rhythms: The theory makes explicit that an abstract plan for action is represented at the upper levels of the output representation. This plan consists of one or more steps or moves, where each move corresponds to a transition between specified states representing some desired end or subgoal. Given this conception of an abstract plan consisting of a series of moves, it seems reasonable to expect that spontaneous speech will be characterized by periods of relative fluency and hesitancy that correspond to the transitions in that plan. That is, we should expect assembly of a move to be accompanied by increased pausing due to the time and processing-capacity requirements of the assembly process. However, once the move is formulated, speech should become more fluent until the move is completed. This tendency toward alternating periods of fluency and hesitation should be attenuated when people have had the opportunity to formulate the move structure of their talk in advance of actual production.

Given this line of reasoning, two essential questions are suggested: (a) Are there periods of fluency and hesitancy in spontaneous speech? and (b) Do these periods correspond to the move structure of the talk? In pursuit of answers to these questions, Greene and Cappella (1986) examined data originally collected in the experiments reported in Greene (1984c). In the first of these studies (Greene & Cappella, 1986, Study 1), we examined the monologues of five people who had been in the control conditions in the previous experiments. These people simply were given the task of arguing in favor of a controversial proposal without the aid of a previously specified organizational structure.

To ascertain the move structure of the monologues examined in this study, coders blind to the research questions were introduced to the concept of a move and asked to demarcate move boundaries in transcripts of the monologues under examination. These move boundaries were then treated as predictor variables in a multiple-regression analog of interrupted time-series analyses (McDowall, Mc-Cleary, Meidinger, & Hay, 1980; Ostrum, 1978), which were applied to each monologue. The results of these analyses revealed that, of the seven move boundaries examined, five were associated with a significant decrease in speech fluency at the $p < .10$ level or better.

In a second study (Greene & Cappella, 1986, Study 2), we sought to determine whether this relationship between the move structure of speech and temporal patterns of fluency would be attenuated when the move structure of the discourse had been prepared in advance. In this study, we examined the monologues of five people from the original experiments who had been provided with an organizational plan for discussing the controversial proposal. As before, coders were used to identify the move boundaries in each monologue, which were then used as predictor terms in the time-series analyses. This procedure revealed that, of the 15 move boundaries, only 3 were associated with a decrease in speech fluency at the $p < .10$ level or better. Taken together, these studies suggest that there are periods of greater and lesser fluency in spontaneous speech, and that these periods tend to correspond to the move structure of the talk. Further, as we would expect from action-assembly theory, this relationship between fluency and speech content is attenuated when the organizational structure of the talk is formulated in advance.

As noted, the opportunity for advance planning has been shown to result in more fluent speech in a number of studies. However, there is a noteworthy exception to this body of findings. Langer and Weinman (1981) reported a familiarity-of-topic-by-opportunity-for-planning interaction in which people given the chance for advance planning on a familiar topic actually exhibited higher filled-pause rates than people speaking without prior planning. In an effort to replicate and further examine this effect, Greene, Smith, Smith, and Cashion (1987) had participants speak on either a familiar or an unfamiliar topic two times. Between these two monologues, one third of the people in the study (planning condition) were told that they would be asked to speak on the same topic again, and they were given an opportunity to plan their talk in advance. A second group (distraction condition) was not told about the second monologue, and instead spent the intermonologue interval reading a passage irrelevant to the topic of discussion. Finally, the last group of participants (no-delay condition) was given the second monologue task immediately upon completion of the first. The result was a 3×2 design (type of preparation by topic familiarity). The dependent variables of interest were changes in speech-onset latency, speech rate, and filled-pause rate from the first to the second monologues.

None of these variables was characterized by a type-of-preparation-by-topic-familiarity interaction of the sort reported by Langer and Weinman. Instead, the analysis of speech-onset latency revealed only a main effect for type of preparation, indicating a tendency toward quicker response latencies in the planning condition and slower responses among members of the distraction group. Similarly, the analysis of change in speech rate produced only a main effect for type of preparation, which again indicated that the planning condition was associated with the most fluent speech and the distraction condition the least fluent, regardless of whether participants were speaking on a familiar or unfamiliar topic. Finally, the analysis of change in filled-pause rate revealed no significant effect for type of preparation, topic familiarity, or their interaction. Other subsequent analyses of filled-pause rate also failed to produce any evidence of an effect like that found by Langer and Weinman.

One final examination of the effects of prior preparation on message production has focused on the nonverbal behaviors accompanying deception (Greene et al., 1985). Due to the demands of formulating a lie and controlling behaviors that might serve as cues to deception, it is reasonable to expect that deceivers will tend to experience heavier cognitive loads than truth tellers (see Zuckerman, DePaulo, & Rosenthal, 1981). However, such demands on processing capacity should be lessened when the deceiver is given the opportunity to plan his or her lie in advance. In this study, participants were provided with a series of 12 questions that they would be asked in a subsequent interview. Prior to that interview, participants in the "deception" condition were privately asked to aid the experimenter by lying in response to the interview question, What is your favorite vacation spot? Thus, these participants were able to prepare their response to this question in advance. However, during the actual interview, a true experimental confederate followed up the focal question with a spontaneous question that did not appear on the interview protocol: Oh, really? What did you do there? In this case, participants in the deception condition were required to deliver a spontaneous lie. Finally, at the end of the 12 questions, the confederate again asked an unscheduled question: Listen, you said you went to _____. What were the people there like?

The videotapes of these interactions were coded for the occurrence of a variety of nonverbal behaviors. These frequency counts were converted to rate data and treated by a multiple discriminant analysis contrasting the behavior of the liars and truth tellers during each response. With respect to the first focal question (i.e., the prepared lie for people in the deception condition), the results indicated that there were several differences in the behavior of liars and truth tellers. Most notably, liars were found to exhibit shorter response latencies than their truth-telling counterparts. Among other differences, the liars were found to have shorter message durations, fewer illustrators, and less eye contact than the truth tellers. In contrast, the analysis of the immediate spontaneous response showed that the liars had longer response latencies than the truth tellers, although this difference was not statistically significant. In this case, the liars were found to exhibit more laughter and smiles, more negative head nodding, and less leg and foot movements. Finally, the analysis of the delayed spontaneous response showed that the deceivers had longer response latencies than the truth tellers, but again, this difference did not reach statistical significance. Among other differences, the liars exhibited more laughter and smiles, less leg and foot movements, less eye contact, and shorter message durations.

Taken together, these results are generally supportive of the notion that planning a lie in advance reduces cognitive load at the time of message production. Further, the evidence of less body movement on the part of deceivers (e.g., foot and leg movements, illustrators, adaptors) was hypothesized to be the result of a general inhibitory command, specified at higher levels of the output representation, and used to suppress leakage and deception cues. Similarly, the use of increased laughter and smiles by deceivers may suggest that such facial expressions are used to suppress the display of other facial cues that might give the liar away.

Studies of Design and Execution
of Multiple-Goal Messages

One of the properties of behavior emphasized in the action-assembly perspective is its multifunctionality: Behavior at any moment is seen to be directed toward a variety of goals and functional requirements. In this regard, the theory can be seen to be a part of the body of recent work focusing on messages developed in pursuit of multiple *social* goals (see Tracy & Coupland, 1990). Research in this area reflects a variety of substantive foci, including: (a) attempts to develop typologies of social goals (e.g., Clark & Delia, 1979; Cody, Canary, & Smith, in press; Dillard, Segrin, & Harden, 1989), (b) exploration of message resources for accommodating competing goals (e.g., Bavelas, Black, Chovil, & Mullett, 1990; McCornack, 1992; O'Keefe, 1988; O'Keefe & Shepherd, 1987; Tracy, 1984), and (c) identification of various social and individual factors that influence the production of such messages (e.g., Baxter, 1984; Hale, 1986; O'Keefe & Delia, 1982; Smith, Cody, LoVette, & Canary, 1990).

The focus of action-assembly theory with respect to multiple social goals is on the processes underlying message production. From the perspective of action-assembly theory, the production of such messages is understood in terms of the two fundamental processes of the output system: the activation process that serves to retrieve procedural records relevant to current goals and situational conditions, and the assembly process whereby output features are combined to produce message specifications. Hence, in the view of action-assembly theory, the pursuit of multiple social goals is simply a special case of the more general operation of the output system.

One implication of the action-assembly perspective is that, relative to those situations in which we pursue a single social end, pursuit of multiple social goals tends to be associated with increased complexity of the assembly process (see Greene & Lindsey, 1989). In part, this increased complexity in formulating output specifications stems from difficulties in combining features relevant to different goals. In other words, the features retrieved in pursuit of one goal may be incompatible or inconsistent with those relevant to a second social end. As a result, it may be necessary to retrieve behavioral specifications that are less readily available in memory, or to assemble more complex output representations that are capable of accommodating features relevant to both goals. Of course, there are a number of situations specified by the theory where this tendency toward more complex assembly during pursuit of multiple social goals would not hold. Most obviously, situations where the behavioral features relevant to current goals are not incompatible should produce little difficulty in assembly. Further, as with other cases of assembly, preparation in advance and unitized assemblies relevant to recurrent, but problematic, situations should permit fluent message production.

Our initial investigation in this domain (Greene, Lindsey, & Hawn, 1990) sought to examine hesitation phenomena associated with pursuit of multiple social goals for evidence of increased difficulty in assembly. In this experiment, the speech of participants given a single interaction goal was contrasted with that of people given two goals. First, each person in the study reviewed the job performance file of a fictitious employee whose work was deficient in several areas. After this, participants in the "single-goal" condition were instructed to report to a third party on the employee's performance, with the goal of being "as clear and direct as possible." In contrast, the instructions for the "multiple-goal" condition were to speak to the employee with the goals of being "clear and direct while also showing concern for his feelings and self-esteem."

Analysis of these monologues revealed several differences between the two experimental groups that are indicative of greater difficulty in assembly for people in the multiple-goal condition. These people were found to exhibit (a) longer speech-onset latencies, (b) more sociocentric sequences, and (c) more frequent repetition of ideas. Further, there was a marginally significant effect ($p = .064$) for pause-phonation ratio, reflecting the fact that multiple-goal participants tended to exhibit more silent pausing after the onset of speech than their single-goal counterparts.

A second study (Greene & Lindsey, 1989) sought to extend these findings by examining the effects of prior preparation on temporal characteristics of message production during pursuit of multiple goals. In this case, which involved a different situation and stimulus materials than those used in the earlier study, participants were again given either the task of providing clear and direct feedback or of being clear and direct while also showing concern for the other. The number-of-goals manipulation was crossed with prior preparation; half of the people in each condition were given the opportunity for advance planning of their messages.

Analysis of speech-onset latency again revealed a significant effect for the number-of-goals manipulation, indicating that participants in the multiple-goal condition took longer to begin their messages. However, there was also a main effect for message planning; people given the opportunity to plan their messages in advance exhibited shorter response latencies than their counterparts who spoke spontaneously. A similar analysis for pause-phonation ratio produced a significant effect for number of goals, again because people attempting to accomplish multiple goals were more hesitant than those pursuing a single goal. There was no significant effect on pause-phonation ratio due to the planning manipulation in this study. Hence, these results are consistent with the idea that production of multiple-goal messages is characterized by greater demand on time and processing capacity, and that these increased processing demands may be partially offset when elements of the message are planned in advance.

A more recent series of studies (Greene, McDaniel, Buksa, & Pavizza, 1993) was conducted to determine whether the increased load associated with multiple-goal message production can be attributed solely to difficulties in assembling incompatible message features. Greene and Lindsey (1989) originally suggested that the cognitive load stemming from production of multiple-goal messages resulted from the difficulty of integrating behavioral features relevant to the goals at hand. They suggested that it is not pursuit of multiple goals, per se, that results in less fluent speech. As long as the behavioral features associated with multiple goals are easily integrated, there should be little evidence of heightened temporal and processing capacity demands, despite the attempt to accomplish multiple goals. They reasoned that it is only when multiple goals result in activation of incompatible features, and subsequent difficulties in assembly, that multiple-goal messages should be characterized by evidence of increased cognitive load.

To explore this line of reasoning, Greene et al. (1993, Experiment 1) contrasted the performance of participants given two compatible goals with that of people given two similar, but incompatible, goals. The results of this experiment indicate that people attempting to accomplish two incompatible goals exhibit (a) longer speech-onset latencies, (b) higher pause-phonation ratios, and (c) greater average-pause durations than their counterparts given the task of accomplishing two compatible social goals.

These results indicate that pursuit of incompatible goals is more difficult than pursuit of corresponding, but compatible, goals. However, these results are limited as a test of the rationale developed by Greene and Lindsey that multiple-goal messages should be characterized by evidence of increased cognitive load only when those goals require assembly of incompatible behavioral features. A more appropriate test of this line of reasoning requires contrasting temporal characteristics of multiple-compatible-goal messages with those of single-goal messages.

Toward this end, Greene et al. (1993, Experiment 2) conducted an experiment in which participants pursued either a single social end, two compatible goals, or two incompatible goals. The analysis of speech-onset latency in this experiment revealed a significant interaction effect: It indicated that participants given the task of accomplishing two compatible goals were as fast to initiate their messages as their counterparts given a single goal, and that longer onset latencies were observed only when people attempted to accomplish two incompatible goals. Thus, this result is consistent with the notion that it is only the pursuit of incompatible goals that results in evidence of increased cognitive load.

However, the results of the analyses of pause-phonation ratio and average-pause duration suggest a very different picture. Both of these variables were characterized by a main effect for number of goals, indicating reduced fluency after the onset of speech for multiple-goal messages, regardless of whether the goals in question were compatible. On the basis of these results, Greene et al. (1993) concluded that, beyond the cognitive load stemming from assembly, there is some other factor contributing to the reduced fluency characteristic of spontaneous, multiple-goal messages.

In the face of such results, we have speculated that there are two sources of cognitive load associated with the production of multiple-goal messages: that stemming from assembly of incompatible message features, and that associated with maintaining more complex, message-relevant specifications while they are executed. Thus, even when assembly associated with multiple goals is relatively easy, the need to maintain more complex message representations relevant to multiple goals may still result in less fluent speech. This idea was subjected to empirical testing in a pair of recent studies (Ravizza & Greene, 1993) that manipulated the amount of information to be conveyed in a message. These studies show no effect for representational complexity on speech-onset latency, but analysis of pause-phonation ratio and average-pause duration indicate that, as the complexity of a message representation (i.e., the amount of information to be communicated) increases, so, too, does pausing after the onset of speech. Further, these studies indicate that these effects can be partially offset when communicating familiar information or when there is opportunity for advance planning.

THE DANCER'S MESSAGE AGAIN: TEMPORAL
INDICES OF MESSAGE-PRODUCTION PROCESSES

A theme running throughout this discussion is that human action is most appropriately seen as a collocation of constituent features, where each feature represents some limited aspect of the whole. In fact, it is possible to distinguish two distinct types of features that characterize message behavior (see Greene, 1989). One of these involves the behavioral features that are represented in procedural records. These long-term memory elements specify behavioral content (defined at many levels of abstraction) as well as the order and timing of those features. Beyond these features deriving from memory representations are properties of messages that reflect the time course of the activation and assembly processes. The focus of this section has been on the latter, but we note that, despite the conceptual distinction to be drawn between content-based and processually based characteristics of a message, in practice it may be difficult to distinguish the two.

To conclude this discussion, I return to my original message and consider the various temporal properties revealed when that message is subjected to the kinds of analyses employed in the experiments reported previously. At the outset of the chapter, we saw one set of properties of the message (i.e., those associated with, and revealed in, its verbal content). An alternative representation of that same message is given as:

111111111111100110011111100000001001100000001111100
000000000001111110100100111000111000000011111100000
001111100011110101100000100000000000001011110001100
011101100111010011111110001111100000111111111101

where each digit represents a 250-msec period of phonation (indicated by a *1*) or silence (indicated by a *0*). In the eyes of the action-assembly researcher, this passage has properties associated with its verbal content, as well as a set of temporal characteristics that stem, in part, from the processes underlying its production. For example, following the question that elicited this utterance, there was a lag of 1.30 sec before the onset of speech. After beginning the speaking turn, there were 27 pause events, with an average-pause duration of .898 sec, in this 49.25-sec message, and the ratio of total duration of silence to total duration of phonation was .970.

CONCLUSION

It is commonly recognized that the conceptual schemes we bring to bear on the world play a key role in determining our perceptions of that world. My aim in this chapter has been to capitalize on this fact by using a single message as a reference point in surveying the conceptual territory illuminated by action-assembly theory, its attendant assumptions, and various empirical applications of the theory.

The treatment given here has focused on the three hierarchical levels of inquiry that comprise the action-assembly perspective. The most fundamental of these is the set of metatheoretical commitments given in generative realism. From that vantage point, the sample message is the result of the mutual causal interaction of a tripartite system of social, physiological, and psychological influences. Explanation is given by specifying the mechanisms that underlie such message behavior. Building from this foundation, action-assembly theory can be viewed as an attempt to develop a model of the generative mechanisms of human action that is sufficiently powerful to incorporate all three elements of the tripartite system. Action-assembly theory leads us to see the sample message as a dynamic, hierarchical collocation of constituent features, creatively organized to satisfy a number of goals and functional constraints. These properties of behavior stem from the characteristics of the activation and assembly processes operating over the store of procedural records. Finally, the procedures established in empirical tests of elements of action-assembly theory can be applied to the sample message as well. These procedures highlight the temporal characteristics of the message, which provides a window on the underlying cognitive processes.

REFERENCES

Allport, D. A. (1979). Conscious and unconscious cognition: A computational metaphor for the mechanism of attention and integration. In L. Hilsson (Eds.), *Perspectives on memory research: Essays in honor of Uppsala University's 500th anniversary* (pp. 61–89). Hillsdale, NJ: Lawrence Erlbaum Associates.

Anderson, J. R. (1976). *Language, memory, and thought*. Hillsdale, NJ: Lawrence Erlbaum Associates.

Anderson, J. R. (1983). *The architecture of cognition*. Cambridge, MA: Harvard University Press.

Anderson, J. R. (1984). Spreading activation. In J. R. Anderson & S. M. Kosslyn (Eds.), *Tutorials in learning and memory: Essays in honor of Gordon Bower* (pp. 61–90). San Francisco: Freeman.

Appel, G., Dechert, H. W., & Raupach, M. (1980). *A selected bibliography on temporal variables in speech*. Tubingen, Germany: Gunter Narr Verlag.

Bavelas, J. B., Black, A., Chovil, N., & Mullett, J. (1990). *Equivocal communication*. Newbury Park, CA: Sage.

Baxter, L. A. (1984). An investigation of compliance-gaining as politeness. *Human Communication Research, 10,* 427–456.

Beattie, G. W. (1979). Planning units in spontaneous speech: Some evidence from hesitation in speech and speaker gaze direction in conversation. *Linguistics, 17,* 61–78.

Beattie, G. W. (1980). The role of language production processes in the organization of behaviour in face-to-face interaction. In B. Butterworth (Ed.), *Language production: Vol. 1. Speech and talk* (pp. 69–107). London: Academic Press.

Bhaskar, R. (1978). *A realist theory of science*. Atlantic Highlands, NJ: Humanities Press.

Bock, J. K. (1982). Toward a cognitive psychology of syntax: Information processing contributions to sentence formulation. *Psychological Review, 89,* 1–47.

Booth-Butterfield, S. (1987). Action-assembly theory and communication apprehension: A psychophysiological study. *Human Communication Research, 13,* 386–398.

Bradley, M. M., & Glenberg, A. M. (1983). Strengthening associations: Duration, attention, or relations? *Journal of Verbal Learning and Verbal Behavior, 22,* 650–666.

Brebner, J. M. T. (1980). Reaction time in personality theory. In A. T. Welford (Ed.), *Reaction times* (pp. 309–320). London: Academic Press.

Bregman, A. S. (1977). Perception and behavior as compositions of ideals. *Cognitive Psychology, 9,* 250–292.

Brown, B. L., Strong, W. J., & Rencher, A. C. (1973). Perceptions of personality from speech: Effects of manipulations of acoustical parameters. *Journal of the Acoustical Society of America, 54,* 29–35.

Butterworth, B. (1975). Hesitation and semantic planning in speech. *Journal of Psycholinguistic Research, 4,* 75–87.

Butterworth, B. (Ed.). (1980a). *Language production: Vol. 1. Speech and talk*. London: Academic Press.

Butterworth, B. (1980b). Evidence from pauses in speech. In B. Butterworth (Ed.), *Language production: Vol. 1. Speech and talk* (pp. 155–176). London: Academic Press.

Butterworth, B., & Goldman-Eisler, F. (1979). Recent studies on cognitive rhythm. In A. W. Siegman & S. Feldstein (Eds.), *Of speech and time: Temporal speech patterns in interpersonal contexts* (pp. 211–224). Hillsdale, NJ: Lawrence Erlbaum Associates.

Campbell, K. B., & Noldy-Cullum, N. (1985). Mental chronometry: Vol. II. Individual differences. In B. D. Kirkcaldy (Ed.), *Individual differences in movement* (pp. 147–167). Lancaster: MTP Press.

Churchland, P. M. (1981). Eliminative materialism and the propositional attitudes. *Journal of Philosophy, 78,* 67–90.

Churchland, P. M. (1984). *Matter and consciousness: A contemporary introduction to the philosophy of mind.* Cambridge, MA: Bradford.

Clark, R. A., & Delia, J. G. (1979). *Topoi* and rhetorical competence. *Quarterly Journal of Speech, 65,* 187–206.

Cody, M. J., Canary, D. J., & Smith, S. W. (1994). Compliance-gaining goals and episodes: An inductive analysis of actor's goal-types, strategies, and successes. In J. Daly & J. Wiemann (Eds.), *Strategic interpersonal communication* (pp. 33–90). Hillsdale, NJ: Lawrence Erlbaum Associates.

Collins, A. M., & Loftus, E. F. (1975). A spreading-activation theory of semantic processing. *Psychological Review, 82,* 407–428.

Dechert, H. W., & Raupach, M. (Eds.). (1980). *Temporal variables in speech: Studies in honour of Frieda Goldman-Eisler.* The Hague: Mouton.

Dennett, D. C. (1971). Intentional systems. *Journal of Philosophy, 68,* 87–106.

Dillard, J. P., Segrin, C., & Harden, J. M. (1980). Primary and secondary goals in the production of interpersonal influence messages. *Communication Monographs, 56,* 19–38.

Dixon, P., & Just, M. A. (1986). A chronometric analysis of strategy preparation in choice reactions. *Memory and Cognition, 14,* 488–500.

Doll, T. J. (1969). Short-term retention: Preparatory set as covert rehearsal. *Journal of Experimental Psychology, 82,* 175–182.

Ekehammar, B. (1974). Interactionism in personality from a historical perspective. *Psychological Bulletin, 81,* 1026–1048.

Endler, N. S. (1983). Interactionism: A personality model but not yet a theory. In M. M. Page (Ed.), *Nebraska symposium on motivation 1982: Personality—Current theory and research* (pp. 155–200). Lincoln, NE: University of Nebraska Press.

Fishbein, M., & Ajzen, I. (1975). *Belief, attitude, intention, and behavior: An introduction to theory and research.* Reading, MA: Addison-Wesley.

Fisk, A. D., & Schneider, W. (1984). Memory as a function of attention, level of processing, and automatization. *Journal of Experimental Psychology: Learning, Memory, and Cognition, 10,* 181–197.

Flanagan, O. J., Jr. (1984). *The science of the mind.* Cambridge, MA: Bradford.

Fodor, J. A. (1975). *The language of thought.* New York: Crowell.

Fowler, C. A., & Turvey, M. T. (1978). Skill acquisition: An event approach with special reference to searching for the optimum of a function of several variables. In G. E. Stelmach (Ed.), *Information processing in motor control and learning* (pp. 2–40). New York: Academic Press.

Fromkin, V. A. (Ed.). (1980). *Errors in linguistic performance: Slips of the tongue, ear, pen, and hand.* New York: Academic Press.

Gardner, H. (1987). *The mind's new science: A history of the cognitive revolution.* New York: Basic Books.

Gergen, K. J. (1985). Social constructionist inquiry: Context and implications. In K. J. Gergen & K. E. Davis (Eds.), *The social construction of the person* (pp. 3–18). New York: Springer-Verlag.

Goldman-Eisler, F. (1961). Hesitation and information in speech. In C. Cherry (Ed.), *Information theory* (pp. 162–174). London: Butterworth.

Goldman-Eisler, F. (1967). Sequential temporal patterns and cognitive processes in speech. *Language and Speech, 10*, 122–132.

Goodman, D., & Kelso, J. A. S. (1980). Are movements prepared in parts? Not under compatible (naturalized) conditions. *Journal of Experimental Psychology: General, 109*, 475–495.

Greene, J. O. (1983). *Development and initial tests of an action assembly theory*. Unpublished doctoral dissertation, University of Wisconsin, Madison.

Greene, J. O. (1984a). Evaluating cognitive explanations of communicative phenomena. *Quarterly Journal of Speech, 70*, 241–254.

Greene, J. O. (1984b). A cognitive approach to human communication: An action assembly theory. *Communication Monographs, 51*, 289–306.

Greene, J. O. (1984c). Speech preparation processes and verbal fluency. *Human Communication Research, 11*, 61–84.

Greene, J. O. (1988). Cognitive processes: Methods for probing the black box. In C. H. Tardy (Ed.), *A handbook for the study of human communication: Methods and instruments for observing, measuring, and assessing communication processes* (pp. 37–66). Norwood, NJ: Ablex.

Greene, J. O. (1989). The stability of nonverbal behavior: An action–production approach to problems of cross-situational consistency and discriminativeness. *Journal of Language and Social Psychology, 8*, 193–220.

Greene, J. O. (1990a, November). *Generative realism: A proposal concerning the nature of human action*. Paper presented at the annual meeting of the Speech Communication Association, Chicago, IL.

Greene, J. O. (1990b). Tactical social action: Towards some strategies for theory. In M. J. Cody & M. L. McLaughlin (Eds.), *The psychology of tactical communication* (pp. 31–47). Clevedon, England: Multilingual Matters.

Greene, J. O., & Cappella, J. N. (1986). Cognition and talk: The relationship of semantic units to temporal patterns of fluency in spontaneous speech. *Language and Speech, 29*, 141–157.

Greene, J. O., & Cody, M. J. (1985). On thinking and doing: Cognitive science and the production of social behaviour. *Journal of Language and Social Psychology, 4*, 157–170.

Greene, J. O., & Geddes, D. (1988). Representation and processing in the self-system: An action-oriented approach to self and self-relevant phenomena. *Communication Monographs, 55*, 287–314.

Greene, J. O., & Geddes, D. (1993). An action assembly perspective on social skill. *Communication Theory, 3*, 26–49.

Greene, J. O., & Lindsey, A. E. (1989). Encoding processes in the production of multiple-goal messages. *Human Communication Research, 16*, 120–140.

Greene, J. O., Lindsey, A. E., & Hawn, J. J. (1990). Social goals and speech production: Effects of multiple goals on pausal phenomena. *Journal of Language and Social Psychology, 9*, 113–128.

Greene, J. O., McDaniel, T. L., Buksa, K., & Ravizza, S. M. (1993). Cognitive processes in the production of multiple-goal messages: Evidence from the temporal characteristics of speech. *Western Journal of Communication, 57*, 65–86.

Greene, J. O., O'Hair, H. D., Cody, M. J., & Yen, C. (1985). Planning and control of behavior during deception. *Human Communication Research, 11*, 335–364.

Greene, J. O., Smith, S. W., Smith, R. C., & Cashion, J. L. (1987). The sound of one mind working: Memory retrieval and response preparation as components of pausing in spontaneous speech. In M. L. McLaughlin (Ed.), *Communication Yearbook 10* (pp. 241–258). Beverly Hills, CA: Sage.

Greene, J. O., & Sparks, G. G. (1983a). Explication and test of a cognitive model of communication apprehension: A new look at an old construct. *Human Communication Research, 9*, 349–366.

Greene, J. O., & Sparks, G. G. (1983b). The role of outcome expectations in the experience of a state of communication apprehension. *Communication Quarterly, 31*, 212–219.

Greene, P. H. (1982). Why is it easy to control your arms? *Journal of Motor Behavior, 14,* 260–286.

Hale, C. L. (1986). Impact of cognitive complexity in a face-threatening context. *Journal of Language and Social Psychology, 5,* 135–143.

Harley, T. A. (1984). A critique of top–down independent levels models of speech production: Evidence from non-plan-internal speech errors. *Cognitive Science, 8,* 191–219.

Harré, R. (1981). Rituals, rhetoric, and social cognition. In J. P. Forgas (Ed.), *Social cognition: Perspectives on everyday understanding* (pp. 211–224). London: Academic Press.

Harré, R., & Secord, P. F. (1973). *The explanation of social behaviour.* Totowa, NJ: Littlefield, Adams.

Hayes, K. C., & Marteniuk, R. G. (1976). Dimensions of motor task complexity. In G. E. Stelmach (Ed.), *Motor control: Issues and trends* (pp. 201–228). New York: Academic Press.

Henderson, A. Goldman-Eisler, F., & Skarbek, A. (1966). Sequential temporal patterns in spontaneous speech. *Language and Speech, 9,* 207–216.

Jaffe, J., Breskin, S., & Gerstman, L. J. (1972). Random generation of apparent speech rhythms. *Language and Speech, 15,* 68–71.

Jaffe, J., & Feldstein, S. (1970). *Rhythms of dialogue.* New York: Academic Press.

Kahneman, D. (1973). *Attention and effort.* Englewood Cliffs, NJ: Prentice-Hall.

Keele, S. W. (1973). *Attention and human performance.* Pacific Palisades, CA: Goodyear.

Kellogg, R. T. (1980). Is conscious attention necessary for long-term storage? *Journal of Experimental Psychology: Human Learning and Memory, 6,* 379–390.

Klein, R. M. (1976). Attention and movement. In G. E. Stelmach (Ed.), *Motor control: Issues and trends* (pp. 143–173). New York: Academic Press.

Langer, E. J., & Weinman, C. (1981). When thinking disrupts intellectual performance: Mindfulness on an overlearned task. *Personality and Social Psychology Bulletin, 7,* 240–243.

Lannamann, J. W. (1991). Interpersonal communication research as ideological practice. *Communication Theory, 1,* 179–203.

Lay, C. H., & Burron, B. F. (1968). Perceptions of the personality of the hesitant speaker. *Perceptual and Motor Skills, 26,* 951–956.

Lewin, K. (1936). *Principles of topological psychology.* New York: McGraw-Hill.

Lindsley, J. R. (1975). Producing simple utterances: How far ahead do we plan? *Cognitive Psychology, 7,* 1–19.

Logan, G. D. (1979). On the use of concurrent memory load to measure attention and automaticity. *Journal of Experimental Psychology: Human Perception and Performance, 5,* 189–207.

MacKay, D. G. (1981). The problem of rehearsal or mental practice. *Journal of Motor Behavior, 13,* 274–285.

MacKay, D. G. (1982). The problems of flexibility, fluency, and speed—accuracy trade-off in skilled behavior. *Psychological Review, 89,* 483–506.

MacKay, D. G. (1983). A theory of the representation and enactment of intentions. In R. A. Magill (Ed.), *Memory and control of action* (pp. 217–230). Amsterdam: North-Holland.

Magnusson, D., & Endler, N. S. (1977). Interactional psychology: Present status and future prospects. In D. Magnusson & N. S. Endler (Eds.), *Personality at the crossroads: Current issues in interactional psychology* (pp. 3–31). Hillsdale, NJ: Lawrence Erlbaum Associates.

Manicas, P. T., & Secord, P. F. (1983). Implications for psychology of the new philosophy of science. *American Psychologist, 37,* 399–413.

Marteniuk, R. G., & MacKenzie, C. L. (1980). Information processing in movement organization and execution. In R. S. Nickerson (Ed.), *Attention and performance VIII* (pp. 29–57). Hillsdale, NJ: Lawrence Erlbaum Associates.

Marteniuk, R. G., & Romanow, S. K. E. (1983). Human movement organization and learning as revealed by variability of movement, use of kinematic information and Fourier analysis. In R. A. Magill (Ed.), *Memory and control of action* (pp. 167–197). Amsterdam: North-Holland.

McClelland, J. L., & Rumelhart, D. E. (1985). Distributed memory and the representation of general and specific information. *Journal of Experimental Psychology: General, 114*, 159–188.

McCornack, S. A. (1992). Information manipulation theory. *Communication Monographs, 59*, 1–16.

McDowall, D., McCleary, R., Meidinger, E. E., & Hay, R. A., Jr. (1980). *Interrupted time series analysis*. Beverly Hills, CA: Sage.

Miller, G. R., deTurck, M. A., & Kalbfleisch, P. J. (1983). Self-monitoring, rehearsal, and deceptive communication. *Human Communication Research, 10*, 97–117.

Mischel, W. (1973). Toward a cognitive social learning reconceptualization of personality. *Psychological Review, 80*, 252–283.

Mischel, W. (1983). Alternatives in the pursuit of predictability and consistency of persons: Stable data that yield unstable interpretations. *Journal of Personality, 51*, 578–604.

Mischel, W., & Peake, P. K. (1982). Beyond déjà vu in the search for cross-situational consistency. *Psychological Review, 89*, 730–755.

Motley, M. T., Baars, B. J., & Camden, C. T. (1983). Experimental verbal slip studies: A review and an editing model of language encoding. *Communication Monographs, 50*, 79–101.

Navon, D., & Gopher, D. (1979). On the economy of the human-processing system. *Psychological Review, 86*, 214–255.

Newell, A., & Rosenbloom, P. S. (1981). Mechanisms of skill acquisition and the law of practice. In J. R. Anderson (Ed.), *Cognitive skills and their acquisition* (pp. 1–55). Hillsdale, NJ: Lawrence Erlbaum Associates.

Norman, D. A. (1981). Categorization of action slips. *Psychological Review, 88*, 1–15.

Norman, D. A., & Bobrow, D. G. (1975). On data-limited and resource-limited processes. *Cognitive Psychology, 7*, 44–64.

O'Hair, H. D., Cody, M. J., & McLaughlin, M. L. (1981). Prepared lies, spontaneous lies, Machiavellianism, and nonverbal communication. *Human Communication Research, 7*, 325–339.

O'Keefe, B. J. (1988). The logic of message design: Individual differences in reasoning about communication. *Communication Monographs, 55*, 80–103.

O'Keefe, B. J., & Delia, J. G. (1982). Impression formation and message production. In M. E. Roloff, & C. R. Berger (Eds.), *Social cognition and communication* (pp. 33–72). Beverly Hills, CA: Sage.

O'Keefe, B. J., & Shepherd, G. J. (1987). The pursuit of multiple objectives in face-to-face interaction: Effects of construct differentiation on message organization. *Communication Monographs, 54*, 396–419.

Ostrum, C. W., Jr. (1978). *Time series analysis: Regression techniques*. Beverly Hills, CA: Sage.

Pervin, L. A. (1978). Theoretical approaches to the analysis of individual–environment interaction. In L. A. Pervin & M. Lewis (Eds.), *Perspectives in interactional psychology* (pp. 67–85). New York: Plenum.

Power, M. J. (1983). Are there cognitive rhythms in speech? *Language and Speech, 26*, 253–261.

Putnam, H. (1973). Reductionism and the nature of psychology. *Cognition, 2*, 131–146.

Pylyshyn, Z. W. (1984). *Computation and cognition: Toward a foundation for cognitive science*. Cambridge, MA: MIT Press.

Raaijmakers, D. G. W., & Shiffrin, R. M. (1981). Search of associative memory. *Psychological Review, 88*, 93–134.

Ravizza, S. M., & Greene, J. O. (1993, May). *The effects of representational complexity on speech fluency*. Paper presented at the annual meeting of the International Communication Association, Washington, DC.

Reason, J. (1979). Actions not as planned: The price of automatization. In G. Underwood & R. Stevens (Eds.), *Aspects of consciousness: Vol. 1. Psychological issues* (pp. 67–89). London: Academic Press.

Reed, E. S. (1982). An outline of a theory of action systems. *Journal of Motor Behavior, 14*, 98–134.

Rey, G. (1980). Functionalism and the emotions. In A. O. Rorty (Ed.), *Explaining emotions* (pp. 163–195). Berkeley, CA: University of California Press.

Rochester, S. R. (1973). The significance of pauses in spontaneous speech. *Journal of Psycholinguistic Research, 4,* 51–81.

Rosenbaum, D. A. (1980). Human movement initiation: Specification of arm, direction, and extent. *Journal of Experimental Psychology: General, 109,* 444–474.

Rosenbaum, D. A. (1984). The planning and control of motor movements. In J. A. Anderson & S. M. Kosslyn (Eds.), *Tutorials in learning and memory: Essays in honor of Gordon Bower* (pp. 219–233). San Francisco: Freeman.

Sabin, E. J., Clemmer, E. J., O'Connell, D. C., & Kowal, S. (1979). A pausological approach to speech development. In A. W. Siegman & S. Feldstein (Eds.), *Of speech and time: Temporal speech patterns in interpersonal contexts* (pp. 35–55). Hillsdale, NJ: Lawrence Erlbaum Associates.

Saltzman, E. (1979). Levels of sensorimotor representation. *Journal of Mathematical Psychology, 20,* 91–163.

Saltzman, E. L., & Kelso, J. A. S. (1983). Toward a dynamical account of motor memory and control. In R. A. Magill (Ed.), *Memory and control of action* (pp. 17–38). Amsterdam: North-Holland.

Saltzman, E. L., & Kelso, J. A. S. (1987). Skilled actions: A task-dynamic approach. *Psychological Review, 94,* 84–106.

Sampson, E. E. (1981). Cognitive psychology as ideology. *American Psychologist, 36,* 703–743.

Sampson, E. E. (1983). Deconstructing psychology's subject. *Journal of Mind and Behavior, 4,* 135–164.

Schmidt, R. A. (1976). The schema as a solution to some persistent problems in motor learning theory. In G. E. Stelmach (Ed.), *Motor control: Issues and trends* (pp. 41–65). New York: Academic Press.

Schneider, W., & Shiffrin, R. M. (1977). Controlled and automatic human information processing: Vol. I. Detection, search, and attention. *Psychological Review, 84,* 1–66.

Schwartz, J., & Jaffe, J. (1968). Markovian prediction of sequential temporal patterns in spontaneous speech. *Language and Speech, 11,* 27–30.

Searle, J. (1980). Minds, brains, and programs. *The Behavioral and Brain Sciences, 3,* 417–424.

Searle, J. (1984). *Minds, brains, and science.* Cambridge, MA: Harvard University Press.

Shiffrin, R. M., & Schneider, W. (1977). Controlled and automatic human information processing: Vol. II. Perceptual learning, automatic attending, and a general theory. *Psychological Review, 84,* 127–190.

Shiffrin, R. M., & Schneider, W. (1984). Automatic and controlled processing revisited. *Psychological Review, 91,* 269–276.

Siegman, A. W., & Feldstein, S. (Eds.). (1979). *Of speech and time: Temporal speech patterns in interpersonal contexts.* Hillsdale, NJ: Lawrence Erlbaum Associates.

Singley, M. K., & Anderson, J. R. (1989). *The transfer of cognitive skill.* Cambridge, MA: Harvard University Press.

Smith, S. M. (1979). Remembering in and out of context. *Journal of Experimental Psychology: Human Learning and Memory, 5,* 460–471.

Smith, S. W., Cody, M. J., LoVette, S., & Canary, D. J. (1990). Self-monitoring, gender, and compliance-gaining goals. In M. J. Cody & M. L. McLaughlin (Eds.), *The psychology of tactical communication* (pp. 91–135). Clevedon, England: Multilingual Matters.

Sparks, G. G. (1986). An action assembly approach to predicting emotional responses to frightening mass media. *Central States Speech Journal, 37,* 102–112.

Stelmach, G. E., & Diggles, V. A. (1982). Control theories in motor behavior. *Acta Psychologica, 50,* 83–105.

Stigen, A. (1970). The concept of human action. *Inquiry, 13,* 1–31.

Street, R. L., Jr., & Brady, R. M. (1982). Speech rate acceptance ranges as a function of evaluative domain, listener speech rate, and communication context. *Communication Monographs, 49,* 290–308.

Tannenbaum, P. H., & Williams, F. (1968). Generation of active and passive sentences as a function of subject or object focus. *Journal of Verbal Learning and Verbal Behavior, 7,* 246–250.

Tracy, K. (1984). The effect of multiple goals on conversational relevance and topic shift. *Communication Monographs, 51,* 274–287.

Tracy, K., & Coupland, N. (Eds.) (1990). Multiple goals in discourse. *Journal of Language and Social Psychology, 9,* 1–170.

Trower, P. (1982). Toward a generative model of social skills: A critique and synthesis. In J. P. Curran & P. M. Monti (Eds.), *Social skills training* (pp. 399–427). New York: Guilford.

Vallacher, R. R., & Wegner, D. M. (1987). What do people think they're doing? Action identification and human behavior. *Psychological Review, 94,* 3–15.

Vernon, P. A. (1987). New developments in reaction time research. In P. A. Vernon (Ed.), *Speed of information-processing and intelligence* (pp. 1–20). Norwood, NJ: Ablex.

Warner, R. M. (1979). Periodic rhythms in conversational speech. *Language and Speech, 22,* 381–396.

Welford, A. T. (1980). Relationships between reaction time and fatigue, stress, age and sex. In A. T. Welford (Ed.), *Reaction times* (pp. 321–354). London: Academic Press.

Wiemann, J. M., & Bradac, J. J. (1988). Metatheoretical issues in the study of communicative competence: Structural and functional approaches. In B. Dervin & M. J. Voight (Eds.), *Progress in communication sciences* (Vol. 9, pp. 261–284). Norwood, NJ: Ablex.

Zuckerman, M., DePaulo, B. M., & Rosenthal, R. (1981). Verbal and nonverbal communication of deception. In L. Berkowitz (Ed.), *Advances in experimental social psychology* (Vol. 14, pp. 2–59). New York: Academic Press.

3 Perceptual Processing of Nonverbal-Relational Messages

Sandi W. Smith
Michigan State University

PERCEPTUAL PROCESSING OF NONVERBAL-RELATIONAL MESSAGES

The premises that humans live in worlds of their own psychological construction and are active, goal-directed social agents undergird cognitive research in communication and psychology (Athay & Darley, 1981; Axley, 1984; Bruner, 1983, 1986; Cody & McLaughlin, 1985; Delia, 1977; Endler, 1982; Greene, 1984; Magnusson & Endler, 1977; Mischel, 1977; Planalp & Hewes, 1982; Rumelhart & Ortony; 1977; Schneider, 1983). If these premises are accepted, communication scholars must address how these separate worlds are constructed, maintained, changed, and enmeshed with the worlds of others through communication. In this view, humans are more than passive receivers of, and responders to, stimuli from the environment. The environment is a function of the perceiver in the sense that the perceiver's cognitive system filters and organizes its own representation of the environment. It is on the basis of social knowledge contained in this representation that humans both interpret and engage in communication to understand, predict, and control their environments (Hewes & Planalp, 1982; Ostrom, 1984). It is important to examine (a) the structures in which social knowledge is represented; (b) the content of these structures; and (c) the cognitive processes that operate as social knowledge is acquired, retained, altered, and acted on as a result of the communication process.

The study of interpersonal communication from a cognitive perspective focuses on the representation and utilization of relational knowledge as interactants interpret and produce relational messages (Planalp, 1989). The focus of this chapter is on the interpretation of relational communication, or input processing, as opposed to the production of relational messages, or output processing. During input processing, persons comprehend relational messages through the interaction of information selected from the stream of behavior with information stored in social-knowledge structures, the results of which are interpretations and inferences derived from the integration process (Planalp, 1989; Sypher & Higgins, 1989). Previous research on interpretation of relational communication employing a cognitive perspective has addressed such topics as (a) the relationship between cognition and communication (Hewes & Planalp, 1982, 1987; Planalp, 1989; Planalp & Hewes, 1982), (b) relational schemata (Planalp, 1985), (c) interpersonal judgment (Pavitt, 1982), (d) second-guessing (Doelger, Hewes, & Graham, 1986; Hewes & Graham, 1989; Hewes, Graham, Doelger, & Pavitt, 1985; Hewes, Graham, Monsour, & Doelger, 1989), (e) social-information gathering (Berger & Kellerman, 1983), (f) inference-generating knowledge structures (Kellerman & Lim, 1989), (g) social cognition and relational development (Berger & Roloff, 1982; Honeycutt, 1991, 1993), (h) events that increase uncertainty in relationships (Planalp & Honeycutt, 1985; Planalp, Rutherford, & Honeycutt, 1988), and (i) perceived intentionality of nonverbal messages (Manusov, 1991; Manusov & Rodriguez, 1989).

The specific phenomenon of interest in this chapter is the perceptual processing of nonverbal-relational messages. The concept of expectancy is central to many theories of nonverbal communication, such as Burgoon's nonverbal expectancy-violations theory (Burgoon, 1978, 1983; Burgoon & Hale, 1988; Burgoon & Walther, 1990), Cappella and Greene's (1982) discrepancy-arousal theory, and Patterson's (1983) sequential-functional model of nonverbal involvement. Communication expectancies have been defined as "cognitions about the anticipated communicative behavior of specific others, as embedded within and shaped by the social norms for the contemporaneous roles, relationships, and context" (Burgoon & Walther, 1990, p. 236). As such, these expectancies consist of representations of social knowledge stored in cognitive structures. They interact with information selected from the stream of behavior in particular ways under different conditions to form interpretations of the meaning of nonverbal behavior (Honeycutt, 1991, 1993).

To study the process of interpretation of nonverbal behavior, the processes by which information held in social-knowledge structures interacts with information selected from the stream of behavior must be analyzed. To examine social knowledge, a full cognitive model that includes a structure of relational knowledge, its content, and the processes by which the structure and content interact with perceptions of nonverbal relational communication must be specified (Greene, 1984; Pavitt, 1989; Planalp & Hewes, 1982). This chapter overviews a cognitive model in which relational schemata are the knowledge structures that hold relational knowledge, and top–down and bottom–up processing are the cognitive processes that drive changes in relational knowledge at different stages of information processing. The input-processing stages of (a) selective attention, (b) encoding, (c) interpretation, and (d) inference are discussed. To determine the relative contributions of social knowledge and information selected from the stream of behavior in the social-judgment process, the Expectation by Situational Information Interactional Framework, previously employed in covariation (Alloy & Tabachnik, 1984) and attribution-perception research (Metalsky & Abramson, 1981), is applied to perceptual processing of nonverbal-relational communication. The results of several studies that employed the cognitive model of relational schemata and top–down and bottom–up processing are reviewed in terms of their implications for the interaction of information held in relational-knowledge structures with current situational data as persons process nonverbal-relational messages and make relevant social judgments.

THE COGNITIVE MODEL: RELATIONAL SCHEMATA AND TOP–DOWN AND BOTTOM–UP PROCESSING

Relational Schemata

Planalp (1985) defined *relational schemata* as "coherent frameworks of relational knowledge that are used to derive relational implications of messages and are modified in accord with ongoing experience with relationships" (p. 9). Relational schemata can exist for any type of interpersonal relationship, such as friendships, romantic relationships, or family relationships. They are a subset of the broad class of schemata that can be explained in general terms.

Schemata are structures of knowledge about a particular domain. Their content includes: (a) general knowledge, (b) relationships among the attributes of the domain, and (c) specific examples or instances of the domain (Taylor & Crocker, 1981). Information in schemata is stored hierarchically, with more abstract information toward the top and more concrete information toward the bottom of the schema. Schemata assume an active, dynamic process; specific instances and abstractions based on exposure to a series of specific instances of the domain over time are stored in these knowledge structures (Fiske & Linville, 1980; McClelland & Rumelhart, 1985; Taylor & Crocker, 1981). Content in these knowledge structures can be altered in the short-term during information processing and in the long-term through repeated experience with different examples of the domain in question. Thus, the structure and content of schemata are based on prior experience.

Schemata are structured along the vertical and horizontal dimensions. The vertical dimension contains three levels (Rosch, 1978): (a) the superordinate, (b) the basic, and (c) the subordinate. Instances of the superordinate level are quite distinct and do not share many features with one another. The basic level is thought to be the optimal level of abstraction, in which an instance of the schema shares more attributes in common with other instances of the schema and is most differentiated from instances of other schemata (Tversky, 1977). This property provides detail and distinctiveness not found at other levels (Pavitt & Haight, 1985). Instances of the subordinate level are thought to be numerous, but tend to overlap with those located in other related schemata.

The horizontal dimension of schemata contains a pattern of overlapping similarities (Tversky, 1977). There is no fixed set of features that determines membership in a particular schema (Anderson, 1980), thus attributes may be shared among schemata creating "fuzzy sets." These fuzzy sets are a class or domain with continuous grades of membership (Zadeh, 1965). Schematic membership is probabilistic in nature as category members vary in their degree of membership from prototypical, best examples, to ambiguous borderline cases at the overlapping and "fuzzy" boundaries (Broughton, 1984; Cantor & Mischel, 1979).

The set of features most commonly associated with schematic membership is abstracted from specific instances and forms a prototypical example of a schema. Knowledge about the particular schema is structured around, and represented in long-term memory as, a prototype. The prototype serves as the symbol and reference point of the schema (Cantor, Mischel, & Schwartz, 1982a, 1982b). Prototypes function as a standard around which a body of input can be compared and in relation to which new input can be assimilated into the previously held social knowledge activated at the time of input. New instances can be compared to the abstracted set of features comprising the prototype. When a sufficiently high degree of similarity exists between the target features and the abstracted features of the prototype, the perceiver classifies the behavior, situation, or person as an instance of that schema (Cantor & Mischel, 1977, 1979).

Research by Davis and Todd (1985) on prototypical dimensions of friendship has shown that the presence or absence and weighting of prototypical features enables finer discriminations than simple determination of gross-category membership. Davis and Todd postulated that (a) success, (b) viability, (c) intimacy, (d) spontaneity, (e) stability, (f) support, and (g) enjoyment are the prototypical features of friendship. Respondents rated these features for different types of friendships, and their ratings served to distinguish (a) best friends, (b) close friends (same gender), (c) close friends (opposite gender), (d) casual acquaintances, and (e) former friends, as well as satisfying from unsatisfying friendships (but, see Planalp, 1985, 1989).

Knowledge stored in schemata interacts with cognitive processes to guide perceptual processing of new information. Expectation concerning the type and location of relevant new information can be provided by schemata in the selective-attention phase of information processing. The knowledge stored in schemata allows persons to make sense of specific new situations by enabling interpretation of them in terms of the general case stored in the schema (Taylor & Crocker, 1981). Schemata can also serve as recognition devices used to evaluate goodness of fit of new interpretations in terms of past social knowledge (Rumelhart, 1984). The processes postulated to interact with relational schemata and their content in perceptual processing are top–down and bottom–up processing.

TOP–DOWN AND BOTTOM–UP PROCESSING

Top–down and bottom–up processing are the control mechanisms specified in this model to account for activation of the content of social knowledge held in relational schemata at different stages of information processing. Top–down processing, also known as contextually driven, hypothesis-driven, and schematic processing, is guided by expectation and preconception based on past social knowledge held in knowledge structures such as relational schemata. Schemata activate their constituent subschemata in a top–down fashion. This derives from an expectation that the subschemata will account for a portion of the input data. Goodness of fit is then evaluated, and satisfaction of these expectations may or may not be found (Rumelhart, 1984; Rumelhart & Ortony, 1977). In this way, perceivers form hypotheses about what data to search out and how to interpret the data that are found. Hypotheses generated by top–down processing can lend (a) focus, (b) structure, and (c) sequence to search behavior and can provide a basis for how information is used (Taylor & Crocker, 1981).

Bottom–up or data-driven processing is initiated as attention is focused on separate features of behavior. In this process, some aspect of the input stimuli suggests or activates schemata, and these schemata activate still higher dominating schemata of which they are constituents (Rumelhart & Ortony, 1977). This process is relatively slow and requires large portions of processing capacity and attention. Top–down and bottom–up processing are thought to occur simultaneously as a person's interpretation of an experience is reinforced by consistency between both levels (McClelland & Rumelhart, 1981; Norman, 1976; Rumelhart, 1984).

This model of relational schemata and top–down and bottom–up processing serves as the basic mechanism by which persons assign meaning to relational communication during the cognitive phases of input processing. The particular ways this model operates during the selective-attention, encoding, interpretation, and inference phases of information processing are addressed in the next section.

COGNITIVE PHASES OF INPUT PROCESSING

Selective Attention and Encoding

The initial phases of information processing involve selective attention and encoding. Selective attention is the operation by which a perceiver focuses on relevant information from his or her environment and/or from his or her body of social knowledge. Encoding is the process by which the information from the environment is translated into an internal symbolic code. It is widely accepted that both incoming data and past social knowledge, held in representational structures such as relational schemata, interact in these initial phases of information processing (Brewer & Nakamura, 1984; Craig, 1978; Fiske & Taylor, 1984; Higgins & Bargh, 1987; Hochberg, 1978; Lord, 1985; McClelland & Rumelhart, 1981; Neisser, 1976; Norman, 1979; Norman & Bobrow, 1976; Ostrom, 1984; Rumelhart, 1984; Taylor & Crocker, 1981; Trope, 1986; Wyer & Carlston, 1979). Particular knowledge structures may be activated in one of several ways through either bottom–up or top–down processing. The new sensory data might activate a particular schema from the bottom–up due to the salience or vividness of the stimuli (Fiske & Taylor, 1984; Higgins & Bargh, 1987; Lord, 1985; Wyer & Carlston, 1979). Top–down activation might result from one of several causes, including (a) recency of activation or priming (Higgins & Bargh, 1987; Johnson & Dark, 1986; Srull & Wyer, 1979; Wyer & Carlston, 1979), (b) frequency of activation (Fiske & Taylor, 1984; Wyer & Carlston, 1979), or (c) observational goal or purpose (Cohen, 1981; Ebbesen, 1980; Fiske & Taylor, 1984).

Once a particular knowledge structure or schema is activated, analysis is likely biased toward instances of that schema if the new data are either ambiguous or congruent with that schema. In this case, (a) stimuli conforming to that active schema are relatively easy to attend to and difficult to ignore (Johnson & Dark, 1986), (b) expectations concerning location and content of new data are likely to be derived from the currently invoked schema, and (c) activated schemata are likely to provide conceptual guidelines used to determine where in the stimulus configuration to search for new data and how to interpret current data (Norman & Bobrow, 1976). Honeycutt (1993) referred to this process as assimilation because the new data are assimilated into the expectation. When data are incongruent with the activated schema, the perceiver may experience cognitive dilemma, which can be resolved either by (a) assimilation; (b) accommodation (Honeycutt, 1993), in which prior beliefs are accommodated to the current incoming data; or (c) interpretation, which involves both assimilation and accommodation.

Interpretation and Inference

Interpretation is the process of integrating new information with previously held knowledge based on the schema activated at the time of processing (Wyer & Gordon, 1984). This schema (a) holds the general knowledge required for comprehension, (b) provides a basis for the interpretation of incoming information, and (c) permits inferences to be made about unstated aspects of the input (Ortony, 1978). Persons make sense of new information by matching it with internal codes, then integrating it with the activated social knowledge. If this match is unclear in some way, inconsistencies are resolved and missing data are filled in by means of inference (Cappella & Street, 1989; Kellerman & Lim, 1989; Lord, 1985; Wyer & Carlston, 1979). In other words, inference making involves "going beyond the information given" (Bruner, 1964) in order to make a judgment about something unknown based on something that is known. The inference process—instantiated when new data are ambiguous, incongruent with expectation, or incomplete, and thus contain missing values—is based on the assignment of default values for those missing. Prototypical values of the activated schema are likely to be assigned as default values. Inferences can be the result of either conscious and controlled or unconscious and automatic processing (Smith, 1984).

Schemata can function in the inference process either from the bottom–up or the top–down. The existence of the whole can be inferred from observation of the parts. In this initially bottom–up process, it is not necessary to observe all aspects of a situation before assuming that the schema currently invoked offers a satisfactory account of the perceived data. Second, aspects of a situation not observed can be filled in based on the assignment of default values about typical attributes of the schema currently invoked in a top–down fashion. As in selective attention and encoding, interpretation and inference are biased toward instances of the currently activated schema, particularly when the current data are either ambiguous or congruent with the activated schema. As Bruner (1986) noted, "It is characteristic of complex perceptual processes that they tend whenever possible to assimilate whatever is seen or heard to what is expected" (p. 47).

The results of input processing are the representations of the specific behaviors or events extrapolated from the stimulus configuration and the interpretation of, and inferences made about, the behaviors or events. This representation is stored as part of the activated schema in long-term memory and forms the basis of subsequent judgments about the original behavior or event, although other related knowledge held in the schema may intrude on the judgment, particularly as the time span between input and judgment widens (Carlston, 1980; Wyer & Carlston, 1979).

A cognitive model in which relational-social knowledge held in relational schemata activated by top–down and bottom–up processing has been postulated to operate in the input-processing stages of (a) selective attention, (b) encoding, (c) interpretation, and (d) inference. Perceptual processing and resulting social judgments are mediated by the relationship between social knowledge and the stimulus configuration at the time of input. It is important to determine the conditions under which perceivers are likely to engage in cognitive processing and to form subsequent judgments that involve assimilation, accommodation, or a combination of the two. The interaction between social knowledge and incoming data that influences these perceptual differences in the social judgment process is set forth in the Expectation by Situational Information Interactional Framework (Alloy & Tabachnik, 1984; Metalsky & Abramson, 1981), which is discussed in the next section. The results of several studies that examine perceptual processing of nonverbal-relational communication and resulting social judgment are then reviewed in terms of the cognitive model and this theoretical framework.

EXPECTATION BY SITUATIONAL INFORMATION INTERACTIONAL FRAMEWORK

The relationship between stored social knowledge and current-situational information is a critical aspect of perceptual processing and resulting social judgment (Higgins & Bargh, 1987). Table 3.1 summarizes the predicted interaction between prior expectation and current-situational information and the resulting nature of the social-judgment process. The joint influence of prior expectation and current-situational information is referred to as an interaction because the relative impact of one factor depends on the level or strength of the other factor; it is this interaction that determines the nature of perceptual processing and resulting social judgment (Alloy & Tabachnik, 1984). The effects of prior expectation should be strong when a schema is activated at the time of perceptual processing by means of priming, frequency of prior activation, or observational

TABLE 3.1
An Expectation by Situational Information Interactional Model of Social Judgment

Prior Expectation	Current Situational Information	
	Low	High
Weak	Cell 1: Refrain from social judgment or social judgment made with low confidence	Cell 3: Social judgment highly influenced by current situational information
Strong	Cell 2: Social judgment highly influenced by prior expectation	Cell 4, Case 1: Both prior expectation and current situational information imply similar social judgment—social judgment made with high confidence
		Cell 4, Case 2: Prior expectation and current situational information imply different judgments—cognitive dilemma

Note.   From "Assessment of Covariation by Humans and Animals: The Joint Influence of Prior Expectations and Current Situational Information" by L. B. Alloy and N. Tabachnik, 1994, *Psychological Review, 91,* p. 115. Copyright 1984 by American Psychological Association. Adapted by permission. Also from "Attributional Styles: Toward a Framework for Conceptualization and Assessment" by G. I. Metalsky and L. Y. Abramson in *Assessment Strategies for Cognitive-Behavioral Interventions* (p. 30) by P. C. Kendall and S. D. Hollon, 1981, New York: Academic Press. Copyright 1981 by Academic Press. Adapted by permission.

goal, and weak when no particular schema is activated. The effects of current-situational information should be strong when the data are nonambiguous, salient, or vivid, and weak when the data are ambiguous or inconsistent (Wyer & Carlston, 1979).

Cell 1 of the Expectation by Situational Information Interactional Framework concerns social judgment under the condition in which both prior expectation and current-situational information are weak. In this case, expectation is weak because the perceiver has not activated a particular schema, and thus has no body of activated social knowledge from which to draw suggestions concerning location or content of relevant features in the stimulus configuration. The current-situational information is also weak, in that it is ambiguous or inconsistent and contains no particularly salient or vivid features that might invoke a particular schema from the bottom–up. It is hypothesized that perceivers will refrain from social judgment or make judgments with a low degree of confidence under these circumstances (Kruglanski & Ajzen, 1989).

Cell 2 concerns social judgment under the condition in which prior expectation is strong, due to the top–down influence of an activated schema, while the influence of current-situational information is weak. The activated schema is likely to direct attention to particular locations and types of content in the stimulus configuration. Interpretation should involve matching the new information with past social knowledge held in the activated schema. Inconsistencies are likely to be resolved and missing data filled in by means of inferences that should conform to prototypical features of the activated schema. Perceivers in this condition are likely to make social judgments that rely on activated social knowledge. Thus, they can be said to have engaged in assimilation because the new information has been assimilated to expectation. Higgins and Bargh (1987) noted that a high proportion of previous research in social cognition, social perception, and attribution falls within this cell, and this has led to the erroneous assumption that perceivers are primarily "theory driven" in all social situations.

Strong current-situational information and weak prior expectation characterize the conditions underlying social judgment in Cell 3. When the stimulus configuration is nonambiguous and no particular schema is activated from the top–down, social judgment should be highly influenced by current-situational data activated in a bottom–up fashion.

Cell 4 concerns the conditions in which strong current-situational data and strong prior knowledge independently suggest a particular social judgment. In Case 1 of Cell 4, both prior expectation and current-situational data are congruent. Social judgments made under this condition should be made with high confidence because a particular schema should be activated both from the top–down and the bottom–up.

Case 2 of Cell 4 is the case in which strong current-situational data and strong prior expectation are incongruent and imply different social judgments. The perceiver is faced with a cognitive dilemma in that different schemata might be activated from the top–down and the bottom–up. Some potential means of resolving this cognitive dilemma are for the perceiver to overlook, distort, or misremember current-situational data and to make a social judgment more in line with prior expectation. The perceiver might also reinterpret or ignore prior expectation based on previous social knowledge to make a social judgment more in favor of current-situational information. In either case, both assimilation and accommodation are likely to occur to a certain extent. In most cases, the perceiver will discount or ignore situational information that disconfirms expectation in favor of a social judgment that is more in line with prior expectation (Alloy & Tabachnik, 1984; Bruner, 1986; Metalsky & Abramson, 1981).

In summary, a cognitive model that specifies relational schemata as knowledge structures employed in top–down and bottom–up processing has been postulated to operate during the input-processing phases of selective attention, encoding, interpretation, and inference as perceivers process relational communication. The representation of specific behaviors or events extrapolated from the stimulus configuration and the interpretation of, and inferences made about, the behaviors or events forms the basis of subsequent social judgments. The degree to which a social judgment (a) is made with confidence, (b) is more or less "theory driven" or "data driven," or (c) stems from cognitive dilemma is a function of the relative strength of prior social knowledge and current-situational information at the time of perceptual processing.

PERCEPTUAL PROCESSING OF NONVERBAL-RELATIONAL COMMUNICATION

The findings from three studies (Smith, 1986, Studies 1 and 2, 1991) concerning the ways in which social actors use knowledge stored in relational schemata as they process and derive meaning from nonverbal-relational communication are reviewed here. They are reviewed in terms of their implications for the relative contributions of prior expectation and current-situational information in the perceptual-processing and social-judgment processes. These studies all assume the cognitive model explicated previously, in which relational schemata, the knowledge structures that hold relational knowledge, and top–down and bottom–up processing interact at the (a) selective-attention, (b) encoding, (c) interpretation, and (d) inference phases of input processing.

Relational Schemata and Nonverbal Behaviors Associated With Intimacy

The expression of nonverbal-relational intimacy was chosen as the communicative domain of interest in these studies because intimacy is a central human function, as well as one in which nonverbal behaviors are prevalent and produced with relative spontaneity. "Intimacy might be described as a bipolar dimension that reflects the degree of union or openness toward another individual" (Patterson, 1983, p. 196). It is commonly held that there are appropriate nonverbal manifestations of intimacy at different relational levels. There are expectations of certain behavioral regularities between those who are just becoming acquainted, and expectations that these constellations of behavior are quite different from those exhibited in a relationship of long and close standing. These expectations of behavioral regularities can be seen as a function of social knowledge stored in relational schemata. Therefore, it is likely that perceivers will hold at least two relational schemata to represent the different poles of the relational-intimacy dimension; one for a dyad that is in the beginning stages of relational development and is just becoming acquainted, and one for a dyad that has developed a long-standing close, personal relationship.

The expected patterns of higher involvement in developed relationships are well documented by empirical research (Patterson, 1983). Research on nonverbal communication as an expression of intimacy has found that certain abstract conceptions such as more trust, depth and breadth, affection, intensity of involvement, and inclusion are associated with greater intimacy (Burgoon, 1985; Burgoon, Buller, Hale, & deTurck, 1984; Burgoon & Hale, 1984). The constellation of nonverbal behaviors associated with greater intimacy includes: (a) more smiling and positive facial expression; (b) greater eye contact, including frequent and longer mutual gaze; (c) more gesturing; (d) forward body lean; (e) direct body orientation and more open body position; (f) more head nods; (g) closer distance or proximity; (h) frequent touch; (i) moderate relaxation; (j) less random body movement; and (k) warmer vocal tones (Burgoon, 1980, 1985). These behaviors are in contrast to nonverbal behaviors associated with the beginning stages of a relationship. This research indicates that persons have certain expectations concerning specific nonverbal behaviors and abstract conceptions associated with different levels of intimate relationships. These expectations are a function of stored social knowledge held in relational schemata.

These findings can be applied to the Expectation by Situational Information Interactional Framework: Prior expectation should be strong when perceivers are primed with either a "becoming acquainted" or a "close, personal" relational schema and weak when no schema is invoked. Current-situational information should be strong when it conforms to the constellation of behaviors expected in either high or low intimate relationships and weak when it is ambiguous along this dimension. The studies described next reflect these conceptions.

The Top–Down Influence of Strong Prior Expectation

The first study (Smith, 1986, Study 1) was designed to test the prediction set forth in Cell 2 of the Expectation by Situational Information Interactional Framework that strong prior expectation will significantly affect social judgment when it interacts with weak current-situational information. In this study, strong prior expectation was operationalized by informing one half of the respondents that they would view a videotape of a couple that was just becoming acquainted and informing the other half they would view a couple that was married ($N = 56$). Weak current-situational information was operationalized by showing respondents one of three videotapes of couples interacting with one another. These tapes had been rated by a separate sample of respondents as ambiguous on an intimacy dimension: Their mean intimacy ratings of 3.49 on a 7-point scale did not differ significantly from one another. After being primed with the prior expectation and watching only the video portion of the tape, respondents were asked to fill out a 14-question 7-point Likert-type scale that asked for a variety of judgments about the couple on the videotape. This scale included five questions concerning the level of intimacy respondents perceived the couple to have exhibited. They were next asked to list the specific nonverbal behaviors they noted in support of their judgments concerning the level of intimacy exhibited by the couple on the videotape.

To analyze the respondents' social judgments of intimacy, a 2 (prior expectation) × 3 (current-situational data) mixed-model analysis of variance (ANOVA) procedure was employed. Prior expectation was treated as a fixed factor, and current-situational information was treated as a random factor. Prior expectation was found to significantly affect the results of the intimacy scale, which was reflected in intimacy scale means of the groups primed with "married" ($M = 2.04$) and "getting acquainted" ($M = 3.34$) prior expectations. Neither current-situational information nor the interaction of prior expectation and current-situational data was found to significantly affect the results of the intimacy scale. Thus, as expected, assimilation occurred: Strong prior expectation significantly overrode the effects of weak current-situational information and affected social judgments of intimacy in this condition.

To determine if respondents primed with different prior expectations reported noting different nonverbal behaviors and making different inferences about equivalent ambiguous data on which they based social judgments of intimacy, responses to the open-ended question "Please note the specific nonverbal behaviors you noted in support of your judgment" were analyzed. All responses were first coded into one of two categories: specific nonverbal behaviors or inferences (responses that went beyond reporting nonverbal behaviors; e.g., "They seemed uncomfortable with one another"). There were 246 instances of nonverbal behaviors and 102 instances of inferences reported, comprising 70.9% and 29.1% of the total responses. Although respondents were asked to report only specific nonverbal behaviors, almost one third of their responses were inferential in nature, a finding that indicates that they made inferences beyond the information given as they integrated prior expectation and current-situational information in the interpretation process.

Next 14 categories of nonverbal behaviors and 9 categories of inferences were found by two coders, and all responses were coded into these categories. Nonverbal categories included: (a) touch, (b) touch missing, (c) smiles, (d) distance close, (e) distance far, (f) nodding, (g) forward lean, (h) gaze toward, (i) gaze away, (j) gestures, (k) leg and arm movements, (l) turn taking, (m) posture, and (n) body orientation. Categories of inferences included: (a) relaxed and comfortable, (b) tense at first but relaxed over time, (c) nervous and uncomfortable, (d) not interested in one another, (e) poor quality of conversation, (f) good quality of conversation, (g) not intimate, (h) relational involvement, and (i) just met. Finally, a "Test of Significance between Two Proportions" (Bruning & Kintz, 1968, p. 199) was performed on all 23 categories of behaviors and inferences. Nonverbal behaviors and inferences that characterized the "becoming acquainted" condition were: (a) gazing away from one another, (b) gestures, (c) leg and arm movements, and (d) the inference that the couple was somewhat tense at first but relaxed over time. The "married" condition was characterized by the nonverbal behavior of nodding, and the inferences that the couple was relaxed, relationally involved, but not interested in one another. These results indicate that respondents primed with different relational schemata noted different nonverbal behaviors and made different types of inferences when making social judgments of intimacy, although they viewed equivalent, ambiguous data.

The results of these analyses show the strong top–down influence of prior expectation when it is coupled with weak current-situational information in perceptual processing. First, perceivers primed with different prior expectations reported noting different nonverbal behaviors on which they based social judgments of intimacy. Next, they made different types of inferences when integrating social knowledge with the behaviors they noted. Finally, they made significantly different social judgments of intimacy, although in all cases they viewed equivalent, ambiguous data. These findings offer support for the predictions set forth in Cell 2 of the Expectation by Situational Information Interactional Framework, although they do not offer evidence as to whether the different nonverbal behaviors and inferences noted by respondents conform to prototypical values of the activated schemata.

The purpose of the next study (Smith, 1986, Study 2) was to determine if the different specific nonverbal behaviors and inferences noted by respondents in the previously described study conformed to the prototypical values of the schemata with which they were primed. To determine the values of each schema, a scale was constructed in which three representative instances of each of the 14 categories of behavior and 9 categories of inferences were drawn from open-ended responses in the previously described study. For instance, for the behavioral category "Gestures," the following items were included:

1. She used a lot of hand gestures to reinforce her words.
2. They tried to find things like fixing clothes and hair to occupy themselves.

3. They sat with their hands clasped in their laps.

For the inferential category "Poor Quality of Conversation," the following items were included:

1. It seemed as if they were having to keep the conversation going.
2. The conversation seemed awkward.
3. They seemed to be in a discussion, not closely associated.

One half of all items were drawn from respondents who had been primed with the "married" condition, and one half were drawn from respondents in the "becoming acquainted" condition. Each item was rated using a 7-point Likert-type scale ranging from 1 (extremely typical that I would see this behavior or make this inference) to 7 (extremely untypical that I would see this behavior or make this inference). This scale was presented to each respondent ($N = 95$) twice: once to rate a couple that was just becoming acquainted and once to rate a married couple. The order of presentation was altered to control for response-order bias.

To determine the values of "becoming acquainted" and "married" relational schemata, the ratings of the three items measuring each category were summed, and mean scores for each category of "becoming acquainted" and "married" schemata groups were calculated. A series of repeated measured t tests were then performed to determine significant differences in the content of "becoming ac-quainted" and "intimate" schemata. Behaviors and inferences most closely asso-ciated with couples that were just "becoming acquainted" were: (a) lack of touch, (b) smiling, (c) sitting far away from one another, (d) gazing away from one another, (e) gesturing, (f) leg and arm movements, (g) body orientation, (h) being tense at first but relaxing over time, (i) nervousness, (j) poor quality of conversation, and (k) having just met. The behaviors and inferences most closely associated with "intimate" couples were: (a) touching, (b) sitting close to one another, (c) gazing toward one another, (d) good posture, (e) relaxation, (f) good quality of conversation, and (g) being relationally involved with one another. Behaviors and inferences not specifically associated with either schema included: (a) nodding, (b) leaning toward one another, (c) turn taking, and (d) not being interested in one another.

To determine whether the different nonverbal behaviors and inferences noted by respondents in the previous study conformed to prototypical values of the schemata with which they were primed, nonverbal behaviors and inferences that characterized the "becoming acquainted" and "married" conditions were con-trasted with the nonverbal behaviors and inferences that were associated with those conditions in this study. The nonverbal behaviors gazing away from one another, gestures, and leg and arm movements, and the inference that the couple was tense at first but relaxed over time, characterized the "becoming acquainted" schema in the first study, and all were found to be prototypical values of the "becoming acquainted" schema in this study. A "Test of Significance between Two Proportions" was performed on this data, and the z score of 2 indicated that this proportion was significant at the .05 level.

The nonverbal behavior of nodding and the inferences that the couple was relaxed, relationally involved, but not interested in one another characterized the "married" condition in the previous study. However, only two of these inferences—relaxation and relational involvement—were found to be prototypical values of this schema in this study. A z score of 0 on a "Test of Significance between Two Proportions" indicates that this is a nonsignificant finding. Nodding and the inference that the couple was not interested in one another were not significantly associated with either schema in this study, which indicated that they were located at the "fuzzy" and overlapping boundaries of the schemata.

These results offer some support for the predictions that schemata are likely to direct attention to particular types of content, and that inconsistencies are likely to be resolved and missing data filled in by means of inferences that conform to prototypical values of activated schemata. The results of these studies also offer some weak evidence that prototypes function as a standard around which a body of input can be compared. In the previous study, poor-quality conversation was more likely to be noted by respondents primed with the "married" schema, whereas good-quality conversation was more likely to be noted by respondents primed with the "becoming acquainted" schema, although the differences were not significant. In this study, good-quality conversation was found to be a value of the "married" schema, and poor-quality conversation was found to be a value of the "becoming acquainted" schema. This suggests that respondents in the previous study primed with the "married" schema (a) expected to find good-quality conversation, (b) compared the data on the videotape with this standard, and (c) made the inference that the quality of conversation was poor. On the other hand, the respondents primed with the "becoming acquainted" schema (a) expected poor-quality conversation, (b) compared the data with this standard, and (c) made the inference that the quality of conversation was good.

The results of these studies reflect the top–down influence of strong prior expectation when it interacts with weak current–situational information. The next study in this series was designed to test the effects of strong current-situational information in perceptual processing of nonverbal-relational communication.

The Bottom-Up Influence of Strong Current-Situational Data

The final study (Smith, 1991) was designed to examine the predictions set forth in Cells 3 and 4 of the Prior Expectation by Situational Information Interactional framework. Cell 3 predicts that when strong current-situational information interacts with weak prior expectation, current-situational information will significantly affect perceptual processing and social judgments of intimacy due to the bottom–up influence of current-situational information. Cell 4, Case 1 predicts that when current-situational information is strong and congruent with strong prior expectation, respondents will experience the highest confidence in their social judgments of intimacy due to the concurrent bottom–up and top–down activation of the same relational schema. Cell 4, Case 2 predicts that strong current-situational information that interacts with incongruent strong prior expectation will result in cognitive dilemma due to the top–down and bottom–up activation of different relational schemata. Previous literature suggests that respondents should resolve this dilemma by reliance on stored social knowledge consistent with prior expectation.

In this study, strong prior expectation was operationalized by informing approximately one third of the respondents that they would view a videotape of a couple that was just becoming acquainted, and by informing another one third of the respondents that they would view a married couple. Weak prior expectation was operationalized by withholding any prime from the final one third of respondents ($N = 137$).

Strong current-situational information was operationalized by showing respondents one of two videotapes of couples interacting with one another. A separate sample of respondents rated these tapes on their level of intimacy, and the mean ratings ($Ms = 2.67, 5.02$) indicated that the tapes were perceived as significantly different from one another on an intimacy dimension.

In each condition, the respondents received one of the three expectation primes, then viewed the video portion of one of the two videotapes. After viewing the videotape, respondents were asked to: (a) indicate how long they believed the couple on the videotape to have known one another, (b) fill out a 15-question 7-point Likert-type scale that asked for a variety of judgments about the couple on the videotape, and (c) rate the degree of confidence with which each judgment was made. The intimacy scale included eight questions concerning the level of intimacy respondents perceived the couple to have exhibited. The confidence of rating scale asked respondents to rate their degree of confidence in each of the intimacy ratings. They were finally asked to list the specific nonverbal behaviors they noted in support of their judgments concerning the level of intimacy exhibited by the couple on the videotape.

To assess the effectiveness of the manipulation of prior expectation and current-situational information, a 3 (prior expectation) × 2 (current-situational data) ANOVA was performed on the amount of time respondents perceived the couples to have known one another. A significant overall effect was found for prior expectation and current-situational data on the amount of time respondents believed the couples to have known one another. There were main effects for prior expectation and current-situational data, although their interaction was nonsignificant. The mean perceived number of days known reported by respondents who viewed the low-intimacy tape were 67.5, 178.2, and 697.4 for "becoming acquainted," control, and "close, personal" primes, respectively. The mean perceived number of days known reported by respondents who viewed the high-intimacy tape were 264.5, 376, and 985.6 for "becoming acquainted," control, and "close, personal" primes, respectively. These results indicate that manipulation of prior expectation and the intimacy level of the tapes was successful.

To test the prediction offered in Cell 3—that strong current-situational data affect social judgments of intimacy when they interact with weak prior expectation—a 3 (prior expectation) × 2 (current-situational data) ANOVA was performed on the results of the intimacy scale. A significant overall effect was found, which was due solely to the main effect for current-situational data. Respondents who viewed the low-intimacy tape in all prior-expectation conditions rated the intimacy level of the couple significantly lower $M = 3.60$) than did respondents who viewed the high-intimacy tape in all prior-expectation conditions ($M = 4.76$). Thus, strong current-situational data were found to significantly affect social judgments of intimacy not only when prior expectation was weak, but also when prior expectation was strong and congruent with the data, and when prior expectation was strong and incongruent with the data.

The prediction set forth in Cell 4, Case 1—that respondents would experience highest confidence in social judgments of intimacy when strong prior expectation interacts with strong congruent current-situational data—was tested by means of a 3 (prior expectation) × 2 (current-situational data) ANOVA on the confidence of success scale. The nonsignificant overall effect, due to an overall mean confidence rating of 5.07, indicates strong current-situational data had a positive effect on confidence in social judgment across all conditions.

The prediction set forth in Cell 4, Case 2—that respondents would experience cognitive dilemma due to the interaction of strong current-situational information and incongruent strong prior expectation and would resolve the dilemma in terms of prior expectation—could be determined in several ways. Perceivers might resolve cognitive dilemma in terms of the (a) number of behaviors they noted, (b) number of inferences they made, (c) type of behaviors they reported, or (d) type of inferences they made. To analyze these data, it was first necessary to analyze responses to the open-ended question, "Please list the specific nonverbal behaviors you noted in support of this judgment (level of intimacy)." As in the first study, all responses were first coded into either specific behavior or inference categories. Next, 15 categories of behaviors and 12 categories of inferences were found by two coders, and all responses were coded into these categories. Categories of nonverbal behavior included: (a) touch, (b) touch missing, (c) smiles, (d) distance close, (e) distance far, (f) nodding, (g) lean, (h) gaze toward, (i) gaze away, (j) gestures, (k) leg and arm movements, (l) turn taking, (m) posture, (n) body orientation toward, and (o) body orientation away. Categories of inferences included: (a) relaxed, (b) nervous, (c) interested in one another, (d) not interested in one another, (e) positive emotions, (f) negative emotions, (g) good conversation, (h) poor conversation, (i) sexual attraction, (j) status difference, (k) familiar, and (l) unfamiliar.

The phenomenon of cognitive dilemma might be indicated by a high number of behaviors noted and inferences made in the social-judgment process as a result of increased attention and perceptual processing due to the necessity of integrating schema-inconsistent information. To test this prediction, two 3 (prior expectation) × 2 (current-situational information) ANOVAs were performed: one on the number of nonverbal behaviors reported, and the second on the number of inferences reported when answering the previously described open-ended question. The nonsignificant overall effect for prior expectation and current-situational data on number of behaviors reported ($M = 4.41$) indicated that number of behaviors respondents noted, on which they based their social judgments of intimacy, was not affected by strong current-situational information or strong prior expectation, nor does it provide evidence of cognitive dilemma.

A significant overall effect was found for prior expectation and current-situational data on number of inferences reported in support of social judgments of intimacy. Main effects for prior expectation, current-situational data, and their interaction indicated that the interaction of incongruent strong current-situational data with strong prior expectation significantly affected the number of inferences reported. To further probe these results, Scheffe's procedure was performed on the number of inferences reported by condition. The results of this test indicated that respondents who were primed to believe they were viewing a married couple, but were shown the low-intimacy tape, made significantly more inferences ($M = 4.89$) than respondents in any other condition ($M = 2.99$). This finding also provides evidence that respondents in that condition were experiencing cognitive dilemma.

To determine the types of behaviors and inferences noted by respondents in the incongruent conditions, two 3 (prior expectation) × 2 (current-situational data) multiple analysis of variances (MANOVAs) were performed: one for positive and negative behaviors, and one for positive and negative inferences noted in support of social judgments of intimacy. Because the MANOVA procedure was sensitive to large numbers of dependent variables, and on the basis of the results of a correlation matrix, it was necessary to place the nonverbal behaviors of (a) touch, (b) smiles, (c) distance close, (d) nodding, (e) gaze toward, (f) gestures, (g) turn taking, and (h) body orientation in one group called *positive behaviors;* and (a) touch missing, (b) distance far, (c) gaze away, and (d) body orientation away in one group called *negative behaviors*. The same procedure was followed for inferences and resulted in one group that included (a) relaxation, (b) interest in one another, (c) good conversation, (d) positive emotions, and (e) familiarity called *positive inferences;* and one group that included (a) nervousness, (b) low interest in one another, (c) poor conversation, (d) negative emotions, and (e) nonfamiliarity called *negative inferences*.

The results of the 3 (prior expectation) $\times$ 2 (current-situational data) MAN-OVA on positive and negative behaviors noted in support of social judgments of intimacy indicated a significant main effect for current-situational data, defined in terms of both negative and positive behaviors, but no effect for prior expectation or the interaction of prior expectation and current-situational data. Contrast procedures indicated that significantly more negative behaviors were noted when respondents were shown the low-intimacy tape ($M = 1.19$) than when they were shown the high-intimacy tape ($M = .50$). Also, significantly more positive behaviors were noted when respondents were shown the high-intimacy tape ($M = 4.03$) than when they were shown the low-intimacy tape ($M = 2.43$). Thus, regardless of prior expectation, respondents viewing the low-intimacy tape were significantly more likely to note that the couple on the videotape (a) did not touch, (b) sat far apart from one another, (c) gazed away from one another, and (d) established body orientation away from one another. Regardless of prior expectation, respondents viewing the high-intimacy tape were significantly more likely to note that the couple (a) touched, (b) smiled, (c) sat close together, (d) nodded, (e) gazed at one another, (f) gestured, (g) took turns in the conversation, and (h) established body orientation toward one another.

The results of a 3 (prior expectation) $\times$ 2 (current-situational data) MANOVA on positive and negative inferences noted in support of social judgments of intimacy indicated a significant main effect for prior expectation, defined in terms of negative inferences, and current-situational data, also defined in terms of negative inferences, but no effect for the interaction of prior expectation and current-situational information. To further probe these results, Scheffe's procedure was performed on negative inferences reported by condition. The results of this test indicate that respondents who viewed the low-intimacy tape and were primed to believe they were viewing a married couple made significantly more inferences that the couple was (a) nervous, (b) not interested in one another, (c) unfamiliar with one another, (d) experienced negative emotions, (e) had a poor quality of conversation, and (f) were unequal in status than respondents in all other conditions—except that in which respondents were primed to believe they were viewing a couple that was just becoming acquainted and viewed the low-intimacy tape.

Taken as a whole, these results indicate that, although respondents in incongruent conditions ultimately made social judgments consistent with the effect of strong current-situational information, incongruent strong prior expectation mediated this outcome and affected perceptual processing in certain ways. Respondents in one incongruent condition who viewed the low-intimacy tape and were primed to believe they were viewing a married couple apparently experienced cognitive dilemma. They did report behaviors consistent with the low-intimacy tape, then made a number of negative inferences such that they were able to resolve inconsistencies between prior expectation and incongruent current-situational data. Finally, they rated the intimacy level of the couple in a manner consistent with current-situational information. Thus, these perceivers engaged in accommodation: They reinterpreted prior expectation based on previous social knowledge to make a judgment in favor of current-situational information. These findings suggest that these perceivers did not overlook, distort, or misremember strong current-situational information and did not resolve cognitive dilemma by reliance on prior expectation, as was hypothesized. Finally, respondents primed to believe they were viewing a couple that was just becoming acquainted and shown the high-intimacy tape apparently did not experience cognitive dilemma because they rated the intimacy level of the couple in a manner consistent with current-situational information without the need to make significantly more inferences. Apparently, they saw this situation as one in which the couple "hit it off" from the start. In summary, prior expectation did not override current-situational information or have the strong effect on perceptual processing and resulting social judgment that was hypothesized in this condition. Salient current-situational information activated from the bottom–up produced the strongest effect on perceptual processing and social judgments of intimacy in the incongruent conditions.

CONCLUSION

A cognitive model that specified relational schemata as the knowledge structures operated on by top–down and bottom–up processing was postulated to operate during the input-processing phases of (a) selective attention, (b) encoding, (c) interpretation, and (d) inference as perceivers process relational communication. The representation of specific behaviors extrapolated from the stimulus configuration and the interpretation of, and inferences made about, these behaviors form the basis of subsequent social judgments. Assimilation occurred when prior expectation was strong and current-situational information was weak. Due to social knowledge held in relational schemata, prior expectation exerted a strong influence from the top–down on perceptual processing of relational-nonverbal communication and subsequent social judgments. However, when current-situational information was strong and prior expectation was weak or congruent with current-situational information, the opposite was the case, and accommodation occurred. Under these conditions, current-situational information exerted a strong influence from the bottom–up on perceptual processing of relational communication and subsequent social judgment. When perceivers experienced cognitive dilemma resulting from incongruence between prior expectation and current-situational information, social judgments were strongly affected by current-situational information, although prior expectation exerted a mediating influence during perceptual processing of relational-nonverbal communication. In this condition, both assimilation and accommodation occurred. Thus, due to their cognitive capacities and the relationship between prior expectation and current-situational information, persons can "both make sense of and impose sense upon the world" (Alloy & Tabachnik, 1984, p. 141).

The benefit of an interpersonal-communication focus on social cognition is that research moves away from "relatively simple and nondemanding information processing situations" to "real world social situations (which) require that information be processed about several different people or events at once" (White & Carlston, 1983, p. 538) and focuses attention on relational-social knowledge. However, it may be difficult to generalize to the perceptual processing and resulting social judgments of interactants engaged in conversation from the results of the studies described here. All respondents in these studies were observers of, not participants in, interaction. Generally, social actors engaged in interaction (a) should be less likely to take their own actions into account (Wyer & Carlston, 1979), (b) should have a greater array of objectives to accomplish, (c) often have access to information about emotions and thoughts that observers do not, and (d) are engaged in dynamic person-perception processes, and, thus, would be likely to process nonverbal-relational communication and make social judgments in a different manner than would observers of that interaction (Cappella & Street, 1989). However, research by Honeycutt (1989, 1990) and Ickes, Patterson, Rajecki, and Tanford (1982) indicated that conversational interactants with strong friendly or unfriendly preinteraction expectancies made postinteraction social judgments that reflected these expectancies, although they tended to sit closer, look at, initiate talk, and talk more to their partners than interactants with no expectancies. Cappella and Palmer (1990) found that both attitude similarity and nonverbal behaviors contribute to attraction and satisfaction. Thus, there is some evidence that both assimilation and accommodation occur for participants in *and* observers of interaction. Future research should attempt to discover how perceptual processing of relational communication and resulting social judgments differ in social actors engaged in communication from social actors who are observers of communication (Cappella & Street, 1989), while taking into account the relationship between data and expectation.

The benefit of a social-cognitive perspective on interpersonal communication is that it can provide insight into the ways that communicators represent and utilize relational knowledge to interpret and produce relational messages. The utilization of a social-cognitive perspective can help communication scholars to answer the *why* and *how* questions that have intrigued us for so long. The union of social cognition and interpersonal communication is one that will benefit scholarship in both areas.

REFERENCES

Alloy, L. B., & Tabachnik, N. (1984). Assessment of covariation by humans and animals: The joint influence of prior expectations and current situational information. *Psychological Review, 91,* 112–149.

Anderson, J. R. (1980). *Cognitive psychology and its implications.* San Francisco: Freeman.

Athay, M., & Darley, J. M. (1981). Toward an interaction centered theory of personality. In N. Cantor & J. F. Kihlstrom (Eds.), *Personality, cognition, and social interaction* (pp. 281–308). Hillsdale, NJ: Lawrence Erlbaum Associates.

Axley, S. R. (1984). Managerial and organizational communication in terms of the conduit metaphor. *Academy of Management Journal, 9,* 428–437.

Berger, C. R., & Kellerman, K. A. (1983). To ask or not to ask: Is that a question? In R. N. Bostrom (Ed.), *Communication Yearbook 7* (pp. 342–368). Beverly Hills, CA: Sage.

Berger, C. R., & Roloff, M. E. (1982). Social cognition and relational trajectories. In R. E. Roloff & C. R. Berger (Eds.), *Social cognition and communication* (pp. 151–192). Beverly Hills, CA: Sage.

Brewer, W. F., & Nakamura, G. V. (1984). The nature and function of schemas. In R. S. Wyer, Jr., & T. K. Srull (Eds.), *Handbook of social cognition* (Vol. 1, pp. 119–160). Hillsdale, NJ: Lawrence Erlbaum Associates.

Broughton, R. (1984). A prototype strategy for the construction of personality scales. *Journal of Personality and Social Psychology, 47,* 1134–1146.

Bruner, J. (1964). On going beyond the information given. In R. J. C. Harper, C. C. Anderson, C. M. Christensen, & S. M. Hunka (Eds.), *The cognitive processes* (pp. 293–311). Englewood Cliffs, NJ: Prentice-Hall.

Bruner, J. (1983). *In search of mind: Essays in autobiography.* New York: Harper Colophon Books.

Bruner, J. (1986). *Actual minds, possible worlds,* Cambridge, MA: Harvard University Press.

Bruning, J. L., & Kintz, B. L. (1968). *Handbook of computational statistics.* Glenview, IL: Scott, Foresman, & Co.

Burgoon, J. K. (1978). A communication model of personal space violations: Explication and an initial test. *Human Communication Research, 13,* 129–142.

Burgoon, J. K. (1980). Nonverbal communication research in the 1970's: An overview. In D. Nimmo (Ed.), *Communication Yearbook 4* (pp. 179–197). Beverly Hills, CA: Sage.

Burgoon, J. K. (1983). Nonverbal violations of expectations. In J. M. Wiemann & R. P. Harrison (Eds.), *Nonverbal interaction* (pp. 77–111). Beverly Hills, CA: Sage.

Burgoon, J. K. (1985). Nonverbal signals. In M. L. Knapp & G. R. Miller (Eds.), *Handbook of interpersonal communication* (pp. 344–390). Beverly Hills, CA: Sage.

Burgoon, J. K., Buller, D. B., Hale, J. L., & deTurck, M. A. (1984). Relational messages associated with nonverbal behaviors. *Human Communication Research, 10,* 351–378.

Burgoon, J. K., & Hale, J. L. (1984). The fundamental *topoi* of relational communication. *Communication Monographs, 51,* 193–214.

Burgoon, J. K., & Hale, J. L. (1988). Nonverbal expectancy violations theory: Model elaboration and application to expectancy behaviors. *Communication Monographs, 55,* 58–79.

Burgoon, J. K., & Walther, J. B. (1990). Nonverbal expectancies and the evaluative consequences of violations. *Human Communication Research, 17,* 232–265.

Cantor, N., & Mischel, W. (1977). Traits as prototypes: Effects on recognition memory. *Journal of Personality and Social Psychology, 35,* 38–48.

Cantor, N., & Mischel, W. (1979). Prototypes in person perception. In L. Berkowitz (Ed.), *Advances in experimental social psychology (Vol. 12,* pp. 3–52). New York: Academic Press.

Cantor, N., Mischel, W., & Schwartz, J. (1982a). Social knowledge: Structure, content, use and abuse. In A. H. Hastorf & A. M. Isen (Eds.), *Cognitive social psychology* (pp. 33–72). New York: Elseiver/North-Holland.

Cantor, N., Mischel, W., & Schwartz, J. (1982b). A prototype analysis of situations. *Cognitive Psychology, 14,* 45–77.

Cappella, J. N., & Greene, J. O. (1982). A discrepancy-arousal explanation of mutual influence in expressive behavior for adult-adult and infant-adult interaction. *Communication Monographs, 49,* 89–114.

Cappella, J. N., & Palmer, M. T. (1990). Attitude similarity, relational history, and attraction: The mediating effects of kinesic and vocal behaviors. *Communication Monographs, 57,* 161–183.

Cappella, J. N., & Street, R. L. (1989). Message effects: Research on mental models of messages. In J. J. Bradac (Ed.), *Message effects in communication science* (pp. 24–51). Newbury Park, CA: Sage.

Carlston, D. E. (1980). Events, inferences and impression formation. In R. Hastie, T. M. Ostrom, E. B. Ebbesen, R. S. Wyer, Jr., D. L. Hamilton, & D. E. Carlston (Eds.), *Person memory: The cognitive basis of social perception* (pp. 89–119). Hillsdale, NJ: Lawrence Erlbaum Associates.

Cody, M. J., & McLaughlin, M. L. (1985). The situation as a construct in interpersonal communication research. In M. L. Knapp & G. R. Miller (Eds.), *Handbook of interpersonal communication* (pp. 263–312). Beverly Hills, CA: Sage.

Cohen, C. E. (1981). Goals and schemata in person perception: Making sense from the stream of behavior. In N. Cantor & J. F. Kihlstrom (Eds.), *Personality, cognition and social interaction* (pp. 45–68). Hillsdale, NJ: Lawrence Erlbaum Associates.

Craig, R. T. (1978). Information systems theory and research: An overview of individual information processing. In D. Nimmo (Ed.), *Communication Yearbook 3* (pp. 99–121). New Brunswick, NJ: Transaction.

Davis, K. E., & Todd, M. J. (1985). Assessing friendship: Prototypes, paradigm cases and relational description. In S. Duck & D. Perlman (Eds.), *Understanding personal relationships: An interdisciplinary approach* (pp. 17–38). Beverly Hills, CA: Sage.

Delia, J. G. (1977). Constructivism and the study of human communication. *Quarterly Journal of Speech, 63,* 66–83.

Doelger, J. A., Hewes, D. E., & Graham, M. L. (1986). Knowing when to "second guess": The mindful analysis of messages. *Human Communication Research, 12,* 301–338.

Ebbesen, E. B. (1980). Cognitive processes in understanding ongoing behavior. In R. Hastie, T. M. Ostrom, E. B. Ebbesen, R. S. Wyer, D. L. Hamilton, & E. L. Carlston (Eds.), *Person memory: The cognitive basis of social perception* (pp. 179–225). Hillsdale, NJ: Lawrence Erlbaum Associates.

Endler, N. S. (1982). Interactionism comes of age. In M. F. Zanna, E. T. Higgins, & E. P. Herman (Eds.), *Consistency in social behavior: The Ontario Symposium (Vol. 2,* pp. 209–249). Hillsdale, NJ: Lawrence Erlbaum Associates.

Fiske, S., & Linville, P. (1980). What does the schema concept buy us? *Personality and Social Psychology Bulletin, 6,* 543–557.

Fiske, S. T., & Taylor, S. E. (1984). *Social cognition.* Reading, MA: Addison-Wesley.

Greene, J. O. (1984). Evaluating cognitive explanations of communicative phenomena. *Quarterly Journal of Speech, 70,* 241–254.

Hewes, D. E., & Graham, M. (1989). Second-guessing. In J. Anderson (Ed.), *Communication Yearbook 12* (pp. 213–248). Newbury Park, CA: Sage.

Hewes, D. E., Graham, M., Doelger, J. A., & Pavitt, C. (1985). Second-guessing: Message interpretation in social networks. *Human Communication Research, 11,* 299–344.

Hewes, D. E., Graham, M., Monsour, M., & Doelger, J. A. (1989). Information-gathering strategies: Reinterpretation assessment in second-guessing. *Human Communication Research, 16,* 297–321.

Hewes, D. E., & Planalp, S. (1982). There is nothing as useful as a good theory: The influence of social knowledge on interpersonal communication. In M. E. Roloff & C. R. Berger (Eds.), *Social cognition and communication* (pp. 107–150). Beverly Hills, CA: Sage.

Hewes, D. E., & Planalp, S. (1987). The individual's place in communication science. In C. R. Berger & S. H. Chaffee (Eds.), *Handbook of communication science* (pp. 146–183) Newbury Park, CA: Sage.

Higgins, E. T., & Bargh, J. A. (1987). Social cognition and social perception. *Annual Review of Psychology, 38,* 369–425.

Hochberg, J. E. (1978). *Perception.* Englewood Cliffs, NJ: Prentice-Hall.

Honeycutt, J. M. (1989). Effects of preinteraction strategies on interaction involvement and behavioral responses to initial interaction. *Journal of Nonverbal Behavior, 13,* 25–35.

Honeycutt, J. M. (1990). An interaction goals perspective on the relationship between preinteraction expectancies, attraction, and attributional confidence in initial interaction. *Journal of Social Behavior and Personality, 5,* 367–383.

Honeycutt, J. M. (1991). The role of nonverbal behaviors in modifying expectancies during initial encounters. *The Southern Communication Journal, 56,* 161–177.

Honeycutt, J. M. (1993). Components and functions of communication during initial interaction with extrapolations to beyond. In S. A. Deetz (Ed.), *Communication Yearbook 16* (pp. 461–490). Newbury Park, CA: Sage.

Ickes, W., Patterson, M. L., Rajecki, D. W., & Tanford, S. (1982). Behavioral and cognitive consequences of reciprocal versus compensatory responses to preinteraction expectancies. *Social Cognition, 1,* 160–190.

Johnson, W.A., & Dark, V. J. (1986). Selective attention. *Annual Review of Psychology, 37,* 43–75.

Kellerman, K., & Lim, T. S. (1989). Inference-generating knowledge structures in message processing. In J. J. Bradac (Ed.), *Message effects in communication science* (pp. 102–128). Newbury Park, CA: Sage.

Kruglanski, A. W., & Ajzen, I. (1989). Bias and error in human judgment. *European Journal of Social Psychology, 13,* 1–44.

Lord, R. G. (1985). An information processing approach to social perceptions, leadership and behavioral measurement in organizations. In L. L. Cummings & B. M. Staw (Eds.), *Research in organizational behavior (Vol. 7,* pp. 87–128). Greenwich, CT: JAI.

Magnusson, D., & Endler, N. S. (1977). Interactional psychology: Present status and future prospects. In D. Magnusson & N. S. Endler (Eds.), *Personality at the crossroads: Current issues in interactional psychology* (pp. 3–31). Hillsdale, NJ: Lawrence Erlbaum Associates.

Manusov, V. (1991). Perceiving nonverbal messages: Effects of immediacy and encoded intent on receiver judgments. *Western Journal of Speech Communication, 55,* 235–253.

Manusov, V., & Rodriguez, J. S. (1989). Intentionality behind nonverbal messages: A perceiver's perspective. *Journal of Nonverbal Behavior, 13,* 15–24.

McClelland, J. L., & Rumelhart, D. E. (1981). An interactive activation model of context effects in letter perception: Part I of an account of basic findings. *Psychological Review, 88,* 375–407.

McClelland, J. L., & Rumelhart, D. E. (1985). Distributed memory and the representation of general and specific information. *Journal of Experimental Psychology: General, 14,* 159–188.

Metalsky, G. I., & Abramson, L. Y. (1981). Attributional styles: Toward a framework for conceptualization and assessment. In P. C. Kendall & S. D. Hollon (Eds.), *Assessment strategies for cognitive-behavioral interventions* (pp. 13–58). New York: Academic Press.

Mischel, W. (1977). The interaction of person and situation. In D. Magnusson & N. S. Endler (Eds.), *Personality at the crossroads: Current issues in interactional psychology* (pp. 333–352). Hillsdale, NJ: Lawrence Erlbaum Associates.

Neisser, U. (1976). *Cognition and reality.* San Francisco: Freeman.

Norman, D. A. (1976). *Memory and attention.* New York: Wiley.

Norman, D. A., & Bobrow, D. G. (1976). On the role of memory processes in perception and cognition. In C. N. Cofer (Ed.), *The structure of human memory* (pp. 114–132). San Francisco: Freeman.

Ortony, A. (1978). Remembering, understanding and representation. *Cognitive Science, 2,* 53–69.

Ostrom, T. M. (1984). The sovereignty of social cognition. In R. S. Wyer, Jr., & T. K. Srull (Eds.), *Handbook of social cognition (Vol. 1,* pp. 1–38). Hillsdale, NJ: Lawrence Erlbaum Associates.

Patterson, M. L. (1983). *Nonverbal behavior: A functional perspective.* New York: Springer-Verlag.

Pavitt, C. (1982). A test of six models of coorientation: The effect of task and disagreement level on judgments of uncertainty, utility, and desired communicative behavior. In M. Burgoon (Ed.), *Communication Yearbook 5* (pp. 303–330). New Brunswick, NJ: Transaction.

Pavitt, C. (1989). Accounting for the process of communicative competence evaluation: A comparison of predictive models. *Communication Research, 16*, 405–433.

Pavitt, C., & Haight, L. (1985). The "competent" communicator as a cognitive prototype. *Human Communication Research, 12*, 225–241.

Planalp, S. (1985). Relational schemata: A test of alternative forms of relational knowledge as guides to communication. *Human Communication Research, 11*, 3–29.

Planalp, S. (1989). Relational communication and cognition. In B. Dervin, L. Grossberg, B. J. O'Keefe, & E. Wartella (Eds.), *Rethinking communication: Paradigm exemplars (Vol. 2*, pp. 269–277). Newbury Park: CA: Sage.

Planalp, S., & Hewes, D. E. (1982). A cognitive approach to communication theory: Cognito ergo dico? In M. Burgoon (Ed.), *Communication Yearbook 5* (pp. 49–77). New Brunswick, NJ: Transaction.

Planalp, S., & Honeycutt, J. M. (1985). Events that increase uncertainty in personal relationships. *Human Communication Research, 11*, 593–604.

Planalp, S., Rutherford, D. K., & Honeycutt, J. M. (1988). Events that increase uncertainty in personal relationships: Vol II. Replication and extension. *Human Communication Research, 14*, 516–547.

Rosch, E. (1978). Principles of categorization. In E. Rosch & B. B. Lloyd (Eds.), *Cognition and categorization* (pp. 27–48. Hillsdale, NJ: Lawrence Erlbaum Associates.

Rumelhart, D. E. (1984). Schemata and the cognitive system. In R. S. Wyer, Jr., & T. K. Srull (Eds.), *Handbook of social cognition (Vol. 1*, pp. 161–185). Hillsdale, NJ: Lawrence Erlbaum Associates.

Rumelhart, D. E., & Ortony, A. (1977). The representation of knowledge in memory. In R. C. Anderson, R. J. Spiro, & W. E. Montague (Eds.), *Schooling and the acquisition of knowledge* (pp. 99–135). Hillsdale, NJ: Lawrence Erlbaum Associates.

Schneider, B. (1983). Interactional psychology and organizational behavior. In L. L. Cummings & B. M. Staw (Eds.), *Research in organizational communication (Vol. 5*, pp. 1–31). Greenwich, CT: JAI.

Smith, E. R. (1984). Model of social inference processes. *Psychological Review, 91*, 392–413.

Smith, S. W. (1986). *A social-cognitive approach to the nature of input processes in reception of nonverbal messages.* Unpublished doctoral dissertation, University of Southern California, Los Angeles.

Smith, S. W. (1991, May). *The effects of strong nonverbal relational data on perceptual processing and resulting social judgments.* Paper presented at the annual meeting of the International Communication Association, Chicago.

Srull, T. K., & Wyer, R. S., Jr. (1979). The role of category accessibility in the interpretation of information about persons: Some determinants and implications. *Journal of Personality and Social Psychology, 37*, 1660–1672.

Sypher, H. E., & Higgins, E. T. (1989). Social cognition and communication: An overview. *Communication Research, 16*, 309–313.

Taylor, S. E., & Crocker, J. (1981). Schematic bases of social information processing. In E. T. Higgins, G. P. Herman, & M. P. Zanna (Eds.), *The Ontario Symposium* (pp. 89–134). Hillsdale, NJ: Lawrence Erlbaum Associates.

Trope, Y. (1986). Identification and inferential processes in dispositional attribution. *Psychological Review, 93*, 239–257.

Tversky, A. (1977). Features of similarity. *Psychological Review, 84*, 327–352.

White, D. J., & Carlston, D. E. (1983). Consequences of schemata for attention, impressions, and recall in complex social interactions. *Journal of Personality and Social Psychology, 45*, 538–549.

Wyer, R. S., Jr., & Carlston, D. E. (1979). *Social cognition, inference, and attribution.* Hillsdale, NJ: Lawrence Erlbaum Associates.

Wyer, R. S., Jr., & Gordon, S. F. (1984). The cognitive representation of social information. In R. S. Wyer, Jr., & T. K. Srull (Eds.), *Handbook of social cognition (Vol. 2,* pp.74–149). Hillsdale, NJ: Lawrence Erlbaum Associates.

Zadeh, L. (1965). Fuzzy sets. *Information and Control, 3,* 338–353.

4

Cognitive Processing of Problematic Messages: Reinterpreting to "Unbias" Texts

Dean E. Hewes
University of Minnesota

Messages exchanged between people build, unravel, secure, and transform personal relationships. Messages can affect people's ability to predict and understand others' intentions and behaviors, i.e., they reduce uncertainty (cf. Berger & Calabrese, 1975; but cf. Planalp & Honeycutt, 1985; Planalp, Rutherford, & Honeycutt, 1988). Messages convey rewards and punishments, and they are the media through which relational fairness is managed or mismanaged (cf. Foa & Foa, 1968). Messages are the tools for ingratiation, self-presentation, and many other social goals (Kellermann, 1988). Although there is some controversy over which of these functions is most fundamental (cf. Berger, 1986; Sunnafrank, 1986), a strong case can be made for uncertainty reduction. Without the ability to predict and understand others, we would live in a confusing world—we would be frozen into inaction because we could anticipate no connections between our endeavors and their social consequences.

Uncertainty reduction reflects at least four different desires: (a) the ability to satisfy simple curiosity, (b) the desire for perceived control, (c) the need to pursue other interpersonal goals effectively (Hewes & Graham, 1988), and, perhaps, (d) an urge to appear objective (Pyszczynski & Greenberg, 1987). Of these, the first, second, and fourth can be satisfied by the uncritical acceptance of information. After all, "inquiring minds want to know," but what satisfies their curiosity may bear little resemblance to the real world. Similarly, the desire for perceived control can be as easily slaked by misattributions as by accurate ones.

To pursue interpersonal goals effectively, the third function, requires some degree of accurate information. Even given the severe limitations on human judgment, oft times we do coordinate interpersonal action successfully (Hewes & Planalp, 1982). Despite our cognitive limitations, we did "make it to the Moon," as an anonymous critic noted in evaluating Nisbett and Ross' (1980) seminal book on cognitive biases. Clearly we need, and can sometimes use effectively, accurate information. But how do we obtain it in complex social world replete with mis-and disinformation cf. Hewes & Graham, 1988)?

I offer a preliminary answer to this question in a theory of the cognitive processing of problematic messages (cf. Hewes & Graham, 1988; Hewes & Planalp, 1982). In this chapter, evidence is presented that suggests the existence of specialized processors for analyzing problematic messages (PPMs). PPMs identify when a message is problematic (i.e., when it contains information that seems to be biased). They identify the likely types of distortion and aid in unbiasing the message. They supply broad strategies for testing the veracity of the newly unbiased message, and they suggest the specific communication tactics to be employed. Moreover, they are guided by quasiscientific norms for assessing the relative plausibility of multiple interpretations of the same message, as well as practical considerations such as conserving effort. Thus, PPMs are tools used by intuitive scientists for living in a complex world (Hewes & Planalp, 1982).

I begin this chapter with Hewes and Graham's (1988) sketch of PPMs, which they labeled Second-Guessing Theory. This sketch is filled with the results of new research. Each of these steps is described. The mechanisms that drive each stage are presented in detail. Let us begin with questions concerning the existence and etiology of PPM's.

IS THE EXISTENCE OF PPMS PLAUSIBLE?

In answering this question, I should note that humans, as social actors, possess an extensive repertoire of message strategies to cope with problematic messages. For instance, we can employ "uncovering strategies" if we believe that crucial information is being hidden (cf. Goffman, 1970; Lyman & Scott, 1970). These strategies might range from observing another's behavior while she or he is alone to the use of relaxation strategies designed to make a person comfortable enough to reveal normally concealed information (Berger, 1987; Berger & Bradac, 1982; Berger & Kellermann, 1983; Kellermann & Berger, 1984). But if these strategies were unguided by elaborate cognitive strategies, they would be enormously inefficient.

The field of information available in any given social situation is potentially infinite. Unless some special cognitive processes existed that (a) generated hypotheses to limit the search for relevant information and (b) directed strategy choices (such as interrogation, strategic self-disclosure, relaxation strategies, etc. (Berger, 1979; Berger & Bradac, 1982; Berger & Kellermann, 1983; Kellermann & Berger, 1984), uncertainty reduction would be nearly impossible (Hewes, Graham, Doelger, & Pavitt, 1985). Furthermore, when active social information-gathering strategies cannot be used or are undesirable, something like PPMs would be necessary to evaluate messages critically (Hewes & Graham, 1988; Hewes et al., 1985). PPMs are a logically plausible part of the uncertainty reduction process in all communication settings.

Viewed in this light, a first step in validating their existence is to establish the conditions that would elicit their development (Hewes et al., 1985). PPMs should arise from the press between personal needs and the demands of the environment. Because they are probably not innate, certain preconditions must exist to foster and sustain their development, preconditions both environmental and personal. Of course, to show that PPMs exist one must directly test them in use.

Do social actors desire the supposed product of PPMs: accurate interpersonal information? Yes, they have expressed this need freely in both open-ended and close-ended survey formats, yielding substantial evidence of convergent validity when the two operationalizations are correlated ($r = .57$, $N = 118$, $p < .001$; Hewes, Graham, Doelger, & Monsour et al., 1988). Moreover, indirect evidence supports the claim that those who express a high need for accurate information engage in several activities, that is, gathering new evidence, critically reevaluating reinterpretations of messages (Hewes et al., 1988), which imply that this need is genuine. Thus, I feel justified in making the need for accurate information a cornerstone of the theory of PPMs.

What conditions provoke the need for accurate information? There is evidence both direct and indirect (Roloff, 1988). We do know that there is a large, positive correlation between social actors' perceived need for accurate information and their desire to take social action based on that information ($r = .90$, $N = 109$, $p < .001$). Kruglanski and Ajzen (1984) and Kruglanski and Freund (1983) also suggested that social actors adopt a more critical stance toward the implications of information when their judgments are open to scrutiny by those they believe are in a better position to know the "truth" (e.g. experts or those who have access to "insider" information).

In addition, stable differences among individuals may be antecedents of the need for accurate information. Consider self-monitoring (Snyder, 1987). In the case of the need for accurate information, there are good reasons to expect such a correlation. Compared to high self-monitors, low self-monitors engage in less strategic self-presentation. Thus, either through lack of skill, lack of motivation, or a counter-motivation to be true to themselves, they do not as readily utilize contextual information to define who they are to others. On the other hand, high self-monitors are very conscious of the demands of social situations, and by motivated, skillful performances, adapt their presented image to the mandates of certain identifiable contexts (Snyder, 1987).

Given this grounding, Hewes and Graham (1988) and Numainville (1993) anticipated that high self-monitors should have higher needs for accurate information than lows, especially in contexts where goals and goal-path linkages are unclear. That difference should decrease in contexts characterized by higher levels of goal clarity. Because high self-monitors have a higher need for information with which to transform their situated identities, they should be more motivated than low self-monitors to seek the requisite information. Indeed, some indirect evidence indicates their willingness to do so (Berger & Douglas, 1981; Bercheid, Graziano, Monson, & Dermer, 1976; Elliot, 1979; Jones & Baumeister, 1976).

Numainville (1993) tested directly the connection between self-monitoring and PPMs, with self-monitoring conceived both as a source of the need for accurate information and as a factor affects the processing of messages. He found modest support for the claim that high self-monitors have a greater general need for accurate information than do low self-monitors ($t = 1.79$, $df = 64$, $p = .04$). Numainville also found a two-way interaction between the type of cue presented (no cue, availability heuristic cue, self-serving motivation cue) and self-monitoring. In the no cue and availability heuristic cue conditions, high self-monitors saw a greater need for accurate information than did lows. When presented with cues that the source might be selfishly motivated, the low self-monitors saw a greater need for accurate information than did the highs ($p < .01$). Thus it appears that self-monitoring may influence the operation of PPMs, but in a complex way. One explanation for this complexity is that self-monitoring not only taps into a general sensitivity toward either the internal or external worlds (Snyder, 1987), but it also reflects certain beliefs about what one can expect from people. Highs recognize that accurate information is useful especially when there is some question concerning the motivations of the senders of that information, but they seem less conscious of the possibility of multiple interpretations when obvious cues are absent or when they are subtle, as in the case of nonmotivational explanations of biases (cf. Hewes & Monsour, 1990). In effect, Nisbett and Ross (1980) appeared to be correct in suggesting that many people intuitively understand the idea of motivations as a cause of human behavior better than they understand cognitive process as causes. On the other hand, they may have been incorrect in that they failed to recognize that a significant subpopulation exists who recognize cognitive factors as naive explanations of human conduct. Thus, self-monitoring offers one promising direction to extend PPM theory through the inclusion of individual-difference variables. Other personality traits associated with the need for information may also prove to be valuable tools for extending our understanding of PPMs.

However, understanding the antecedents of the need for accurate information is insufficient to explain the etiology of PPMs. If we focus on social information-gathering, social actors would have to believe that they needed to know about persons and/or events outside their direct experience for PPMs to be developed. Further, they would have to recognize that such information is available through other people, and that such information is not irredeemably tainted. Strong evidence supports the existence of all three of these beliefs as obtained in two distinct populations: college students and members in formal organizational settings (Hewes et al., 1986). Thus, the preconditions necessary to foster the development of PPMs exist in the press between a real need for accurate information and perceived environmental barriers to the flow of accurate information. However, this does not guarantee that PPMs have actually developed.

THE STRUCTURE AND PROCESSING OF PPMS

To determine if PPMs function in the social life, we must first consider their inner workings. To do so, let us begin with a verbal introduction to PPMs. I first describe the nature of PPMs, and then I trace through each stage in these processes.

Sketch of PPMs in Action

Virtually every day we encounter people who misrepresent events they have observed, or the attributes of others they have met, because of intentional or unintentional errors in human judgment (cf. Hewes & Graham, 1988; Kahneman, Slovic, & Tversky, 1982). Whether messages are distorted intentionally or not, receivers of those messages sometimes fail to accept them at face value. In fact, receivers often go to great lengths to see behind the literal or intended meanings of messages to understand what is "really going on." For instance, they not only attempt to identify deception (although, objectively, they do so inaccurately), but they may also attempt to identify the truth behind the lie (Zuckerman, DePaulo, & Rosenthal, 1981). Jurors do not always accept eyewitness testimony as sacrosanct; they can specify how such testimony may go awry both intentionally and unintentionally (Loftus, 1979). Counselors question their clients' accounts of their lives and try to construct more viable explanations of those lives based on their knowledge of the human mind (cf. Labov & Fanshel, 1977). People in everyday life attempt to winnow the truth from messages that they feel are biased (Hewes & Planalp, 1982).

In each of these cases, social actors are employing PPMs (Hewes & Planalp, 1982). As noted earlier, PPMs are cognitive processes by which social actors, upon identifying what they believe to be a biased message, attempt to correct for the bias by means of specialized forms of social knowledge. Social actors are assumed to attempt to "unbias" messages consciously in order to identify what they hope to be a "truer" account of the topics discussed therein.

PPMs are hypothesized to activate in reaction to a perceived bias only when there is some threshold need for accurate information (Hewes et al., 1985; Hewes et al., 1988). Further, the reinterpretations of those messages that result from the use of PPMs are assumed theoretically to be approximately "normatively adequate" (Hewes et al., 1985). That is, I assume that social actors actually do arrive at a "truer" account of the topic covered in a message is when their reinterpretations are compared to more objective assessments based on socially sanctioned methods of gathering and evaluating evidence.

To make this sketch of the functions of PPMs more concrete, consider a commonplace example provided by Hewes and Graham (1988). A friend (the source) comes to you upset over a conflict he has just had with his wife (the target). He tells you that his wife is an uncaring and abusive person who will never change. He sees no hope for the relationship (message). Since you (the receiver) wish to offer your friend good counsel, you reflect on his message critically, hoping to attain a better, "truer," understanding of the situation that he faces than he can manage at this moment. In other words, you need accurate information.

There are several claims in this message that you might question. For instance, in the simplest case, you might have reason to doubt that his wife is either an uncaring or an abusive person based on your prior experiences with her, leading you to reject your friend's claim. Alternatively, you might reinterpret the same claim based on your knowledge that people tend to see others as more consistent and unchangeable than they really are. Thus, you may reason that what is really going on here is that your friend is blaming his wife for being an abusive and uncaring person, when she is only reacting to the immediate difficulties she faces in the relationship. You might go further, questioning your friends' imputation of her personality as the cause of the conflict. You know him to be a demanding, insecure person who may provoke others to keep their distance from him and who responds angrily when he asks for too much. Consequently, you may feel that the message is really a reflection of his own insecurity and that he is really the cause of the conflict.

This example illustrates certain general properties or PPMs. First, messages that trigger them are salient to the receiver. They may be salient either because they have serious consequences for the receiver's goals ("I want to advise my friend well"). Although not illustrated here, they may also simply be striking in their own right (Doelger, Hewes, & Graham, 1986), as in the case of a rumor of a scandal or a Presidential address on a politically awkward topic. Second, the messages make synthetic, attributional truth claims. These claims may concern *existence* of people or events, and/or their *attributes* ("he is insecure; "*Wild at Heart* is a great film"), and/or the *causes* of, or *reasons* for, states of affairs ("she is abusive because . . ."), and/or the *imputation of cognitive or emotional states* ("He loves me, he loves me not"; or "mind reading" as in Gottman, 1979). Third, something about the message—its *form* (e.g., manifestations of unusual levels of tension) or, as in the example, its *content*—gives the receiver reason to question the attribution made in the message. Fourth, *prior knowledge,* either general ("people generally blame others more than themselves for conflicts") or specific to the target ("my friend is an insecure person"), is brought to bear in the process of reinterpreting the message in order to construct one or more satisfying, useful reinterpretations. These reinterpretations may be checked by the receiver to determine plausibility or veracity.

A Sketch of the Stages in PPM Operation

Our model of PPMs includes the reinterpretive aspects of PPMs (Doelger et al., 1986; Hewes et al., 1985; Hewes & Planalp, 1982) and reinterpretation assessment (Hewes et al., 1988) evaluated in previous research with social information-gathering tactic selection speculated on only briefly in Hewes and Graham (1988). This model is necessarily described in strictly linear terms as it might operate if a social actor were evaluating only one message claim, rather than a set of partially unrelated claims. In this latter case, a social actor might be operating simultaneously at a number of different stages in the process and be faced with the additional cognitive demands this might entail (Hewes & Graham, 1988). Given this one proviso, the model operates as follows. (see Figure 4.1).

In the first phase of PPM operation, *Vigilance Phase,* a message is received from a source in a particular context. That message is given an initial interpretation that involves accepting the meaning of the message at face value. Then, depending on the cues contained in the message and/or context, and the importance of obtaining accurate information, some degree of doubt may be generated concerning the veracity of the initial interpretation of the message (Doelger et al., 1986). If there is insufficient reason to doubt, the initial interpretation of the message is accepted at face value. If there is reason to doubt that interpretation, but the importance of accuracy is not sufficiently high, no effort is made to extract the "true" state of affairs behind the message, although it might be recalled if its importance became greater. However, if there are cues that raise questions about the veracity of the initial interpretation of the message, and accuracy is important, the social actor enters what Hewes and Graham (1988) called the second phase of PPM operation.

In this phase, the *Reinterpretation Assessment Phase,* the social actor engages in the reflective, controlled process of reinterpreting the message. Earlier discussions of PPMs, under the guise of "Second-Guessing Theory", implied that there is an essentially dichotomous reaction to doubts about the truth of a message (see Doelger et al., 1986; Hewes et al., 1985). That is, because social actors could be in only two states, reflective (controlled) or nonreflective (automated), with respect to the message, they either accept the message at face value or reinterpret it. Hewes and Graham (1988) concluded that there is a third possibility: Social actors may have doubts about the veridicality of a message, and thus be in a "mindful" state, but may conclude that discovering the truth behind the message is not important enough to activate PPMs.

The outcome of this reinterpretive process is one or more interpretations of the "truth" behind the message, each of which is assigned some *level of confidence*

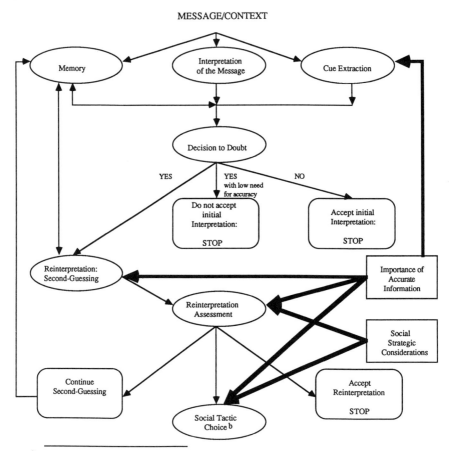

MESSAGE/CONTEXT

a   The ellipses represent cognitive processes. Narrow arrows initiating in these processes carry the results of each process to the next stage in processing or to some exit point represented by the rounded rectangles. The standard rectangles represent causal variables, with the wide arrows indicating the causal influence of those variables on some cognitive process.

b   Upon choosing and deploying some social tactic, receivers may be faced with another message/context which re-initiates the whole process described in Figure 1.

FIG. 4.1.   A pictorial model of second-guessing.a

and each of which may provide a more or less detailed explanation of the subjectively "true" state of affairs behind the message called the *level of clarity* of the reinterpretation. The results of this reinterpretive process are approximately "normatively adequate." That is, the reinterpretations are assumed to be closer to the truth about the target than the initial face-value interpretation of the message (Hewes et al., 1985), although it is still possible that upon reflection in a subsequent phase, a social actor may return to the original interpretation.

At this point, the social actor enters the *Reinterpretation Assessment Phase*

(Hewes et al., 1988). Depending on the importance of accurate information, the mental difficulty (cognitive load) involved in assessing the reinterpretations, and certain social strategic considerations, the social actor may adopt one or more alternative strategies for assessing the adequacy of each reinterpretation as judged against the original interpretation and other reinterpretations of the same claim. The social actor may decide to accept the best, or only, reinterpretation (or even the original interpretation, although this occurs infrequently) and top further analysis of the message. Alternatively, he or she may opt to continue processing the message by returning to the may remain of the original message and context as stored in memory. Finally, she or he may decide to employ some social tactic designed to test the logical consistency of the reinterpretations or to provide new information that will generate more confidence and/or clarity in one of the reinterpretations, or both. If the social actor desires to seek new information in the social realm, the fourth and final phase is entered.

In the *Social Tactic Choice Phase* (Hewes et al., 1989), the choice of some social tactic is guided by the importance of accurate information, social strategic considerations and the cognitive load involved in the *Reinterpretation Phase*. Tactics choices are arrayed along a number of manifolds, including (a) who one might turn to for more information, (b) how one might approach them, and (c) what kinds of information one wants to obtain. The fruits of these tactics are then used to improve the quality of the reinterpretations or to generate new and better ones.

EMPIRICAL TESTS OF PPMS

Having sketched the phases in the operation of PPMs, let us consider in greater detail how each phase functions theoretically and what evidence there is to support these claims.

Phase 1: Vigilance

For the Vigilance Phase to operate as I described it, social actors must be able to identify potentially biased messages before, during, or after the message is transmitted. To do so, social actors must have a set of cues that permit them to discriminate subjectively between the presence and absence of potentially biased messages. Doelger et al. (1986) undertook the process of identifying these cues. Key to that effort is their conception of what cues are. Cues are elements of the message content, form, and context conjointly through which a social actor privileges certain interpretations of the message. A cue is not simply an objective property of a message (Ostrom, 1984). It is a receiver's interpretation of the message content, form, and such contextual factors as the immediate definition of the situation and background knowledge, relational history, and any implicit goals attributed to the participants in the exchange.

The process by which these interpretations are made is labeled *cue extraction* in Figure 4.1. Cue extraction has not been the focus of much research on PPMs. Instead, research has provided evidence supporting the existence of cues utilized to identify potentially biased messages (Doelger et al., 1986). Table 1 summarizes the current list of eighteen cues (Hewes & Graham, 1988). Following Doelger et al., four sets of cues are presented: cues attributable to (a) the receiver of the message, (b) the source of the message, (c) message form or content, and (d) the receiver.

Independent support for the existence of some of these cues is available in Hewes et al. (1985) in which subjects demonstrated clear, conscious knowledge of sources of biased messages. Surprisingly, each source of bias (the availability heuristic, the representativeness heuristic, and the fundamental attribution error) is supposed to be reflectively inaccessible to social actors under normal circumstances (cf. Fiske & Taylor, 1990; Nisbett & Ross, 1980), although there is isolated evidence to the contrary (cf. Isen, Means, Patrick, & Nowicki, 1982, on the representativeness heuristic; Kruglanski, Hamel, Maides, & Schwartz, 1978, on the fundamental attribution error). Overall, we have good support for the existence of cues that could trigger the operation of PPMs.

Having shown that the preconditions exist for the development of PPMs, let us turn to the two theoretical linkages posited in the Vigilance Phase: that between need for accurate information and cue extraction, and that between cue extraction and the decision to doubt. PPM theory implies that the higher the need for accuracy, the more vigilant social actors should be in identifying sources of biased information that might prevent them from taking appropriate social action to attain their goals; however, increased vigilance does not necessarily have the obvious effect of increasing a social actor's sensitivity to the occurrence of cues. Increasing the need for accuracy could decrease the detection rate for cues. Increasing accuracy can be accomplished by increasing the social actor's awareness of cues otherwise undetected (increasing sensitivity) or by decreasing the ambiguity of cues used in judgments (discounting normally observed but ambiguous cues).

Social actors tend to prefer the latter alternative, at least in experimental signal detection tasks. The reporting rate of cue detection for very simple objective cues decreases as motivation to identify those increases (Davenport, 1968, 1969; Levine, 1966). The explanation for these findings is that under task conditions in which the task is open-ended and is rewarding in its own right, increases in motivation lead social actors to report having detected cues more conservatively, thus avoiding errors (cf. Eysenck, 1982; McGraw, 1978). Thus, PPM theory predicts that as the need for accurate information increases, the perceived number of cues that activate PPMs will decrease.

Preliminary evidence obtained by, Monsour, and Rutherford (1989) provides some support for this prediction. They obtained the predicted significant negative correlation between need for accurate information and the number of cues identified ($r = -.16$, $N = 111$, $p < .05$). The regression of the need for accurate information on the occurrence of the eighteen kinds of cues described in Table 4.1 determined that an increase in the need for accurate information resulted in a near significant multiple R of .50 (F (18, 920 = 1.65, $p = .064$) for the whole model. Of the eighteen cues, only one, background consistency cues, had an unstandardized regression coefficient significantly different than zero (standardized beta = 0.22, $t = 2.15$, $df = 110$, $p < .05$). Thus, as the need for accurate information increases, the number of perceived cues that trigger PPMs decreases, with one exception. In high need situations, social actors shift their focus away from cues specific to the message, sender, or receiver and assume that what they already know to be true is still true. This is the most conservative, effort-saving strategy they could use, and, perhaps, the most accurate one if the weight of evidence favors their established beliefs.

PPM theory also posits that the presence of any of the eighteen cues in a message will produce more doubt in the minds of social actors about the accuracy of that message than will the absence of such cues. Direct support for this claim appeared in Doelger et al. (1986) and was replicated in Numainville (1993). In both studies, three cues were manipulated: (a) cues to the presence of self-serving motivational biases in the source's message, (b) background cues in which the receiver's knowledge of the target could lead to a different interpretation than the source's, and (c) cues to the presence of the availability heuristic in the sources reasoning. Both studies contrasted the effects of these three cues with a no cue condition over four widely differing everyday contexts. They found that, when asked to evaluate the reasonableness of the face value of a message from the source, subjects reported significantly more reason to doubt it in all the cued than in the no cue conditions. No significant effects, neither main effects nor interactions, were obtained for the gender of the receiver or the context in which the message was embedded.

The strengths and weaknesses of these studies are both clear. On the one hand, there is strong evidence linking cues that trigger PPMs to the reason to doubt. On the other, only three of the posited eighteen cues (see Table 4.1) have been used to test this relationship. Tests of the other fifteen cues is essential to rigorously evaluate the claims of PPM theory.

In conclusion, there is good preliminary support for, and replication of, the hypothesized relationships posited to function in the Vigilance Phase. In addition, the linkages between memory and both cue extraction and the preliminary interpretation of messages should be explored. Because memory is an active, constructive process (Bartlett, 1932; Hastie, Park, & Weber, 1984), rather than a dust bin filled with the past, it can affect and be affected by cue extraction and interpretation (cf. van Dijk & Kintsch, 1983). Although the implications of this view of memory have not been worked out for the PPMs, those implications will undoubtedly be important to future extensions of PPM theory.

TABLE 4.1
Coding Scheme for Second-Guessing Cues: Category Descriptions and Reliability Estimates

	Category Descriptions	Average Percentage Agreement	

(1) Target Cues

(1.1)	Inconsistency (specific to target): Message from the source is inconsistent with prior knowledge of the target. (This includes baseline probabilities on events as related to the target as an individual.)	.88	.83
(1.2)	Inconsistency (general): Message from the source is inconsistent with prior knowledge of the target. (This includes baseline probabilities on events as related to norms or information concerning events and/or people like the target.)		

(2) Source Cues

(2.1)	Motivational Cues		
(2.1a)	Source distorts for his or her own benefit.	.85	.73
(2.1b)	Source distorts for altruistic reasons: for example, to avoid embarrassing the target or some other person.	.98	1.00
(2.1c)	Consistency bias: Distortion resorts from source's attempts to keep his/her attitudes and/or beliefs consistent.	1.00	.93

(2.2) Dispositional Cues

(2.2a)	Rigid use of knowledge structures: Source always sees things in a particular way (e.g., from a constructivist, Marxist, right wing, or religious perspective) even when such a perspective is inappropriate. Could be the implied result of the source's group membership.	.96	.98
(2.2b)	Dispositional distortions: Source is a habitual liar, exaggerator, distorter, and so on. [Or source has distorted information in similar contents previously.]	.90	.80
(2.2c)	Personal preferences: Not necessarily implying bias or distortion, but acknowledging the role of personal tastes. Source holds different judgmental criteria when evaluating the target. Therefore, he or she cannot provide accurate information for me.	.94	.95
(2.2d)	Diagnosticity: Source is not skilled in identifying or using discriminal clues to reach a conclusion.	.93	.98

(2.3) Consistency Cues

(2.3a)	Behavioral consistency: Source's typical behavior patterns are deviated from (would not be a cue for anyone though: These are deviations particular to this source's typical behavior). [Uses *this* source's typical behavior as a baseline, not a baseline of all human behavior (for the latter, see 4.1b).]	.88	.95

(2.4) Informational Cues

(2.4a)	Availability heuristic: Source's account of the target was influenced by the availability of objects or events, for example, their accessibility in the processes of perception, memory, or recall; not their actual occurrence. Specific type: Ecocentric bias—One's own efforts and actions may be disproportionately available and their frequency compared to those of others may be overestimated ("I helped the group more than they did").	.95	1.00
(2.4b)	Representativeness heuristic: Application of simple resemblance or goodness of fit criteria to problems of categorization. Deals with the degree to which salient features	.98	1.00

TABLE 4.1
Coding Scheme for Second-Guessing Cues: Category Descriptions and Reliability Estimates

	Category Descriptions	Average Percentage Agreement	
	of the object are representative of, or similar to features presumed to be characteristic of the category. Source has not considered the relevant base-rate information in drawing conclusions about the target.		
(2.4c)	Fundamental attribution error: Source's comment on the target reflects his or her view that behavior is caused by enduring dispositions of the actor rather than characteristics of the situation.	.99	.98
	Data sufficiency: Source does not have sufficient data to reach the stated conclusion about the target. (This includes the area of expertise normally associated with source credibility.)	.92	.98
(3) Receiver Cues			
(3.1)	Dispositional traits: Receiver makes a global self-attribution concerning his or her own tendencies to question the face interpretations of messages, for example, "I just distrust people."	.92	1.00
(3.2)	Specific tendencies: Receiver makes a specific self-attribution concerning her or his tendency to question messages of a specific kind or messages received in a specific context" "I don't accept flattery well." Excluded from this category are attributions made about others, for example,"Salesmen are untrustworthy."	n.a.	.95
(4) Message Cues			
(4.1)	Message is internally inconsistent: Components of the message are contradictory. Anyone could hear the inconsistency; not based on prior knowledge of the specific source or target. (May also include inconsistencies between claims or between data and claims for specific types of messages.)	.83	.85
(4.2)	Message deviates from expected form: Represents clues that would be evident if provided by *any* source, for example, the delivery was too smooth, too confident, too hesitant, and so on.	.91	.93

Source. The first column of agreement figures is derived from Doelger et al., 1986; the second column from Hewes et al., 1988.
Note. Two categories were not used in the study by Doelger et al., 1986, but were in the study by Hewes et al., 1988. Those two categories—1.2 and 3.2—obviously have no reliability estimates in the first column, as indicated by n.a. (not available) designation.

Phase 2: Reinterpretation

Two theoretical relationships are posited during the Reinterpretation Phase. The first is a choice inspired by the reason to doubt and the need for accurate information (see Figure 4.1). Faced with sufficient reason to doubt the face value of the message and a sufficient need for accurate information, the social actor will attempt to reinterpret the message so as to winnow the truth behind the message. If there is reason to doubt but insufficient need for accurate information, the social actor will ignore the message and make no attempt to reinterpret it, or at least not until the perceived bias becomes important. Should there be insufficient reason to doubt and an insufficient need for accurate information, the social actor will accept the message at face value. Thus, we anticipate an interaction between doubt and need for accurate information in predicting the choice among three reactions to the message (Hewes et al., 1985; Hewes & Planalp, 1982; but see Note 1). No direct evidence exists to support this hypothesis though some indirect support appears in Langer's (1978) early work on "mindlessness."

As originally conceived, mindlessness was the complementary process to PPMs. In Langer's early work was a nonreflective state in which messages were accepted and acted upon without conscious processing of their meaning. Conversely, PPMs operate in a mindful state in which the content of messages are examined critically with an eye to reinterpretation. (Also note the parallels to Petty and Cacioppo's (1986) "direct" and "peripheral" processing routes; cf. Roloff, 1989). Langer demonstrated that compliance-gaining messages with unusual form or content trigger more critical processing and less compliance than more typical messages (Langer & Abelson, 1972; Langer, Blank, & Chanowitz, 1978). Her results are entirely in line with the notion that doubt and reinterpretation are triggered by the distinctive properties of messages (see Cues 1.1, 1.2, 2.3, 4.1, and 4.2 in Table 4.1 and generally in Doelger et al., 1986). However, as Doelger et al. noted, mindfulness is a necessary, but not a sufficient, precondition for PPMs to be invoked. Social actors do not attribute bias to all messages while in a mindful state. Thus, Langer's evidence is only partially relevant to our predictions concerning the relationship of both the need for accuracy and cue extraction to the reinterpretation of the message.

More direct support is available for the second theoretical linkage in the Reinterpretation Phase. PPM theory predicts that, when confronted with a message displaying cues to either potential cognitive or motivational biases on the part of some source, receivers will adjust their inferences about the target in the normatively correct fashion (Hewes et al., 1985). Thus, PPM theory claims that not only will social actors attempt to reinterpret messages in a way that seems more accurate to them, but also their reinterpretations will in fact be closer to the "truth" than those who do not employ PPMs. The truth in this claim is defined by external observers employing both methods and well established results of careful inquiry to examine critically the social actors' reinterpretations.

If social actors' reinterpretations are normatively adequate, they should adjust their own judgments about the true state of the affairs referred to in the message so as to reflect an understanding of scientifically validated sources of biases in human judgment. Hewes et al. (1985) undertook to address this criterion for determining the normative adequacy of PPMs, Hewes and Monsour (1990) and Numainville (1993) replicated their results. All three studies manipulated four validated versions of three cues to biases in human judgment, biases whose effects have been documented in the research literature. Those cues were to: (a) background inconsistencies (only in et al. 1985), (b) self-serving motivational biases, and (c) availability heuristic biases. Reinterpretations of messages con taining one of these three types of cues were each contrasted to a no-cue condition. Each of the cue types were embedded in a minimum of two different contexts. The gender of the subject was also included in the design as an independent variable.

The relevant dependent variable in these study was the subjects' assessment of the likelihood that the source's impression of the target was correct. To reflect the normative adequacy of their reinterpretations, subjects needed to respond to cues to bias by judging that the source's impression of the target was less likely than in the no-cue situation. This is precisely what happened for all three cues ($p < .01$). No significant effects for context or gender were obtained, nor were there any significant interactions among the independent variables ($p > 0.10$). Hewes and Monsour (1990) hypothesized that social actors in general would show less facility in using the cognitive, in comparison with the motivational, cues to trigger PPMs. They found support for this hypothesis which was replicated by Numainville (1993).

These results, though supportive of the normative adequacy of PPMs, are not without their limitations. Beyond the obvious criticism that they only relate to three out of eighteen cues that are supposed to trigger and aid in reinterpretation, there lurks a much more serious potential problem. These same results might reflect only a certain cynicism toward the source's conclusions about the target without implying that the target can correct for different biases in ways consistent with the particular distortions associated with each kind of bias. However, Doelger et al. (1986) demonstrated that subjects' reasons for reinterpreting sources' messages were consistent with the manipulations of the message cues conducted in the aforementioned design. For example, although subjects mentioned background inconsistency as an explanation for reinterpreting the message in all four cue conditions, they almost doubled the percentage of times they mentioned it in the background-consistency cue condition (44.9% in this condition vs. 25.6% in the no-cue condition). Even more striking, 24.6% of the subjects explained the concept of "the availability heuristic" in nontechnical terms in their accounts of why they reinterpreted the message in the availability-heuristic cue condition, but only 2.3% mentioned it in the no-cue condition. No effects of gender on the identification of cues or in the accuracy with which cues were integrated into accounts of the reinterpretation were found. Hewes and Monsour (1990) replicated this finding and added to it that the accuracy with which social actors perceive cues is greater for motivational cues than for cognitive cues. Numainville did not replicate either Doelger et al. or and Monsour on accuracy but did find that high self-monitors as compared with low self-monitors are more sensitive to, although no more accurate in identifying, cognitive cues. Lows were more sensitive to, but no more accurate in identifying, motivational cues, especially altruistic reasons that a source might have for distorting the truth.

In addition, Doelger et al. found that certain contexts provoked the use of some kinds of explanations more than others regardless of the cues that were manipulated. For instance, in highly emotion-laden interpersonal situations, recall of other situations in which similar emotions dominated should be greater than recall for emotionally different situations (Forgas, Bower, & Krantz, 1984; Isen, 1984; Martins, 1982). Recalling these easily remembered instances should influence one's judgment even when they are not truly relevant to the issue at hand. This is an occasion ripe for the availability heuristic bias (Nisbett & Ross, 1980). If social actors understand this bias, they should view such interpersonal situations as likely to produce this bias regardless of the cues contained in a message. Post hoc analyses of the Doelger et al. data revealed this pattern.

In summary, these results lend credence to the normative adequacy thesis that plays such a major part in PPM theory, especially in the Reinterpretation Phase. Subjects in these studies displayed a range and depth of nontechnical understanding of biasing strategies that cannot be explained by conventional theories of human judgment (cf. Nisbett & Ross, 1980; Sherman & Corty, 1984; Fiske & Taylor, 1991). The evidence could be stronger. If it could be shown either that social actors are highly selective in which portion of a complex message they choose to reinterpret, based on the presence of cues to bias, or that qualitative changes in the reinterpretation of the same message arise out of different combinations of multiple cues to bias, the evidence for normative adequacy would be more persuasive. Nevertheless, with the evidence at hand, normative adequacy is a very plausible hypothesis.

Phase 3: Reinterpretation Assessment

Social actors need to assess the plausibility of their reinterpretations arrived at during the previous stage. During the Reinterpretation Assessment Phase, the need for accurate information, both directly and indirectly, affects the ways in which social actors choose to determine if their reinterpretations of a message are perceived to be adequate for their needs. In addition, two other classes of factors, cognitive load and social strategic considerations, also influence this assessment (Hewes et al., 1988). The sketch of PPM theory presented earlier and Figure 4.1 both indicate that the first theoretical link to be tested in this phase is the connection between need for accurate information and cognitive load. Hewes et al. hypothesized that the greater the need for accurate information, the more alternative reinterpretations social actors would consider, the less confidence they would feel globally in their reinterpretations, and the less clear they would think their reinterpretations were. The number of reinterpretations, the confidence with which they are held, and their clarity are all indices of cognitive load during the Reinterpretation Assessment Phase. For example, if social actors hold two or more incompatible reinterpretations of a message, they must choose among them—a more demanding cognitive task than if there is only one reinterpretation. Even two potentially compatible reinterpretations could increase cognitive load because their compatibility must be assessed. Similarly, greater reflection is required to reach an acceptable reinterpretation if it is held with little confidence or its implications are unclear.

Support for this prediction was obtained by Hewes et al. (1988) in a nonexperimental study of 118 subjects who were asked to recall their most recent instance of rethinking the meaning of a message. Hewes et al. (1989) replicated these findings in a nonexperimental diary study in which subjects recorded similar instances as they occurred. Correlations of the predicted sign between an index of need for accurate information and each of the cognitive-load variables were obtained. One of those correlations, between need for accurate information and confidence, approached significance ($r = .23$, $p = 0.07$) in Hewes et al. (1988) and achieved significance in Hewes et al. (1989); the rest were significant at the .05 level. Given the small magnitude of the correlations obtained in these studies, and the high reliability of the operationalizations of each of the variables, cognitive load probably has antecedents in addition to the need for accurate information. In all likelihood these other factors as include such things as: (a) the ambiguity of the message, (b) the available cognitive capacity during processing, (c) the speed with which an assessment is needed, and (d) the social actor's facility at using PPMs.

The Reinterpretation Assessment Phase also contains another theoretical link—this one directed toward the social actors' subjective (as opposed to "normative") evaluation of their reinterpretation(s). According to the theory (cf. Hewes et al., 1988), social actors must choose among three options to assess the subjective adequacy of their reinterpretations: (a) to stop reinterpreting the message and accept the results of the Reinterpretation Phase, (b) to continue to reinterpret the message relying on information already stored in memory, or (c) to seek new information from others by selecting and implementing a social information-gathering tactic. Considered in this choice are: (a) the need for accurate information, (b) the cognitive load under which the social actor is operating, and (c) social strategic considerations affecting the accessibility and potential accuracy of new information. These three considerations are reflected in three theoretically interrelated predictions posited by Hewes et al. (1989). First, the greater the need for accurate information, the more likely are social actors to engage in social information gathering. The less the need for accurate information, the more likely will they be to settle with their extant reinterpretations or to continue to employ PPMs using information stored in memory; however, social actors will continue to use PPMs in preference to stopping. Results of a nonexperimental test of this hypothesis were supportive, although caution must be exercised in the interpretation of predictions concerning the decision to accept extant reinterpretations because only 9% of the sample reported employing this assessment strategy.

Why these results? According to the theory, in the ideal case where social-strategic considerations and cognitive limitations play no part in social actors' decisions, new relevant information is always desirable, its gathering limited only by the motivation to obtain it. Even when that motivation is low, social actors should prefer to utilize PPMs than to stop because some initially unnoticed information could be obtained. However, the choice of assessment strategies seldom takes place under ideal conditions. Social actors are limited in the cognitive capacity that they can devote to any task (Fiske & Taylor, 1992; Mischel, 1981; Navon & Gopher, 1979; Planalp & Hewes, 1982), including the reinterpretation assessment. Whatever the level of motivation, social actors must shepherd their limited cognitive capacities carefully, lest those capacities become overloaded, resulting in decrements in performance (Eysenck, 1982). Thus, the Hewes et al. (1988) second hypothesis was that the greater the cognitive load, the more likely social actors will be to conserve cognitive effort. As a consequence, the greater the number of reinterpretations, the less confident social actors would be in their reinterpretations, the less clear are those reinterpretations would be, the more likely would social actors be to stop using PPMs, and the less likely would they be to engage in social information gathering.

Partial support for this prediction was obtained in the same nonexperimental study (Hewes et al., 1988) and replicated in the diary study (Hewes et al., 1989). Contrary to the Hewes et al. (1988) predictions, the number of reinterpretations did not discriminate among assessment strategy choices, a result they attributed to operational problems with this independent variable (see Hewes et al., 1988). However, this prediction was supported by Hewes et al. (1989). Social actors' confidence in their own reinterpretations did discriminate significantly among reassessment strategies. The perceived clarity of those reinterpretations also discriminated significantly with one anomalous finding. At the lowest levels of clarity, social actors preferred to employ social information-gathering tactics, suggesting that, although cognitive load is an important factor in the operation of PPMs, it may be overridden by the need for accurate information.

According to PPM theory, one other factor affects assessment strategy choice, social strategic considerations. Social strategic considerations concern those costs and constraints that affect the availability or usefulness of information obtained in the social realm. For example, the time or effort needed to gather assessment information are costs. The social appropriateness of turning to a particular source on a given topic, the credibility, or the accessibility of that source represent constraints on either the availability or the usefulness of assessment information (Hewes et al., 1988).

Taken together, these costs and constraints are social strategic considerations that affect the amount of social effort needed to evaluate social actors' reinterpretations. Because social actors are thought to work on a principle of conservation of social effort (Hewes et al., 1988; McDougall, 1911) that parallels the principle of conservation of cognitive effort discussed previously, we anticipated that the less the social effort to be expended in assessing the adequacy of the results of second-guessing, the more inclined social actors would be to employ social information-gathering tactics and the less inclined they would be to continue to employing PPMs or their initial interpretations.

Results obtained by Hewes et al. (1988) lend partial support to this prediction as do those of the aforementioned diary study (Hewes et al., 1989). Neither time nor credibility predicted reinterpretation assessment strategy choice due to high multicollinearity with other independent variables. The effort needed to obtain more information, considerations of social appropriateness, and accessibility, all anticipated reinterpretation strategy choice.

In sum, PPM theory received some support in Phase 3, although experimental evidence for this phase is sorely needed. Still, PPMs appear to operate as anticipated. They not only lead to reinterpretations of messages, but they also serve as antecedents to speaker-oriented strategies associated with social information-seeking. In every case examined in Hewes et al. (1988) and Hewes et al. (1989), reinterpretation of the meaning of the message preceded the use of social information-gathering tactics. In all but one case, social actors reported having relatively well-formulated reinterpretations in mind before engaging in the interactive quest for new data (Hewes & Graham, 1988). Even granting the general tendency of subjects to make themselves look good in the eyes of the researcher, these results are simply too forceful to ignore (Hewes et al., 1988). Social actors must be seen as potentially thoughtful naive scientists who use theories of bias to explore the social world (cf. Hewes & Planalp, 1982).

Phase 4: Social Tactic Choice

If social actors decide to evaluate their reinterpretations by means of new information, they must select, consciously or not, social tactics for doing so. All that is required is that the choice be derived from the activation of a goal to obtain accurate information and that it serve social actors in their reflective examination of a message (cf. Graham et al., 1989; also see Greene, 1984, and Norman, 1981, on goals and the activation of cognitive processes). Moreover, as both Figure 4.1 and our sketch of PPM theory indicate, the use of PPMs need not stop with the application of social information-gathering tactics. Those tactics may provoke messages that are themselves subject to analysis via PPMs (Hewes & Graham, 1988).

To understand Phase 4, two questions must be answered. First, what driving principle forces the operation of this phase? Second, what social tactics are there and how might they be portrayed? Social tactics reflect practical choices made by social actors in the pursuit of accurate information while trying to conserve cognitive and social effort. These tactics take into account aspects of the social context, including (a) *who* can supply the requisite information, (b) *how* will that source (or sources) will be approached, and (c) *what* kind of information probes might prove most useful.

Graham et al. (1989) developed a list of social tactics based on two considerations. First, they attempted to make a direct connection between those tactics
and existing and demonstrably useful typologies of social information-seeking,
i.e. Berger (1979). Second, since information-seeking takes place within social
networks (Hewes & Planalp, 1982; Hewes *et al.*, 1985), Graham et al. needed to
ensure that their typology encompassed the possibility of multiple sources of
information, including the original source of the message, the target if the target
were a person and not an event, and others outside the original message exchange.

Berger's typology also differentiates uncertainty reduction tactics in terms of
who is the source of the information. For example, "interactive" strategies involve talk with the target of the uncertainty reduction, whereas one of the
"active" strategies involves asking others about the target. Graham et al. incorporated this distinction into their own typology, expanding it to cover the more
numerous sources of new information gathering available in a social network.
Thus, from *whom* to seek follow-up information, includes five descriptors: (a)
returning to the original source, (b) interacting with the target, (c) seeking
information from someone other than either the source or the target, (d) employing some form of triangulation which involves crosschecking with multiple
sources of new information including any of those mentioned heretofore, and (e)
contacting causal agents or the events. This last descriptor is needed to handle the
situation when the target of the problematic message is an event, such as a party
or an argument, rather than an attribute of a person. In the former cases, the
receiver must return to the event as recorded (tapes, photographs, etc.), unless
the event is ongoing, or seek out a person or persons responsible for the event.

The issue of *how* to pursue reinterpretation assessment with social tactics also
reflects distinctions drawn by Berger, again with modifications. In discussing his
interactive strategies, Berger implied that interrogation (direct questioning of the
target) may be more direct and less subtle than strategically self-disclosing on a
topic of interest to provoke a related self-disclosure from the target (Berger,
1979). In Berger and Kellermann (1983), similar emphasis is given to the directness or indirectness of uncertainty reduction strategies.

Graham et al. agreed with the importance of directness in differentiating
among social information-gathering tactics. A concern for the directness of a
tactic is especially important because PPMs are likely to be provoked precisely in
those circumstances when a receiver has reason to believe that a source may be
unwilling or unable to provide accurate information (Hewes & Graham, 1988).
Further, direct, confrontive tactics may be deemed socially inappropriate in
many circumstances (Berger & Kellermann, 1983; Hewes & Graham, 1988).
Thus, as descriptors for the "how" facet of tactics, we included direct, indirect,
or both where the directness of a tactic is determined by whether the specific
tactical message contains an explicit statement of the specific information needed
by the receiver in re-interpretation assessment.

Finally, social information-gathering tactics may be distinguished from one another in terms of *what* kinds of information are being sought. Although there are many specific kinds of information for which a receiver might seek relevant concrete goals, there is one general approach that dominates the social information-gathering research, hypothesis testing. The notion of hypothesis testing flows naturally from any research grounded on the metaphors of the intuitive scientist (cf. Heider, 1958; Kelley, 1967; Kelly, 1955), including research of both listener and speaker oriented tactics for social information-gathering. Social actors are said to form hypotheses about the target and to assess those hypotheses more or less accurately.

However, the metaphor of the intuitive scientist suggests that hypothesis testing is not the only method by which social actors assess intuitive theories. Theories are also evaluated in terms of their internal consistence and fidelity to the available evidence (Kaplan, 1964). If applied to social information-gathering tactics, the analog of the professional scientific enterprise is what Graham et al. labeled plausibility testing. This tactic is exemplified by "tell me if I'm crazy" discussions in which a receiver turns to someone else to see if his or her reinterpretation of a message is sensible. The other person may not know any more about the target than the receiver. Still, that person may be able to perform a kind of reality check on the receiver's reinterpretation(s). Of course, the other person may have new information to give the receiver in which she or he is performing both a hypothesis and a plausibility testing function.

Each of the social tactics associated with who, how, and what questions combine into triplets called *tactical stances,* such as source-indirect-hypothesis testing or other-direct-plausibility testing, that provide the framework within which specific messages are produced. Graham et al. did not hazard to guess if there are specific preferred tactical stances or, if so, what their antecedents might be. Nevertheless, finding out if there were preferred patterns of tactical stances is of some importance both theoretically and methodologically: theoretically, because preference for certain tactical stances over others would require explanations not yet formulated; statistically because substantial dependence among the tactics in forming tactical stances would make tactical stances, rather than tactics, the appropriate unit of analysis for testing hypotheses about the antecedents and consequences of tactic choice. Graham et al. found that, for all practical purposes, social tactics, rather than tactical stances, were the proper units of analysis for testing hypotheses concerning the Social Tactic Phase [X^2 (35) = 33.54, p = .54].

Graham et al. tested several hypotheses concerning the antecedents of social tactic choice. Data were employed from subjects who chose to employ a social tactic in recalled instances of the use of PPMs. Their open-ended responses were categorized in to the three tactic types (*who, how,* and *what*). Each type was used as the criterion measure in a series of multiple discriminant analyses with need for accurate information and the social strategic consideration variables as predictors.

Graham et al. argued that PPMs are activated in situations where the need for accurate information is both high and in jeopardy. Consequently, the greater the need for accurate information, the more often social actors would employ quasi-scientific norms to pick tactics for gathering information. For instance, they would prefer to triangulate information or talk to others rather than restrict their data-gathering to the target or the source (*who* tactics). They would prefer hypothesis testing or both hypothesis testing and plausibility testing to plausibility testing alone because new information is used in the first two tactics but not the latter (*what* tactics). Only in the case of *how* tactics (direct, indirect, or both) was social appropriateness expected to play a determining role in tactic choice.

These predictions were born out by the data. The Social Tactic Phase, like the other three phases in the operation of PPMs, is governed by a set of three principles: (a) obtain accurate information; (b) conserve cognitive effort; and (c) conserve social effort. Although the tradeoffs among these three principles are not completely understood, the principles seem plausible enough. Unlike more mundane interactions where issues of social position and politeness (appropriateness) seem to be major factors controlling social interaction strategies and tactics (Berger, chapter 5, this volume; Kellermann, chapter 6, this volume), social actors perform more like truth seekers when they activate PPMs.

CONCLUSIONS

All of this research points to the existence of something very like PPMs that operates, at least partly, according to the processes previously described. Although the evidence is mostly consistent with theory, the type of evidence employed here needs to be bolstered with more experimental studies of on-line cognitive processing of messages. The reliance on nonexperimental studies, especially for the latter two phases, both limits and expands the conclusions that can be drawn about the theory. It limits the conclusions because such studies give us no definitive access to causal, cognitive processes as they occur, although in the case of salient, reflective cognitive processes, self-report data on process should be given some credence (Ericsson & Simon, 1993). These nonexperimental studies expand the possible conclusions because they suggest the PPMs are robust enough to operate in real life settings, not just in the laboratory.

The theory of PPMs also offers us an unusual opportunity. Socially oriented cognitive research, as represented by many of the chapters in this book, often reflects an implicit division between two kinds of theories: theories of message production and theories of message interpretation/storage (Littlejohn, 1992). Message production theories focus primarily on the processes by which messages are created or selected from a repertoire and the processes by which those messages are enacted (cf. Berger, chapter 5, this volume; Greene, chapter 2, this volume; Kellermann, chapter 6, this volume). Message interpretation/storage theories address questions of the attention paid to messages, the inferences drawn from them, and how those inferences are stored and retrieved (cf. Smith, chapter 3, this volume; Wyer & Gruenfeld, chapter 1, this volume).

PPM theory is unusual because it crosses the boundaries between the two kinds. It follows a message from its interpretation and through the cognitive system to message production. Although PPM theory is limited to the contexts in which it applies and the kinds of cognitive processes it describes, the general tactic of connecting inputs to outputs is crucial to developing truly social theories of cognition. One of the primary criteria by which one can judge a cognitive theory of human communication is by how much it helps us understand the flow of social interaction. Connecting message inputs to message outputs is a necessary, although not a sufficient, condition to meet this criterion.

Finally, within the boundaries to which it applies, the theory of PPMs sheds light on the appropriate metaphors to guide cognitive research. Fiske and Taylor (1991) typify modern cognitive social psychological research as moving away of a "cognitive miser" model of the social actor and toward a model of the "motivated tactician." The danger of this move is that the latter model often loses too much of the parsimony so characteristic of "miserly" explanations. What I have tried to do in PPM theory is to retain as much of the desirable simplicity of cognitive models which rely on cognitive capacity/efficiency for explanations, while recognizing the thoughtful, socially oriented tactician in all of us. In short, the explanatory power of "cognitive miser" model, like the limitations of cognitive capacity, must be balanced with the real contribution of thoughtful, goal-driven action.

Where does PPM theory go from here? Hopefully, the directions are clear. Much more needs to be known about the details of the cognitive operations captured by PPMs. What, if any, are the hierarchical relationships among the three principles that seems to guide PPMs: (a) obtain accurate information; (b) conserve cognitive effort; and (c) conserve social effort? Are there other strategies for managing capacity limitations that do not require tradeoffs among these three principles? What are the costs of the overuse or underuse of PPMs? How are multiple, contradictory cues pressed? These questions and others yet unasked point to a busy life for those who study PPMs. But the rewards for answering these questions are great if they make it possible to communicate more effectively in an ever more complex social world.

REFERENCES

Bartlett, F. C. (1932). *Remembering.* Cambridge, England: Cambridge University Press.

Berger, C. R. (1979). Beyond initial interaction: Uncertainty, understanding, and the development of interpersonal relationships. In H. Giles & R. St. Clair (Eds.), *Language and social psychology.* Baltimore, MD: University Park Press.

Berger C. R. (1986). Uncertain outcome values in predicted relationships: Uncertainty reduction theory then and now. *Human Communication Research, 13,* 34–38.

Berger, C. R. (1987). Communicating under uncertainty. In M. R. Roloff & G. R. Miller (Eds.), *Interpersonal processes* (pp. 129–145). Newbury Park, CA: Sage.

Berger, C. R., & Bradac, J. J. (1982). *Language and social knowledge.* London: Edward Arnold.

Berger, C. R., & Douglas, W. (1981). Studies in interpersonal epistemology: III. Anticapated interaction, self-monitoring, and observational context selection. *Communication Monographs, 48,* 183–196.

Berger, C. R., & Calabrese, R. (1975). Some explorations in initial interaction and beyond: Toward a developmental theory of interpersonal communication. *Human Communication Research, 1,* 99–112.

Berger, C. R., & Kellermann, K. A. (1983). To ask or not to ask: Is that a question? In R. N. Bostrom (Ed.), *Communication Yearbook 7* (pp. 342–368). Beverly Hills: Sage.

Berscheid, E., & Graziano, W. (1979). The initiation of social relationships and interpersonal attraction. In R. L. Burgess & T. L. Huston (Eds.), *Social exchange in developing relationships.* New York: Academic.

Berscheid, E., Graziano, W., Monson, T., & Derman, M. (1976). Outcome Dependency: Attention, attribution, and attraction. *Journal of Personality and Social Psychology, 34,* 978–989.

Davenport, W. G. (1968). Auditory vigilance: The effects of costs and values on signals. *Australian Journal of Psychology, 20,* 213–218.

Davenport, W. G. (1969). Vibrotactile vigilance: The effects of costs and values on signals. *Perception and Psychophysiology, 5,* 25–28.

Doelger, J. A., Hewes, D. E., & Graham, M. L. (1986). Knowing when to "second-guess": The mindful analysis of messages. *Human Communication Research, 12,* 301–338.

Elliot, G. C. (1979). Some effects of deception and level of self-monitoring on planning and reacting to a self-presentation. *Journal of Personality and Social Psychology, 37,* 1282–1292.

Ericsson, K. A., & Simon, H. A. (1993). *Protocol analysis* (2nd ed). Cambridge, MA: The MIT Press.

Eysenck, M. W. (1982). *Attention and arousal.* Berlin: Springer-Verlag.

Fiske, S. T., & Taylor, S. E. (1991). *Social cognition* (2nd ed.) Reading, MA: Addison-Wesley.

Forgas, J. P., Bower, G. H., & Krantz, S. E. (1984). The influence of mood on perceptions of social interactions. *Journal of Experimental Social Psychology, 20,* 497–513.

Graham, M., Hewes, D. E., Doelger, J., & Monsour, M. (1989). *From cognition to social information-gathering: II. Social Tactic Choice.* Unpublished manuscript, University of Minnesota, Minneapolis.

Greene, J. O. (1984). A cognitive approach to human communication: An action assembly theory. *Communication Monographs, 51,* 289–306.

Hastie, R., Park, B., & Weber, R. (1984). Social memory. In R. S. Wyer, Jr., & T. K. Srull (Eds.), *Handbook of social cognition* (Vol. 2., pp. 152–212). Hillsdale, NJ: Lawrence Erlbaum Associates.

Heider, F. (1958). *The psychology of interpersonal relations.* New York: Wiley.

Hewes, D. E., & Graham, M. L. (1988). Second-guessing theory: Review and extension. In J. A. Anderson (Ed.), *Communication Yearbook 12.* Newbury Park, CA: Sage.

Hewes, D. E., Graham, M. L., Doelger, J., & Pavitt, C. (1985). "Second-guessing": Message interpretation in social networks. *Human Communication Research, 2,* 299–334.

Hewes, D. E., Graham, M. L., Monsour, M., & Doelger, J. A. (1988). *From cognition to social information-getting tactics: I. Re-interpretation assessment in second-guessing.* Paper presented to the annual meeting of the International Communication Association, New Orleans, LA.

Hewes, D. E., & Monsour, M. (1990). *The innerworkings of Second-guessing: Differential Cue Effectiveness.* Unpublished manuscript, University of Minnesota, Minneapolis.

Hewes, D. E., Monsour, M., & Rutherford, D. K. (1989). *Second-guessing: The effects of need for accuracy on cue extraction, doubt, and normative adequacy.* Unpublished manuscript, University of Minnesota, Minneapolis.

Hewes, D. E., & Planalp, S. (1982). There is nothing as useful as a good theory . . . : The influence of social knowledge on interpersonal communication. In M. E. Roloff & C. R. Berger (Eds.), *Social cognition and communication* (pp. 56–78). Beverly Hills, CA: Sage.

Isen, A. M. (1984). Toward understanding the role of affect in cognition. In R. S. Wyer, Jr. & T. K. Srull (Eds.), *Handbook of social cognition* (Vol. 3, pp. 179–236). Hillsdale, NJ: Lawrence Erlbaum Associates.

Isen, A. M., Means, B., Patrick, R., & Nowicki, G. (1982). Some factors influencing decision-making strategy and risk-taking. In M. S. Clark & S. T. Fisk (Eds.), *Affect and cognition* (pp. 231–254). Hillsdale, NJ: Lawrence Erlbaum Associates.

Jones, E. E., & Baumeister, R. (1976). The self-monitor looks as the ingratiator. *Journal of Personality, 44,* 654–674.

Kahneman, D., Slovic, P., & Tversky, A. (Eds.) (1982). *Judgment under uncertainty.* Cambridge, England: Cambridge University Press.

Kaplan, A. (1964). *The conduct of inquiry.* San Francisco, CA: Chandler.

Kellermann, K. A., & Berger, C. R. (1984). Affect and social information acquisition: Sit back, relax, and tell me about yourself. In R. Bostrom (Ed.), *Communication yearbook 8* (pp. 412–445). Beverly Hills, CA: Sage.

Kelley, H. H. (1967). Attribution theory in social psychology. In D. Levine (Ed.), *Nebraska Symposium on motivation* (Vol. 15, pp. 25–67). Lincoln, NB: University of Nebraska.

Kelly, G. A. (1955). *A theory of personality.* New York: W. H. Norton.

Kruglanski, A. W., & Ajzen, I. (1983). Bias and error in human judgment. *European Journal of Social Psychology, 13,* 1–44.

Kruglanski, A. W., & Freund, T. (1983). The freezing and unfreezing of lay-inferences: Effects on impressional primacy, ethnic stereotyping, and numerical anchoring. *Journal of Experimental Social Psychology, 19,* 448–468.

Kruglanski, A. W., Hamel, I. A., Maides, S. A., & Schwartz, J. M. (1978). Attribution theory as a special case of lay epistemology. In J. H. Harvey, W. Ickes, & R. F. Kidd (Eds.), *New direction in attribution research* (Vol. 2, pp. 299–333). Hillsdale, NJ: Lawrence Erlbaum Associates.

Labov, W., & Fanshel, D. (1977). *Therapeutic discourse.* New York: Academic.

Langer, E. J. (1978). Rethinking the role of thought in social interaction. In J. Harvey, W. Ickes, & R. Kidd (Eds.), *New directions in attribution research* (Vol. 2., pp. 36–58) Hillsdale, NJ: Lawrence Erlbaum Associates.

Langer, E. J., & Abelson, R. P. (1972). The semantics of asking a favor: How to succeed in getting help without really dying. *Journal of Personality and Social Psychology, 24,* 26–32.

Langer, E. J., Blank, A., & Chanowitz, B. (1978). The mindlessness of obstensibly thoughtful action: The role of "placebic" information in interpersonal interaction. *Journal of Personality and Social Psychology, 36,* 635–642.

Levine, J. M. (1966). The effects of values and costs in the detection and identification of signals in auditory vigilance. *Human Factors, 8,* 525–537.

Littlejohn, S. W. (1992). *Theories of human communication* (4th ed.). Belmont, CA: Wadsworth.

Loftus, E. E. (1979). *Eyewitness testimony.* Cambridge, MA: Harvard University Press.

Lyman, S. M., & Scott. (1970). *A sociology of the absurd.* Pacific Palisades, CA: Goodyear.

Martins, D. (1982). Influence of affect on comprehension of a text. *Text, 2,* 141–154.

McDougall, W. (1911). *Body and mind: A history and a defense of animism.* London: Methuen.

McGraw, K. O. (1978). The detrimental effects of reward on performance: A literature review and a prediction model. In M. R. Lepper & D. Greene (Eds.), *The hidden costs of reward* (pp. 42–68). Hillsdale, NJ: Lawrence Erlbaum Associates.

Mischel, W. (1981). Personality and cognition: Something borrowed, something new? In N. Cantor

& J. F. Kihlstrom (Eds.), *Personality, cognition, and social interaction* (pp. 3–19). Hillsdale, NJ: Lawrence Erlbaum Associates.

Navon, D., & Gopher, D. (1979). On the economy of the human processing system. *Psychological Review, 86,* 214–255.

Nisbett, R., & Ross, L. (1980). *Human inference.* Englewood Cliffs, NJ: Prentice-Hall.

Numaninville, B. E. (1993). *Second-guessing and self-monitoring: Monitoring the need for accurate information in second-guessing.* M. A. Thesis, University of Minnesota, Minneapolis.

Norman, D. A. (1981). Categorization of action slips. *Psychological Review, 88,* 1–15.

Ostrom, T. M. (1984). The sovereignty of social cognition. In R. S. Wyer, Jr. & T. K. Srull (Eds.), *Handbook of social cognition* (Vol. 1, pp. 3–38). Hillsdale, NJ: Lawrence Erlbaum Associates.

Petty, R. E., & Cacioppo, J. T. (1986). *Communication and persuasion: Central and peripheral routes to attitude change.* New York: Springer-Verlag.

Planalp, S., & Hewes, D. E. (1982). A cognitive approach to communication theory: *Cogito Ergo Dico?* In M. Burgoon (Ed.), *Communication Yearbook 5* (pp. 49–77). New Brunswick, NJ: Transaction-International Communication Association.

Planalp, S., & Honeycutt, J. M. (1985). Events that increase uncertainty personal relationships. *Human Communication Research, 11,* 593–604.

Planalp, S., Rutherford, D. K., & Honeycutt, J. M. (1988). Events that increase uncertainty in personal relationships II: Replication and extension. *Human Communication Research, 14,* 516–547.

Pyszczynski, T., & Greenberg, J. (1987). Toward an integration of cognitive and motivational perspectives on social inference: A biased hypothesis-testing model. In L. Berkowitz (Ed.), *Advances in experimental social psychology* (Vol. 20, pp. 210–235). San Diego, CA: Academic Press.

Roloff, M. (1898). On second-guessing the theory of second-guessing: A comment. In J. A. Anderson (Ed.), *Communication Yearbook 12* (pp. 249–265). Newbury park, CA: Sage.

Sherman, S. J., & Corty, E. (1984). Cognitive heuristics. In R. S. Wyer & T. K. Srull (Eds.), *Handbook of social cognition* (Vol. 2, pp. 190–286). Hillsdale, NJ: Lawrence Erlbaum Associates.

Snyder, M. (1987). *Public appearances/private relatities.* New York: Freeman.

Sunnafrank. (1986). Predicted outcome values: Just now and then? *Human Communication Research, 13,* 39–40.

Van Dijk, T. A., & Kintsch, W. (1983). *Strategies of discourse comprehension.* New York: Academic Press.

Zuckerman, M., DePaulo, B. M., & Rosenthal, R. (1981). Verbal and nonverbal communication of deception. In L. Berkowitz (Ed.), *Advances in experimental social psychology* (Vol. 14, pp. 124–156). New York: Academic Press.

INTERPERSONAL COMMUNICATION FROM AN ARTIFICIAL INTELLINGENCE PERSPECTIVE

5 A Plan-Based Approach to Strategic Communication

Charles R. Berger
University of California, Davis

Interpersonal-communication researchers and social psychologists have shown increasing interest in understanding the communication strategies that persons use to achieve a variety of social goals, especially those involving compliance (Boster & Stiff, 1984; Cody, McLaughlin, & Jordan, 1980; Cody, McLaughlin, & Schneider, 1981; deTurck, 1985; Dillard & Burgoon, 1985; Falbo, 1977; Falbo & Peplau, 1981; McLaughlin, Cody, & Robey, 1980; Miller, 1987; Miller, Boster, Roloff, & Seibold, 1977, 1987; Rule & Bisanz, 1987; Rule, Bisanz, & Kohn, 1985; Schenck-Hamlin, Wiseman, & Georgacarakos, 1982; Tracy, Craig, Smith, & Spisak, 1984; Wheeless, Barraciough, & Stewart, 1983). Considerably less attention has been paid to strategies employed to attain other social goals. Strategies used for affinity seeking or ingratiation have been isolated (Bell & Daly, 1984; Berger & Bell, 1988; Douglas, 1987; Jones, 1964; Jones & Wortman, 1973), and some work has been done on strategies used to gain personal information from others and to assess the state of relationships (Baxter & Wilmot, 1984; Berger & Kellermann, 1994; Goffman, 1969; Snyder, 1981; Trope & Bassok, 1982). Still, the amount of research done to explore various strategies is so great that two volumes have appeared on the topic (Cody & McLaughlin, 1990; Daly & Wiemann, 1994). Although this body of research has provided valuable characterizations of the strategies used to attain some social goals, it generally has not advanced beyond description. Some studies (e.g., Miller et al., 1977) have explored how variables such as *type of relationship* and *consequences to the relationship* affect the propensity to deploy alternative compliance-gaining strategies. But, as Berger, Karol, and Jordan (1989) pointed out, the variables used to predict strategy selection in these studies have been chosen on an ad hoc basis. The great outpouring of communication-strategies research has not been matched with equally impressive advances in the construction of theories that explain strategy development and strategy use.

Researchers' excessive preoccupation with descriptions of various communication strategies, and the conditions under which they may or may not be deployed, has diverted attention away from the more fundamental questions of how individuals devise strategies for reaching social goals and how ready-made strategies are instantiated from long-term memory. Strategies are taken as givens. For example, work linking person-impression and message-production processes has been virtually mute on this issue (O'Keefe & Delia, 1982). Although these constructivist researchers hypothesize with reference to the interpersonal construct system that "increases in differentiation and abstractness influence the *availability* of strategies for addressing obstacles and subsidiary aims" of communicators, they do not specify the cognitive structures and processes responsible for generating these strategies (O'Keefe & Delia, 1982, p. 61, emphasis added). Subsequent work in this tradition (O'Keefe & McCornack, 1987; O'Keefe & Shepard, 1987) has not specified in detail such generative mechanisms. Studying covariation between the complexity of person impressions and the complexity of messages is not likely to shed light on strategy-generation structures and processes.

The general lack of concern for strategy generation has produced additional negative consequences for both communication theory and communication praxis. At the theory level, explaining how persons fabricate strategies to reach social goals enables a better understanding of how and why persons finally deploy particular strategies at the level of tactical action. Specifically, because attributes of the immediate situation in which a goal is being pursued may affect strategy formulation and strategy selection, it is important to understand how these situational attributes are integrated into formulation and selection processes. This understanding is only possible if these formulation and selection processes are well understood. As for communication practice, with few notable exceptions (e.g., Donohue, 1978, 1981; Hirokawa, 1982; 1983; 1985; Hirokawa & Pace, 1983), it is remarkable that communication-strategies researchers have virtually ignored the question of how persons who are effective at reaching various social goals differ from those who are relatively ineffective at so doing. Understanding how persons formulate and select communication strategies may help explain variations in interaction effectiveness. Taxonomies of strategies alone or in combination with the knowledge of the conditions under which various strategies are selected cannot address the effectiveness issue. Simply because persons who differ on personality traits, or who find themselves in different situations, tend to choose different tactics when pursuing a compliance-gaining goal says little about the relative effectiveness of the tactics chosen. Finding reliable predictors of strategy choice begs the question of how the strategies were generated in order to be selected. Moreover, unless theoretical accounts are constructed to explain these reliable relationships, the processes subserving strategy selection remain obscure. The aim of the present chapter, then, is to begin to redress this lack of theory by focusing on the question of how strategies are generated.

TOWARD A PLANNING THEORY

Some Preliminary Considerations

The perspective presented here rests on the assumption that the communication process is the linking of two or more mental representations through verbal and nonverbal symbol systems. This view of communication in general and interpersonal communication in particular suggests that, to understand the communication processes, it is not only necessary to study exchanges of symbols, but it is also crucial to understand the cognitive processes that subserve the interpretation and generation of these symbols. This assertion echoes those made by Hewes and Planalp (1982, 1987) and Planalp and Hewes (1982) in their persuasive presentations supporting a cognitive approach to the study of interpersonal communication. But it obviously extends beyond the limited domain of interpersonal communication to include all forms of communication.

Although this general assumption points the way toward potentially fruitful approaches to the study of communication, it does not constitute a detailed theory that accounts for the formation and realization of goal-oriented strategies. Fortunately, considerable work has already been done on knowledge structures that may, in part, be responsible for the interpretation and generation of goal-directed social action. In particular, the constructs of *goal* and *plan* have frequently been invoked to explain how persons understand the actions of others and symbolic representations of these actions in narrative texts (Abbott & Black, 1986; Black & Bower, 1979; Green, 1989; Lichtenstein & Brewer, 1980; Schank & Abelson, 1977; Schmidt, 1976; Seifert, Robertson, & Black, 1985; von Cranach, Kalbermatten, Indermuhle, & Gugler, 1982). In addition, these constructs have been implicated in the production of action by artificial-intelligence (AI) researchers (Sacerdoti, 1977), philosophers (Brand, 1984; Bratman, 1987), and psychologists (Ajzen, 1985; De Lisi, 1987; Dorner, 1985; Kluwe & Friedrichsen, 1985; Kreitler & Kreitler, 1987; Miller, Galanter, & Pribram, 1960; Nuttin, 1984; Read & Miller, 1989; von Cranach et al., 1982). Given the roles played by goals and plans in action comprehension and action production, it is natural to look to these constructs and the bodies of research embodying them for guidance in shaping a theory of strategic communication. Before embarking on an explication of the outline of such a theory, it is necessary to define the two key constructs of *goal* and *plan*.

Goals. Goals are desired end states toward which persons strive. Goals may be both explicit or implicit; that is, at any given point in time, persons may be able to articulate the goal or goals they are trying to attain. However, at the same time, persons may be pursuing other implicit goals about which they are unable to verbalize. There are at least two different senses of the term *implicit goal*. In the first sense, an implicit goal is one that is only temporarily out of a person's awareness. For example, on the way to the store to purchase a pack of gum, a person encounters a neighborhood friend and proceeds to catch up on the latest neighborhood gossip. If the person was asked about his or her current goal during the conversation, he or she might reply that his or her goal was to obtain neighborhood gossip and *not* mention the gum-purchasing goal. In this example, the gum-purchasing goal has receded temporarily into the background and presumably will become explicit when the conversation ends—assuming, of course, that the person remembers where he or she was going and why he or she was going there, which is not necessarily a good assumption (Norman, 1981; Reason, 1990).

A second sense of the term *implicit goal* involves the possibility that, within a given encounter, an individual may pursue multiple goals simultaneously, only a subset of which may be accessible to the person's conscious awareness. The notion that persons pursue multiple goals in their interactions with others recently has achieved the status of a truism among interpersonal-communication researchers (O'Keefe & Shepard, 1987; Tracy & Eisenberg, 1989), although the coding problems created by the multifunctionality of specific interaction behaviors was discussed in considerable detail by Hewes (1979) and was alluded to by Sillars (1980) over a decade ago. In the previous example, the explicit goal of the person may be to acquire certain information about neighbors. However, implicitly the person may also be pursuing the goal of maintaining the friendship. Such preservation goals (Schank & Abelson, 1977) are frequently not accessed verbally to explain current conduct. When persons are asked why they are eating, they are most likely to reply that they are hungry or that it is time to eat, rather than to say that they are eating because they wish to preserve their life. Given that conscious attention is a relatively scarce cognitive resource, it is almost a certainty that, in any social-interaction situation, several goals will be implicit for the actors involved, and that goals at the focal point of conscious awareness will change during the course of most social-interaction episodes (Berger, 1988a).

Plans and Planning.   Several definitions of the plan construct have been advanced over the years (Miller et al., 1960; Schank & Abelson, 1977; Wilensky, 1983). Berger (1988a) reviewed these definitions and proposed the following synthetic definition: "A plan specifies the actions that are necessary for the attainment of a goal or several goals. Plans vary in their levels of abstraction. Highly abstract plans can spawn more detailed plans. Plans can contain alternative paths for goal attainment from which the social actor can choose" (p. 96). Plans are not actions, but conceptual representations of actions. Plans differ from knowledge structures like scripts: They contain general knowledge and are considerably more flexible (Galambos, Abelson, & Black, 1986; Schank & Abelson, 1977). Plans become scripts through repeated enactment. One would not speak of *a* plan of ingratiating one's self to another, as if there was only one way to accomplish this goal.

Although this definition of *plan* seems to be straightforward, there are those whose conceptions of plan differ. Bratman (1987, 1990) argued that the notion of plan implies a commitment to action; that is, when persons assert that they "plan to do" something, they are indicating a commitment to perform the action. For Bratman, a plan is an intention "writ large." Contrast Bratman's view of a plan with De Lisi's (1987) "Type 4" plan, which he defines as "an individual or collective deliberate effort to devise a plan; that is, construction of an acceptable plan is now an end unto itself rather than serving as a means toward a goal" (p. 103). These hypothetical plans may be formulated by persons who are fully aware that their plans may never be acted upon. Plans devised to cope with potential personal and public disasters frequently display these attributes.

Given Bratman's (1987) interest in the personal and social criteria for judging the rationality of reconsideration or nonreconsideration of planned actions, it is clear why he has highlighted the behavior-commitment aspect of plans. If no commitment to action is present in plans, there is nothing to reconsider or not reconsider at a later time. Although this future commitment assumption is convenient for Bratman's purposes, it is overly restrictive in the present context. Persons can and do mentally rehearse alternative social-interaction plans that may never be realized when the interaction takes place. Persons may devise interaction plans involving aggressive acts that they know they would never deploy in an actual encounter with another. The distinct advantage of including the notion of hypothetical plans within the definition of the plan construct is that the ability to formulate hypothetical plans may be related both to other planning abilities and to interaction skills (Edwards, Honeycutt, & Zagacki, 1988). To exclude this type of plan from consideration would be to engage in an overzealous application of Occam's razor.

The *plan* concept can and should be differentiated from the construct of *planning*. Planning is a process in which persons (a) devise action sequences, (b) anticipate the outcomes of action sequences, (c) adjust projected actions in terms of anticipated outcomes, and (d) finally realize their plans in actions. Planning can occur in advance of action, or it can take place on-line as action unfolds (Rogoff, Gauvain, & Gardner, 1987). Observation of plans in action may lead the social actor to modify plans. Although planning may be the focus of conscious attention, planning may also occur outside of conscious awareness, just as goals that are not at the focus of attention may be pursued.

Planning may be carried out using either a top–down (Sacerdoti, 1977) or a bottom–up approach (Hayes-Roth & Hayes-Roth, 1979). Top–down planning begins with an abstract plan from which progressively more detailed actions are deduced. Presumably, as this type of planning takes place, the more specific, deduced actions are checked against the desired-goal state to determine their consistency. Sacerdoti embodied these consistency checks in the form of "critics" as part of his computer program *NOAH* that is designed to guide a robot arm. Bottom–up planning is data drive; that is, the planner devises an abstract plan through induction by using cues that are supplied by the environment. It is reasonable to suppose that both approaches to planning are used by social inter-actants. Persons may enter interaction situations with abstract plans from which specific actions may be deduced. However, as interaction episodes unfold and feedback is received, plans may be revised to fit the situation. Hayes-Roth and Hayes-Roth labeled this approach to planning *opportunistic* and argued that, in many instances of problem solving, planners use this approach to develop plans. Nevertheless, although there is opportunistic planning during interactions, it is implausible to suppose that goal-directed human interactants plan, *de novo,* for each different situation they encounter. Devising new interaction plans for each interaction episode is most likely beyond the capabilities of virtually all human planners. Some abstract plan, no matter how tenuously related to current interaction goals, is no doubt brought to bear in the situation.

Metagoals and Metaplans.   Given the energy and time constraints of social actors, it is assumed that the metagoal of efficiency guides the planning processes in order to avoid squandering these scarce resources (Berger, 1987, 1988a; Kellermann, 1988). Wilensky (1983) invoked a similar metagoal in his AI work on planning. The efficiency metagoal implies that planners seek to devise plans that will minimize the amount of time and effort expended to reach goals, although this ideal may not be realized. Moreover, it is assumed that persons may devise metaplans to help them attain their metagoals. Such metaplans might include the belief that one should devise plans that "kill two (or more) birds with one stone." That is, efficient plans are those in which several goals are achieved simultaneously by deploying the same action. In this regard, the concept of *while* assumes critical importance. In many arenas of everyday action, including social interaction, it is possible to plan to pursue goals while other goals are being pursued. Doing errands while on the way to a particular locale or trying to persuade the Dean on an important issue while enjoying a faculty party are examples of the application of the while metaplan. Other efficiency metaplans might involve attributes of the plans. Such metaplans might direct the planner to devise the least complex plan that will work. These metaplans would act to reduce the time, energy, and cognitive capacity that persons must expend to make and carry out plans.

A second metagoal that is vitally important in most social-interaction situations concerns the *social appropriateness* of actions (Berger, 1987, 1988a; Berger & Kellermann, 1983, 1994; Brown & Levinson, 1978; Kellermann, 1988; Kellermann & Berger, 1984; Spitzberg & Cupach, 1984). When planning to achieve goals involving social interaction, persons must take into account the social appropriateness of their projected actions. In general, because persons prefer conflict-free interactions and interactions in which their faces will be maintained, they will try to minimize the amount of disruption in their interactions with others (Goffman, 1959). The *social appropriateness* metagoal may also spawn metaplans designed to guide planners toward constructing plans that will not offend others. Such plans might include such admonitions as "be friendly," "compliment the other person," "don't dominate the conversation," and "smile a lot."

The efficiency and social appropriateness metagoals may bear several different relationships with each other (Berger & Kellermann, 1983, 1994; Kellermann, 1988; Kellermann & Berger, 1984). Under certain conditions, the two goals may be in conflict; that is, the most efficient way to reach a social goal may be the least appropriate. Kellermann and Berger observed this tension between the two goals in a study where persons attempted to acquire personal information from a stranger. Research participants reported using question asking, self-disclosure, and relaxing the target as ways to gather information. As listed here, these strategies are ranked from most to least efficient. However, considering the possibility that question asking can become both intrusive and obnoxious, it has the potential for being the least socially appropriate of the three strategies, whereas deploying actions to relax the target implies acting in a socially appropriate manner.

Other social goals may force the efficiency and appropriateness metagoals into conflict. The most efficient ways to induce behavioral compliance may be low in social appropriateness. The use of threat and physical force come to mind as examples. There is evidence that when persons pursue behavioral-compliance goals, their first influence attempts tend to be relatively socially appropriate. However, if they fail to gain compliance, their later influence attempts become less socially appropriate by becoming progressively more coercive (deTurck, 1985; Goodstadt & Kipnis, 1970; Kipnis & Consentino, 1969). Efficiency considerations may override the social appropriateness metagoal in extreme circumstances (e.g., where persons' lives are in danger). One would not expect parents to speak politely to their children if their children were in the path of an oncoming automobile.

It is also possible for the efficiency and social appropriateness metagoals to be compatible with each other. For example, when persons pursue ingratiation goals, the most efficient ways to accomplish these goals may also be the most appropriate socially (Bell & Daly, 1984; Jones, 1964; Jones & Wortman, 1973). Of course, plans for inducing another person to like one could be of close to equal social appropriateness but quite variable in terms of their efficiency. Giving compliments might be less effortful and time-consuming than rendering favors, but both of these plans for ingratiation might be of similar levels of social appropriateness. Having explicated the nature of goals, plans, planning, metagoals, and meta-plans, it is now time to make good on the promissory note issued earlier in this chapter; that is, to provide an account of how social actors formulate plans to reach social goals.

Searching for Plans

This theory begins with the general proposition that when persons are trying to achieve social goals, their first tendency is to search their long-term memories for plans they have used in the past to reach similar goals. As was pointed out earlier, being able to employ a previously used plan to reach a social goal is considerably more efficient, both in physical and cognitive terms, than constructing plans from the ground up each time a goal is pursued. Hewes (1986) made a similar assumption in his socioegocentric model of group decision making, and AI work on case-based planning is predicated on the same assumption (Hammond, 1989; Riesbeck & Schank, 1989). Given the conception of plans developed in this chapter, and the general proposition that persons prefer to utilize old plans when possible rather than develop new ones, one might ask whether plans that are stored in long-term memory are not merely scripts (Abelson, 1976, 1981; Schank, 1982; Schank & Abelson, 1977).

Although the line between plans and scripts is a fuzzy one (Galambos, Abelson, & Black, 1986), the term *script* has been reserved for highly rountinized action sequences that allow for little flexibility. This is true in both early (Schank & Abelson, 1977) and later (Schank, 1982) work involving the construct, although Schank and Abelson did invoke the notion of *tracks* to allow for possible variations in scripts (e.g., a fast-food restaurant track vs. an expensive restaurant track in the restaurant script). Although such a move may make sense for eating routines, which in these contexts tend to be quite predictable, this move makes less sense in the domain of social-interaction goals. For instance, when two persons are mutually attempting to influence one another, it is safe to assume that, in general, there is likely to be considerably greater potential for variability in the actions persons deploy in such a situation, compared with the level of variability of actions that are typically manifested by actors in the restaurant context. After all, within a given track of the restaurant script, how many different ways are there to achieve the goal of obtaining food? Bratman (1987) argued that in their everyday planning, persons devise partially formulated plans that are filled in with details as the day progresses. He argued persuasively that devising detailed daily plans is inefficient because it is impossible to anticipate events that may occur during the day that will cause reconsideration of plans or goals. Plan flexibility is a natural response to a highly variable environment, and the environment of social interaction is usually highly variable. As a consequence, although persons may develop scripts for attaining some social goals, for the most part more flexible plans are required to reach social goals because of the inherent variability that social actors encounter when trying to achieve them. In fact, reducing the actions necessary to reach social goals to a rigid, script-like formula may produce relatively ineffective social action.

Having taken this necessary small diversion to distinguish between plans and scripts, it is now time to return to the question of how plans are selected from memory, assuming they are available. Cappella and Folger (1980) argued that situational cues may activate tags associated with information stored in episodic memory, leading to the recall of specific episodes. Similarly, Schank (1982) asserted that persons may base their understanding of present situations on re-mindings from prior experiences. However, the notion of *reminding* implies that information processors have applied a similarity criterion to their memories for events and found a prior situation that matches or is similar enough to the present situation to remind them of the present situation. Although Schank's theory of reminding aims to explain action comprehension, persons could use remindings of prior experiences in which they attempted to reach similar goals to guide their present actions. The question is, do recalled specific episodes constitute plans? There appear to be at least two answers to this question. First, prior specific episodes could become plans for future action if social actors decided to copy their memory for the episode and use the copy to guide present action. Second, a prior specific episode could be used as the basis for forming a new plan. Under this second alternative, the actor might evaluate the outcomes of the recalled specific episode and, on the basis of such an evaluation, modify actions taken previously to form a new plan. Or the actor might augment the prior episode with knowledge from other sources without any evaluation of the previous episode. In either case, the intent here is not to argue that actors necessarily first search memory for specific prior episodes to use for present planning purposes. As we shall see, this is one possibility among many.

In their search for plans to reach current goals, actors may not retrieve specific episodes that remind them of their current situation. This may happen for a number of reasons. Most obviously, there may be no specific episode to retrieve. In addition, the actor may have experienced so many similar episodes that all that is available in memory is a generalized representation of the episode, much like Schank's (1982) scenes. As was the case with specific episodes, recall of gener-alized episodes may be copied directly and used as a plan for current action, or comparison of the generalized episode with current circumstances may reveal the need for making adjustments in the generalized episode to form a plan for attaining current goals.

Both specific and generalized episodes involve recollections of actions that were used to attain the goal in question in the past. There are additional sources of knowledge on which planners can draw. First, persons may have formulated a plan in the past to achieve goals that are similar to present goals, but never actually carried out the plan. What is available in memory is the plan itself, rather than a representation of the social situation in which the goal was actually pursued, as in the cases of generalized and specific episodes. Second, persons may have received direct instruction in how to reach the goal, and thus have general knowledge available to them concerning how to achieve certain goals. Students who have taken public-speaking classes may acquire knowledge of how to devise plans for persuading others, or persons who have participated in financial-planning seminars may obtain the knowledge necessary for devising get-rich-quick plans. Such instruction may or may not give persons the plans, but many provide them with metaplanning knowledge that can be used to formulate plans.

Given that specific episodes, generalized episodes, previous plans, and knowledge gained by instruction can be retrieved to aid in the formulation of present plans, it is difficult to imagine a situation in which persons have no plan available to them for pursuing a specific goal or goals. When normal adults are thrust into what are seemingly novel social circumstances, they do not remain unable to act for a prolonged period of time. Finding oneself in a new situation might increase the latencies with which one responds, but most persons seem capable of "figuring out" what is socially appropriate and at least moderately efficient to do without formal instruction. The apparent ability of most adults to deploy at least somewhat meaningful actions in new situations indicates the considerable range of schemata for interpreting and generating action available to most adults (Brewer & Nakamura, 1984).

It is still true that, under certain circumstances, normal adults may initially assert that they do not know what to do in a given set of circumstances. To take such verbalizations as "I don't know what to do" or "I don't know how to do that" as evidence of a lack of a plan for achieving the goal or goals in question may be misleading for the following reasons. First, if the situation involves some kind of an emergency and the planner is under stress, it is possible that the planner has a perfectly good plan for meeting the emergency but is currently unable to retrieve the plan because of the stress-induced interference being experienced. Second, in such stressful situations, persons may experience temporary "inaction" because too many alternative plans occur to them at once. Consider the plight of a lone father who finds his small child choking on some food and does not know whether he should begin the Heimlich Maneuver or call "911" first. Whereas a father in this situation might cry "I don't know what to do," this statement does not imply a complete lack of knowledge about how to save his child. Alternatively, increased stress may lower the ability of an individual to process complex environmental stimuli in the first place, thus reducing the range of alternative actions he or she can generate (Schroder, Driver, & Streufert, 1967). Third, in situations where stress is not an important factor, planners may be unable or unwilling to expend the time or effort needed to retrieve or construct potentially relevant plans. On some reflection, such persons may have very good plans for reaching goals, yet say that they have no idea how they would go about reaching a particular goal.

Although adults who have been exposed to a range of experiences throughout their lives may encounter situations in which they find it very difficult to initiate actions toward social goals, it is difficult to imagine such persons being thrown into a state of profound inaction because of a complete lack of requisite plan knowledge. Detecting even a few similarities between the present situation and prior situations enables the planner to retrieve a sketchy plan that can be filled in as the interaction sequence unfolds. In the previous example of the father and the choking child, assume that the father does not know the Heimlich Maneuver and also knows that emergency help from "911" will probably not arrive in time to save his child. However, also assume that from a recent television show in the hospital genre, the father remembers the statement "Get those air passages clear" being made in an emergency-room scene. This kind of cue might provide the father with a sketchy plan for saving his child. The father will have to fill in such details as reaching down his child's throat or turning the child upside down, but the retrieval of the sketchy plan provides an initial path to the goal. For adults, who have large stores of world knowledge, minimal cuing from the environment generally will produce retrieval of at least some relevant plan knowledge. As a result, persons are rarely left with the alternative of not knowing how to reach a social goal or goals, at least in an absolute sense.

PLANNING FOR SOCIAL GOALS

To determine the knowledge sources that persons use to develop current plans, undergraduate students were asked to devise plans for reaching the following four goals: (a) asking a person at a party for a date for the next weekend, (b) ingratiating oneself to a new roommate, (c) persuading another student to accept one's opinion on a current campus issue, and (d) becoming a millionaire. The specific instructions for each goal were as follows:

Date Request: Assume that you have met someone to whom you are very attracted for the first time at a party. You would like to ask this person out for the next weekend. How would you go about asking this person for a date?

Roommate Ingratiation: You are about to meet your new roommate at the beginning of the year. You are interested in getting this person to like you. How would you go about getting your new roommate to like you?

Persuasion: You are interested in persuading another person to accept your personal opinion about whether alcohol consumption in dormitories should or should not be banned. How would you go about getting the person to agree with your opinion on this issue?

Millionaire: How would you go about becoming a millionaire?

The first three goals were chosen because of their presumed relevance to under-graduate students. The date-requesting and roommate-ingratiation goals are similar to some of the college-life tasks used by Cantor, Norem, Niedenthal, Langston, and Brower (1987) in their study of cognitive strategies for coping with life transitions (see Cantor & Kihlstrom, 1987). At the time of the study, the alcohol-ban issue was highly salient among students in the study. The millionaire goal was included because it is both a nonsocial goal and one about which most students would not have thought too much. Each student responded to each of the goals. Plans were generated using the think-aloud procedure with retrospective reports outlined by Ericsson and Simon (1984). Participants were asked to indicate how they would go about reaching the goal while telling everything about which they were thinking. Participants were then asked to report everything about which they were thinking while solving the problem. In general, the first part of the think-aloud procedure yielded a plan; during the retrospective reports, the participants revealed the sources of their plans. Given the current interest in planning sources, the retrospective reports will be of primary concern rather than the content of the plans. Although statistical summaries of these sources have been made (Berger & Jordan, 1992), the focus here is on individual protocol responses.

Specific Episodes

Single episodes in which the participants had actually taken part were frequently used as a basis for planning, especially in the case of the roommate-ingratiation goal. The following responses illustrate this planning source:

> *Subject 003:* "I guess I related this to my roommate this year and tried to realize how I got her to like me."
>
> *Subject 016:* "Ok. Again !-I pictured back to my situation meeting my—very first roommate ah because we had a lot of differences ah just in background and life and everything, and we still got along."
>
> *Subject 031:* "Ah, right back to freshman year again at Elder. Um, seeing my, ah, roommate the first day."
>
> *Subject 064:* "First thing that came to mind without any effort was ah, mental images and recollections of meeting my ah, first college roommate, and what that was like, and ah, then in reporting that and thinking about that and reflecting on it. . . ."

As the previous responses indicate, persons frequently recalled the specific episode of meeting their freshman roommate for the first time as a guide to formulating their current roommate-ingratiation plan.

Specific episodes were recalled as a basis for planning for some of the other goals as well. The following responses were given for the date-requesting goal:

Subject 004: "Ok. I was thinking about being at a party one time and seeing somebody that I was attracted to, but didn't know, and I can remember being with friends of mine and asking, you know, what they thought about him, what they knew about him, if he had a girlfriend. And, uh, trying to decide whether I knew him well enough to go up and ask him out or whether I had enough guts to go up and talk to him without knowing him very well."

Subject 039: "Uh, I remember thinking, huh, about ah being at a party where someone that I've known for a long time was there, and I wanted to ask her out and, ah, a half hour it took two friends to convince me to actually go ask her, and ah remembering th- I just remember thinking, you know, what a big deal it was, and I manipulated in my own mind into this huge event, and then when I actually ask her it's no big deal."

In the cases of both the roommate-ingratiation and date-requesting goals, some participants had vivid memories of prior situations in which they had been key social actors. In fact, in the case of specific episodes, participants never took the perspective of a detached observer of the scene. Apparently, participants did not recall relevant episodes they may have witnessed, but episodes in which they were not a central character. The specific episodes recalled by these participants involved themselves seeking the goal in the situation.

Aggregated Episodes

Participants also provided responses indicating that they based their current planning on collections of single, specific episodes. Evidence for aggregation was manifested in the following sample of protocol responses:

Subject 016: "Ok. I remember first picturing party or picturing situations that had happened to me like similar to this you know so—going back and trying to remember more what I did. . . ."

Subject 023: "I was going back on past experiences. Ah, how I've met a person at a party."

Subject 026: "I just thought about things in the past, maybe since I've been here at college when I've been at a fr-fraternity party and you see somebody, or I was in the Bahamas and you meet people and you don't really know how to go about them—you don't know them very well.

Subject 031: "Um, thinking that that this is ah, a pretty, um—common situation, and, um—that I'm no—I'm not shy. . . Um—just images came in my mind of the bar and different social places on campus."

Subject 036: "Ah, I—believe my thinking was a direct extension of my debating experience. Um, a rigid format of—first of all, as I had said, my strategy for ad-addressing the problem on a large level."

In some instances, persons examined each episode they recalled individually, as Subjects 023 and 026 seem to have done. By contrast, other respondents (e.g., Subject 036) appeared to have recalled a more generalized representation of their similar experiences. Apparently, Subject 036 had debated so many times that he had induced an abstract structure for changing persons' opinions on issues. However, as these excerpts from the protocols demonstrate, in some cases it is difficult to make this distinction.

Hypothetical Episodes

In addition to specific episodes and aggregations of specific episodes, some participants based their plans on imagined episodes that they apparently had never experienced directly. The following protocol responses illustrate this type of episode:

> *Subject 002:* "I was thinking that I was at a party, and that there was somebody who I just met who, um, who I really, like, seemed to like, and then I could imagine myself going up to them and saying. 'What are you doing, um, next weekend?'"
>
> *Subject 017:* "All I can remember about my thinking is first I tried to visualize that I was at a party and a dis—and a person was at some sort of distance away from me. Um, and I was picturing the person—intermingling er, uh, mixing with a bunch of other people, and I thought of approaching the person; when I would, um, do it, and would it be an appropriate time to do it, and then asking the person out."
>
> *Subject 056:* "I could imagine me being in a situation talking to someone and what I would do in that situation. I was invisioning the situation talking to someone."
>
> *Subject 066:* "I was—ah—pr-a-probably invisioning—I was invisioning someone—g-ah-giving me the opposing point of view and countering with my argument."

In these examples, respondents gave no indication that they actually experienced the particular episode they recalled. These hypothetical episodes appeared to be based on generalizations from previous experiences verbalized in such a way that no mention was made of the specific episodes subsumed under them. These hypothetical episodes frequently included references to visualization of oneself in the situation.

The Plan Sources Hierarchy

The think-aloud protocol responses provide strong evidence for this general proposition: When persons are faced with the task of planning to reach social goals, their first tendency is to search long-term memory for plans that they have used to achieve similar social goals in the past. Retrieving specific episodes, aggregated episodes, and hypothetical episodes provides planners with ready-made plans for the present situation and reduces cognitive load.

In addition to providing evidence for the basic proposition, the think-aloud data suggest that previous plans may be arranged in a hierarchy, just as scripts are alleged to be (Abelson, 1976). It appears that persons can conceptualize similar specific episodes as aggregates and search these aggregations for common plan actions that might be used to formulate plans for the present situation. Furthermore, these aggregated episodes can be abstracted further into hypothetical episodes. At this level, recall of specific episodes is difficult, yet planners have no difficulty imagining themselves, and in some cases visualizing themselves, attempting to achieve the social goal.

On Not Knowing What to Do

The think-aloud data also provide some insights into the problem of not knowing what to do when faced with the task of reaching a specific goal. As was noted previously, even in novel situations it is difficult for adults not to have at least sketchy plans for achieving goals because of their extensive store of world knowledge. Subjects were presented with the millionaire goal to see how they would plan for a relatively unfamiliar goal. Our intuitions about the unfamiliarity of the millionaire goal were supported by the fact that 32% of the subjects spontaneously indicated that they did not know how to go about reaching this goal. By contrast, the rates of "don't know how to reach the goal" responses for the other three goals were each less than 9%.

Although subjects asserted that they did not know how to go about becoming a millionaire, they frequently generated sketchy plans to achieve the millionaire goal as the following protocol responses indicate (C.B. is chapter author).

Subject 001: "Oh my God! How would I go about becoming a millionaire? I wouldn't play the lottery. I would—wow, I don't—I guess I wouldn't want to work for it because it would just take too long. I guess probably I would learn to invest money, and I would take—I would take as much money as I could spare that, you know, if I lost it I wouldn't die and be poor, but—and I would just try to invest it in-in I guess currency or—not stocks—probably foreign currency or something, and-and try to build it up that way."

C.B.: "Now, tell me all you can remember about your thinking."

Subject 001: "That I'll never be a millionaire. I would have no idea how to go about it, so I ws shootin' in the dark. Just kinda brain storming."

Subject 039: "I'm not thinking anything! How would I go about becoming a millionaire? I would—probably give a little bit of money to my dad and—let him invest it in stocks and bonds, and just wait."

C.B.: Now, tell me all you can remember about your thinking."

Subject 039: "Um, first just a blankness, am emptiness. Not—knowing, um what—what the answer would be, or how I would do it. Cause I don't think it's something that I aspire to so it's never something I've thought about, but, um—then the logical thing would—to me, would be to give it somebody else and let them handle it. So, that's what I thought."

Subject 066: "I would go about becoming a millionaire the easiest way possible. Um. . .ah. . .um. . .p-probably start a b-ah do something that I like using, you know, a business or something based on what—I do well or like doing, and then work hard at that, a-aaa-har-til I became a millionaire."

C.B.: "Now, tell me all you can remember about your thinking."

Subject 066: "Uh, it—I remember drawing a blank because I'd never really been as-b-eahh-been asked a question like that before, and ah—it was hard— ah what I had—w-I had visions of like just being a millionaire, and ah, so I had to work my mind backwards to figure out how I would get there. It was hard to get—thoughts of already being there out of my mind."

In the first two cases, subjects indicated that they have no idea of how to become a millionaire, yet both of them advanced plausible, sketchy plans for doing so. Although Subject 066 did not specifically state that he does not know how to reach the millionaire goal, he indicated that he has never been asked the question before. This subject also came up with the sketchy plan of starting a business. However, he also reported that preoccupation with visualizing the goal interfered with developing a plan.

Although many subjects exhibited the kinds of responses illustrated by the three cases previously described, a few subjects indicated that they had given considerable thought to the goal of becoming a millionaire. The protocol responses displayed next show a sharp contrast to those just considered:

Subject 031: "How, would I go about becoming a millionaire? Um, well, um—tch first of all, um, um-um I guess I'm very money oriented so this question is appropriate. Um, I want to go into broadcast—sales, um selling air time, ah, for a radio station. Um, which I'll be doing next year. Um, I plan to work my way up into a in management, ah, of a radio station, and then, ah, I'd like to, um, get into ownership, and then that's where becoming a millionaire comes in because if you get into some kind of ownership of a broadcast property, um, and later sell, ah, this property, um, the-the prices these days are very much inflated. Um, so, ah, that's that's would be my route to becoming a millionaire."

C.B.: "Now, tell me all you can remember about your thinking."

Subject 031: "Um, it was—easy cause, um, as I said I was money or-um, money conscious and-and I have a very definite career plan. Um, so I just thought of my, you know, personal experience."

Subject 037: "How would I go about becoming a millionaire? Huh, an excellent question, huh. Something I think about quite a bit. Um, I would graduate with a high grade point and hopefully go to business school, perhaps law school in personal injury because I know that's how to make the most money in law school, but business school is what I'm probably gonna do, and ah—I think I'd work in the State Department for a couple of years because I know the government gives you a lot of responsibility right away, and from the people I've talked to that's very good experience. Um, try to work in a corporation or a small business firm for a couple of years, gain some more experience there, and ah start up my own company which is—almost everyone I've talked to who seems to know, in my opinion, everyone's convinced that's the only way to become a millionaire these days."

C.B.: "Now, tell me all you can remember about your thinking."

Subject 037: "Um, I've th- I've thought about that one a lot so it's pretty similar to what I just said, but ah, I've-I've discussed that with my-my parents and my grandparents, and I-every business person that I know that I consider to be knowledgeable. Um, just because I think that th-their obviously gonna know quite a bit more than I am about ah—that subject, and ah just ah went through my conversations with them and-and what they thought and put them into kind of a conglomeration that already existed in my head, so there really wasn't much thought about it."

In both of these protocols, the subjects proposed plans for becoming a millionaire that are considerably more complex than those in the previous group. Moreover, both of these subjects explicitly indicated that they have spent considerable time thinking about making money in the future. Although both of these subjects' protocols shared these attributes, the structure of their proposed plans differed. In the case of Subject 031, a step-by-step progression was offered. This is made possible, in part, by the fact that this person has decided on a specific occupational trajectory and apparently knows how to maximize income within that occupation. In contrast, Subject 037 is still considering a number of alternative occupational possibilities, although Subject 037 seemed to be aware that specific subspecialities of law are likely to prove more lucrative than others. It is obvious that Subject 037 has spent considerable time seeking information about alternative career possibilities from a number of different sources. However, his plans are still not as well structured as those of Subject 031—the plan does not include a coherent progression of steps to the goal.

The millionaire-goal responses demonstrate that adults can devise sketchy plans to reach novel goals. Despite that subjects faced with the unfamiliar millionaire goal said that they "didn't know how to reach the goal," they were able to retrieve very general and relatively plausible plans for becoming millionaires. One possible explanation for the seeming contradiction between saying "I have no idea of how to become a millionaire" and then presenting a general plan for so doing lies in the interpretation of the phrase, "I don't know how. . . ." There are several alternative meanings that might be implied by the use of this and similar phrases. First, the phrase could mean, "I don't know how to do this well," implying that the person has some knowledge of how to achieve the goal, but probably does not have the requisite skill for reaching the goal. Second, the phrase could also mean that, although the person has a general idea of how to achieve the goal, he or she does not have the necessary information to enable him or her to devise a detailed plan. The question here is not so much how well the person might achieve the goal, but how complex a plan her or her is capable of developing. Third, the phrase "I don't know how" may reflect lack of both knowledge and skill.

Finally, when persons have no plans for reaching goals or when they perceive their plans to be inadequate for reaching goals, they can either seek out an agent who has the necessary knowledge and have that agent attain the goal on their behalf, or they can seek out the information necessary to formulate a plan for themselves. There are examples of both of these options in the millionaire responses. Some respondents asserted that they would go to a good financial adviser, give the adviser their money, and let the adviser make the critical decisions. Others suggested that they would acquire information from various sources, including financial advisers, and then formulate their own plans for investing. These responses provide evidence for two different kinds of meta-plans: one having to do with agents and the other having to do with information seeking. Such a metaplan might read something like, "I don't know how to become a millionaire myself, but I do know a person who does," implying that the subject can either find out how to become one or have the person act as an agent. Apparently, then, the phrase "I don't know how" can also indicate that the person uttering it not only has an inadequate plan but does not have a metaplan for generating a more adequate plan.

Desire and Plan Complexity

It was argued previously that, in contrast to Bratman's (1987) position, the actions contained in plans do not necessarily imply commitments to future action. In his naturalized theory of action, Brand (1984) took a position sympathetic to that advocated here: He asserted that, by themselves, plans are not capable of supplying an exhaustive explanation of intentional conduct. He opined that a desire component is needed as well. He chooses the term *desire* instead of *motivation* because of what he sees as a number of inadequacies in current psychological theories of motivation. Although the status of the desire and motivation constructs in contemporary philosophical discussions of action theory is somewhat unclear, there is little doubt that desire to attain goals exerts considerable influence on the extent to which persons plan to reach goals. In support of this claim, Nuttin (1984) argued that need states not only activate behavior but also stimulate such cognitive processes as goal setting and planning. The think-aloud data provide indirect support for this proposition. Of the 72 persons who devised plans for the millionaire goal, 23% spontaneously indicated that this was a goal that they really were not interested in pursuing. Thus, in addition to the relative lack of knowledge explanation discussed earlier, this fact may explain why many persons devised sketchy plans for the millionaire goal. Furthermore, 29% of the respondents stated that they had no desire to pursue the date-requesting goal, with significantly more females than males spontaneously providing this response. Previous research using the same population (Berger, 1988a; Berger & Bell, 1988) revealed that females infrequently ask males for dates. As a consequence, one would not expect females to have high levels of desire to reach this goal. By contrast, only 7% of the respondents indicated a lack of desire for pursuing the ingratiation and persuasion goals. In addition to these findings, Berger and diBattista (1992a) reported that individuals who sought more person and situation information before developing plans to reach social goals developed more complex plans than did those who requested less information. Presumably, those who sought more information had higher levels of desire to reach the goals in question. Persons also may hold general beliefs about the desirability and efficacy of planning as an activity. Krietler and Krietler (1987) found that children who believed it was a good idea to devise plans before embarking on certain hypothetical activities, rather than letting the activities happen spontaneously, developed plans that contained more steps and contingencies designed to meet unanticipated circumstances than did children who generally devalued planning as an activity.

Taken as a whole, these findings suggest two different kinds of desire. *Goal desire* indexes the strength of desire to reach the focal goal. For example, Kuhl (1986) distinguished among wishes, wants, and intentions as three levels of increasing commitment along this goal-desire continuum. The think-aloud protocol data previously cited are directly related to this type of desire. In contrast, *planning desire* refers to one's overall level of commitment to the activity of planning (Krietler & Krietler, 1987). This desire component is tied to the meta-planning activity that must be engaged in when one has no plan or a plan that is inadequate. Both goal desire and planning desire affect the complexity with which persons plan, but these relationships are potentially complex. A person may have a high level of planning desire but a low level of goal desire; that is, the person believes in the efficacy of planning in general, but has no particular desire to reach a specific goal. Under these conditions, one would not expect complex plans to be generated. When a person has a high level of goal desire but a low level of planning desire, one would also not expect complex plans to be generated, even though desire to reach the focal goal is high. It is when both desires are high that complex plans are likely to be developed.

Adjusting Plans to Changing Circumstances

The following verse from Burns' (1785/1819) poem, "To a Mouse," offers considerable wisdom concerning the potential utility of planning:

> But Mousie, thou art no thy lane,
> In proving foresight my be in vain:
> The best-laid schemes o' mice an' men
> Gang aft a-gley,
> An' lea'e us nought but grief and pain,
> For promis'd joy! (p. 133)

Persons may enter social situations with well-articulated goals and detailed plans for achieving them, only to find that the circumstances are such that the plan most likely will not succeed (Alterman, 1988). Circumstances could include attributes of the social situation or characteristics of the social actors in the situation. Given this broad conception of circumstances, it is important to delineate specific elements that might induce planners to modify or, in the extreme, abandon their plans in favor of new ones.

Assuming that planners have well-defined goals and well-articulated plans for achieving them before they enter a particular situation, it is possible that significant modifications of plans may be rendered necessary by some specific attribute of the situation, independent of the target person or persons in the situation. The mere presence of others may force planners to abandon their plans. In addition to attributes of the social situation, attributes of the target may interfere with the tactical deployment of a plan. Planners may perceive targets to be unreceptive to their planned actions, and thus abandon their plans before they begin to act on them. Situational and personal sources of goal blockage may have different effects on the nature of contingent actions generated for pursuing a specific goal. Actor–observer differences in attribution are produced, in part, by the tendency for observers to focus their attention on actors at the expense of heeding information provided by the environment surrounding the actor (Heider, 1958; Jones & Nisbett, 1972). Hence, it follows that planners should be more focused on goal blocks that arise from targets of their goal striving than from sources of goal blockage that reside in the environment or in themselves. This hypothesis implies that, in attributional terms, plans for reaching social goals may be more vulnerable to interference from the environment than to interference from targets, at least in terms of being able to engage in alternative actions to achieve the goal.

In addition to the circumstances that may abort the deployment of a plan, another set of possible events may force planners to adjust their plans while they are being carried out. The question is, how do persons modify plans that are not working while they are engaged in actions directed toward achieving the goal or goals for which the plan was developed? One possibility is that when plans are not successful, persons simply abandon them and search for new ones. However, such a strategy would increase processing demands on the planner because the planner must devise a new plan. Another possibility is that when planners are thwarted during their interactions with others, they continue to deploy actions that normally produce successful goal achievement. In addition, however, they augment these actions with new ones. In support of this latter possibility, Berger and Kellermann (1986) found that persons who were trying to find out as much as they could about their conversational partners, but who were paired with persons who were instructed to reveal as little as possible about themselves to their partners, continued to ask questions directed at obtaining information about their partners at the same rate. However, they also began to use other tactics to try to induce their reticent partners to reveal personal information. The information seekers tried to focus the conversation on their partners; when their partners spoke, they encouraged them to continue talking by using verbal prompts of various kinds. These findings suggest an accretive model of plan alteration in which actions that are parts of previous plans are maintained and augmented with other actions.

Although an accretive model might provide a plausible account of plan alteration in the face of thwarting, there are still other possible responses to thwarting, aside from abandoning the goal. First, the planner might simply reiterate the plan with minimal or no modifications. Repetition may be done for strategic purposes, or it might indicate that the planner has no alternative plan available. Second, the hierarchical nature of plans suggests several potential alteration strategies. Action units lower in the plan hierarchy might be altered, whereas the higher level, more abstract units of the plan are left intact. Using this strategy, the abstract plan would be reiterated, but the surface manifestations of the plan in action would change. For example, an abstract plan unit like threat, which might be part of a compliance-gaining plan, could be realized at the level of social action using an extremely large number of combinations of verbal and nonverbal behavior. If threat is an integral part of a compliance-gaining plan that is being thwarted, the planner might modify the verbal and nonverbal means being used to represent threat in action. These lower level alterations probably would be accomplished outside of conscious awareness. Moreover, such low-level changes are less taxing on the cognitive system because they do not require the complete reorganization of the superstructure of the plan.

This reasoning has been embodied in the hierarchy hypothesis. This hypothesis asserts that when goal-directed actions are thwarted, and individuals continue to pursue the goals in question, their first tendency is to alter low-level plan elements, rather than more abstract plan elements, because such modifications require fewer cognitive resources for their implementation. Two studies, employing a geographic direction-giving task, revealed that when direction givers were misunderstood by their partners and asked to give their directions again, they showed significant increases in vocal intensity during the second rendition of the directions, but very little propensity to change the route on which they based their directions when they gave them the second time (Berger & diBattista, 1992b, 1993). Thus, such low-level modifications to message plans as the vocal intensity at which they are delivered were considerably more likely to occur than such high-level alterations as route changes. Two additional studies found direct support for the postulate that higher level message-plan alterations produce higher levels of cognitive load than do lower level alterations (Berger, 1993; Berger & Abrahams, 1993). Again, within the direction-giving paradigm, direction givers who were asked to provide a different route in the second rendition of their directions showed speech-onset latencies that were three to four times longer than direction givers who were asked to reduce their speech rate during the second renditions of their directions. These findings provide direct support for the assumption that higher level plan alterations demand more scarce cognitive resources than do lower level massage-plan modifications.

Action-identification theory (Vallacher & Wegner, 1985; Wegner & Vallacher, 1986) makes a similar prediction concerning the relationship between the disruption of action and the conceptual level at which persons think about their actions. Specifically, their theory suggests that persons are more likely to pay attention to the details of what they are doing when an act is disrupted. When no disruption occurs, and the act is well practiced, persons are likely to think about their action in more molar terms. Thus, for example, when persons intend to persuade others and they experience success, they are likely to think about what they are doing as an abstract act of persuasion. However, if they encounter difficulties while attempting persuasion, they are likely to become more aware of the lower level actions such as vocal intensity, vocal intonation, and verbal fluency that are being used to realize the abstract strategy at the tactical level. However, action-identification theory does not deal with the issues of how action plans are generated, how they are realized at the tactical level, and how they are altered.

As the research investigating the hierarchy hypothesis suggests, when goal failure occurs, alterations of the lower level message-plan units—rather than the more abstract, higher level units—are the rule. However, the relationships posited in the hierarchy hypothesis might be modulated by the two desires discussed previously. Persons have high levels of both goal desire and planning desire might have a greater propensity to alter higher level plan units in response to goal failure. In addition to the effects of different desire levels, it is possible that some persons might enter strategic-communication situations with both more alternative actions in a given plan or more alternative plans to reach the goal in question. Such planners would find it easier to alter thwarted plans at higher levels of abstraction than would planners with relatively few contingencies within a plan or with few alternative plans.

Plans, Planning, and Affect

Up to this point, the discussion has focused on the role that "cold," procedurally oriented cognitive processes play in the development and deployment of plans. Given that cognitive representations of interpersonal-communication episodes are frequently organized around "hot," affect-laden cognitions, it is important for any theory purported to explain the relationships between cognitive processes and social interaction to give serious attention to the relationships among cognition, affect, and action. The present concern regards the question of the roles that goals, plans, and planning play in the generation of affect.

Building on the seminal work of Mandler (1975), several investigators have suggested that one condition promoting affect is the interruption of action sequences being used to pursue goals (Berscheid, 1983; Ortony, Clore, & Collins, 1988; Srull & Wyer, 1986; Sternberg, 1986). Both Berscheid and Sternberg employed this general principle to explain the extreme levels of positive affect that persons experience when they are involved in the initial stages of romantic relationships. For example, Berscheid argued that when persons do not know each other well in the early stages of romantic relationships, they are likely to be confronted with unexpected actions on the part of their romantic partner (e.g., surprise gifts). According to Berscheid, these unpredictable events give rise to autonomic nervous system (ANS) arousal. In turn, ANS arousal is interpreted as the special romantic feeling of being in love. In his triangular theory of love, Sternberg postulated a similar explanation for the appearance of feelings of romantic love.

In their computationally oriented cognitive theory of emotions, Ortony et al. (1988) stressed that thwarted progress toward goals gives rise to the experience of emotions. Srull and Wyer (1986) made the same assumption in their discussion of the role of goals in social-information processing. They also presented a detailed analysis of the variables that are likely to affect the intensity of affect experienced when plans are thwarted. Specifically, they hypothesized that the intensity of affect produced when planned actions are blocked is influenced by: (a) the importance of the superordinate goal, (b) the psychological distance from the attainment of the superordinate goal, and (c) the amount of time and energy that has been invested in vain as a result of the thwarting event. Srull and Wyer's first factor is much the same as goal desire—the degree to which the planner desires to reach the focal goal. They pointed out that the third factor is partially a function of how much of the blocked plan has been completed and partially a function of the availability of alternative plans or subplans to achieve the same goal. Their analysis suggests that when low-level, initial actions in plans are thwarted, relatively little affect will be generated. However, if the blockage occurs at later stages in the plan, especially when the thwarted actions are at a relatively high level of abstraction and close to the ultimate goal, then considerable affect should be generated. They argued, that, in general, thwarting of planned actions gives rise to negative affect, and that this negative affect will be magnified not only as the psychological distance remaining to be traversed to the goal decreases, but also as the goal becomes more important and the investment of resources in terms of time and energy increases. They also assumed that attainment of goals generally gives rise to positive affect.

Although this analysis has considerable intuitive appeal, there are some conditions that might potentially limit its generality. In the case of interrupted plans, Srull and Wyer aver that the existence of alternative plans to reach subgoals or the superordinate goal will reduce the negative affect experienced by the thwarted planner because the planner still has some potential means for attaining the goal. However, it is also possible that the existence of readily substitutable superordinate goals might also eliminate the experience of negative affect. For example, assume that the goal of a particular social actor is to persuade a friend to change his or her opinion on a social issue. The person begins to execute a persuasion plan that is thwarted in its latter stages. As a way of avoiding the experience of negative affect, the planner might redefine the goal of the interaction to one of simply having a conversation with the friend to pass time. As a result, failure to reach the persuasion goal does not give rise to negative affect. This scenario is extremely plausible given that a multiplicity of goals are generally pursued more or less simultaneously in any given interaction, and that goals may be extremely fluid in social situations.

On the other side of the coin, is it possible for the attainment of a goal to produce negative affect? Clearly, this can happen when an individual thinks retrospectively; in some cases, *retrospectively* may be almost immediately after achieving the goal. Persons who expend considerable time and effort to achieve what are prospectively valued goals sometimes experience disappointment when they finally achieve the goal. Such disappointment may stem from the fact that, before achieving the desired goal, persons were not aware of all the consequences or conditions that accompany the sought-after state. Persons who choose an academic career over a corporate one (because they believe that there are more political machinations in corporate life than in academic life and that intellectual acumen is always valued more than political prowess in the academic community) are bound to be disappointed. Of course, this example does not exclude the possibility that the immediate response to learning that one has landed a highly desired university position could generate considerable positive affect. Nevertheless, even elation is sometimes very short-lived, as persons become aware of all the implications of their goal attainment (Janis & Mann, 1977).

Metagoals such as efficiency may also be implicated in the generation of affect. In addition to wanting to attain a particular goal, when individuals wish to do so quickly or with minimal effort, thwarting of initial low-level actions may give rise to considerable negative affect, even though persons are far from achieving the goal. Furthermore, if goals are achieved in a relatively inefficient manner and the efficiency metagoal is salient, negative affect may be generated.

Similarly, the social appropriateness metagoal might also determine the valence and intensity of affect experienced after goal blockage or goal attainment. If one attains a compliance goal, but in a way that alienates the person complying, one may not feel particularly positive about achieving the goal. Given the same compliance behaviors and a lessened concern for social appropriateness, one might feel quite positive about attaining the goal. In general, then, affective responses to goal blockage and goal attainment cannot be determined simply by focusing on the sequence of actions leading to the primary goal and potential alternative-action sequences. The salience of metagoals, the availability of alternative primary goals, and the unanticipated consequences of both goal attainment and goal blockage also play a role in shaping affective responses.

Clearly, interruptions of planned, goal-direction action sequences can have affective consequences, as can the attainment of goals. However, goal attainment and the thwarting of action sequences are not the only sources of affect in strategic communication. It is also possible that affective states may be part of plans; that is, particular affective states may be attached to plans. To lay the groundwork for successful compliance gaining, planners may try to induce themselves to experience more positive affective states so that when they interact with the targets of their compliance-gaining attempts, the targets will be more likely to respond in a positive way to their requests. This process is not merely an instance of self-presentation, in which planners purposely manipulate behaviors to induce positive mood states in their targets (Berger, 1988a; Berger & Bell, 1988; Rosenfeld, 1966), although such actions can also be planned (Berger, 1988a). Rather, in this case, planners actually modify their affective states with the hope that social contagion will produce similar affective states in their targets. Planners attempting to cheer up infirmed persons may try to get themselves into a "positive frame of mind" before interacting with the ill individuals. Frijda (1986) presented an extended discussion of the processes by which individuals may achieve such regulation of their emotional states. Of course, at the level of social action, it may be difficult to determine the causal locus for a particular act. Smiling may be the consequence of a positive affective state, or it may be an action that is deployed without reference to an underlying affective state. Nevertheless, plans may call for affective states of varying valences and intensities.

FROM PLANS TO SOCIAL ACTION

As discussed previously, when persons decide to pursue social goals, their first tendency is to try to retrieve a plan from long-term memory that "fits" the present situation. As the protocol-analysis data revealed, for adults there appears to be at least some kind of rudimentary plan that can be retrieved even for relatively unfamiliar goals. Assuming that a plan has been instantiated and is being held in a working memory, how is that plan translated into action? There are at least two approaches to answering this question. One focuses on how plan content is represented in action; that is, the degree of correspondence between planned actions and actions deployed in the situation (Hjelmquist, 1991; Hjelmquist & Gidlund, 1984). A second way to explore this question concerns how the projected actions that make up the plan are processed and how that processing affects the fluency with which the plan is realized in action. Relatively little work has been done on the first of these two approaches, and some initial work examining plan processing and its relationship to action fluency has been reported. This latter approach is the focus of the following discussion.

The rationale underlying this process-oriented research is that, given a particular social goal, there will be considerable individual differences in the complexity of plans that social actors have for reaching that goal. Plan complexity is the number of alternative actions for reaching subgoals and the main goal of plans; the greater the number of alternatives contained in the plan, the greater its complexity. Furthermore, it is postulated that when persons' progress toward goals is thwarted, plan complexity becomes critical to their ability to continue to pursue the goals. Persons with more complex plans that contain alternative actions for achieving goals should be able to persist for a greater length of time in the face of thwarted progress toward these goals. Furthermore, persons with complex plans should be able to maintain higher levels of action fluency in the face of thwarting than those with less complex plans. These relationships between plan complexity, on the one hand, and persistence and action fluency, on the other hand, are of course predicated on the assumption that persons maintain the requisite level of goal desire. As noted previously, action-identification theory (Vallacher & Wegner, 1985; Wegner & Vallacher, 1986) postulates that, when actions are thwarted, persons tend to think about their actions in greater detail (low-level identification). Vallacher, Wegner, and Somoza (1989) reported that persons who anticipated trying to persuade a highly resistant audience showed greater verbal fluency when they were induced to identify their actions at a lower level. Those who identified their actions at a higher conceptual level (i.e., attempting persuasion) were less fluent. Persons who believed that their audience would be easily persuaded showed exactly the opposite pattern of relationships between identification level and fluency; persons who identified their actions at a lower level were less fluent than those who identified their actions at a more abstract level. Although this particular study was concerned with the fluency with which speech is produced and the conceptual level at which actions are identified, persons in the study neither created their own persuasion plans, because they were given a prepared speech to read, nor did they experience thwarting in terms of their progress toward the persuasion goal; that is, they were not provided with feedback concerning their persuasive effectiveness while they read their speech. Nevertheless, it is possible that, in addition to plan complexity, the level at which an action is identified and the perceived difficulty of attaining the goal may affect the degree to which persons perform their actions fluently.

Although the relationship between plan complexity and action fluency under conditions of thwarting appears to be straightforward, persons whose plans are extremely complex might show reduced levels of action fluency in the face of goal blockage because, at any given point at which the plan is thwarted, they may have a relatively large number of alternative actions from which to choose. This large number of alternatives might lead to increased decision times and thus to decreased fluency. Persons with fewer alternative actions would presumably take less time to choose an alternative to the action that was thwarted. Of course, persons with no alternative actions to the blocked action would be faced with the problem of what to do next and would probably show reduced fluency, although, such persons might simply repeat previous actions.

These possibilities were examined in a series of experiments in which students devised plans to reach the goal of persuading their conversational partner to accept their opinion on a controversial campus issue (Berger et al., 1989). In the first experiment, some persons wrote a plan and then immediately entered the persuasion situation (Plan Only). A second group wrote a plan about which they were subsequently questioned (Plan Question). Persons in this condition were asked what they would do if four different actions contained in their plan failed to bring about the desired goal. It was assumed that this questioning procedure would induce persons to generate more specific arguments on the issue, and that, as a result, persons whose plans initially contained numerous arguments would be more likely to experience overload and reduced fluency. After being subjected to the questioning, the persons then entered the persuasion situation. Finally, a third group simply entered the persuasion situation with no prior planning (No Plan). Unbeknownst to participants in all conditions, the conversational partners had been instructed to begin by being neutral on the controversial issue, but to disagree with the position advocated by the subject as the conversation progressed.

Subjects' speech was rated for its overall fluency. In addition, other judges scored the following behavioral measures of speech that have been linked with uncertainty in linguistic decision making and linguistic planning in previous research (Butterworth & Goldman-Eisler, 1979; Greene, 1984; Siegman, 1979): (a) vocalized pause rate, (b) nonvocalized pause rate, (c) average nonvocalized pause duration, and (d) false starts rate. Consistent with the previous predictions, between-condition comparisons revealed that persons whose plans were questioned were judged to be significantly less fluent than persons who had only written a plan before the conversation. The difference between the Plan-Question and No-Plan conditions fell just short of being significant, but was in the same direction. All of the behavioral indicators except for false starts showed the same pattern of relationships. More importantly, within the Plan-Question condition, a significant inverse partial correlation ($r = -.62$), which controlled for protocol length, was observed between the number of specific arguments included in the persuasion plan and judges' fluency ratings: The greater the number of specific arguments, the less the fluency. The same correlation within the Plan-Only condition was also negative, but not significant ($r = -.26$). Partial correlations between the number of specific arguments and the behavioral measures of fluency, with the two nonvocalized pausing measures combined, revealed a similar pattern of results between the two conditions. Within the Plan-Question condition, planners with more arguments were significantly less fluent on all measures except for vocalized pauses. However, the same correlations within the Plan-Only condition were generally nonsignificant, with the exception of the nonvocalized pausing variable. Apparently, the questioning procedure debilitated the fluency of those with more complex plans, presumably because the procedure induced them to create unique arguments over and above those generated in their initial plans.

The second experiment in this series demonstrated that the lowered fluency of Plan-Question participants of Experiment 1 could not be attributed to the fact that their self-confidence was undermined by being questioned about planned actions that might fail. Persons whose planned actions were subjected to questioning were no less confident of their ability to persuade a potential conversational partner than persons who wrote a plan but were not questioned. The third experiment demonstrated that questioning persons about their plans induces them to think up new arguments that were not included in the original plan, even though postquestioning plans contain no more actions than plans written before questioning. This experiment also showed that persons whose plans were questioned were no less confident of their ability to persuade a potential partner than were persons who were subjected to questioning that was not focused on their plan.

When people's actions are questioned with respect to what they would do in the event of action failure, they generate unique alternative actions. In the case of Experiment 1, these actions were specific arguments. However, in doing so, when social actors try to realize their plans in action, they may experience cognitive overload that debilitates their verbal fluency when they encounter thwarting. This debilitation of verbal fluency is especially apparent for persons who have relatively complex plans before they are questioned. As Experiments 2 and 3 demonstrated, these effects cannot be accounted for by recourse to the notion that questioning undermines self-confidence, thus reducing fluency. Moreover, a measure of subjective difficulty in persuading the confederate given to participants in Experiment 1 showed no significant difference among the three conditions. Apparently, questioning persons does not alter felt ability to persuade. Interviews conducted after Experiment 3 suggest why unique actions might be generated by questioning. During these interviews, some participants indicated that when they developed their first plans, they failed to focus on the actions of their potential interaction partners. By contrast, after being questioned about their initial plans, they were more likely to anticipate the potential responses of their partner's when developing a second plan. This shift from an egocentric to a sociocentric planning mode makes resulting plans more complex by default. However, this increased complexity may debilitate verbal fluency because of the availability of more action alternatives.

One alternative explanation for the fluency differences observed in Experiment 1 is that, whereas questioning plans induces persons to generate unique actions not contained in their initial plans (Experiment 3), the decrements in fluency observed in Experiment 1 were not due to cognitive overload but to the fact that persons may have enacted alternative actions that were less well rehearsed than actions included in the original plan, thus lowering their fluency. This explanation is predicated on the assumption that arguments included in the initial plans were better rehearsed than arguments generated as the result of questioning. This possibility needs to be evaluated in future research.

As the discussed studies demonstrate, when persons' planned actions are thwarted, they may have varying numbers of contingent actions to deploy to continue pursuing their goal or goals. Consider the case in which two persons have the same number of alternative actions available to them, but one of them is able to retrieve alternatives more quickly than the other; that is, the alternatives are more readily available to the one person than to the other. Given these circumstances, one would expect the person whose alternatives are more readily accessible to display greater verbal fluency than the person whose accessibility to alternative actions is slower. This relationship was examined in another study in which persons each wrote two persuasion plans on different issues (Berger, 1988b). One issue involved divestment from South Africa, and the other concerned undergraduate drinking in dormitories. After writing their plans, an interviewer questioned each action in the plans by asking what the person would do if the action failed. Responses to these questions were tape-recorded. One week later, subjects argued their position on one of the two issues for which they had planned during the previous week's session. Half of the subjects were paired with a disagreeing confederate, whereas the other half were faced with a confederate who ultimately showed agreement with the position they advocated.

Response-onset latencies were computed for each question asked during the first session, when plans were subjected to questioning. In addition, other judges rated the verbal fluency with which each subject performed during the persuasive interaction that took place during the second session. Correlations computed between the response-onset-latency measure for the issue argued and the fluency measure consistently revealed negative relationships between the two variables. Specifically, within the condition in which the confederate ultimately agreed with the subject (Acquiescence), a correlation of $-.33$ ($p < .03$) was found, whereas in the condition where the confederate consistently disagreed with the subject (Dissent), the correlation was $-.39$ ($p < .02$). The correlation for both conditions combined was $-.36$ ($p < .001$). Regardless of condition, persons who had more difficulty retrieving action alternatives when their plans were confronted with potential failure were less fluent when enacting their plans 1 week later.

A potential alternative explanation for the correlations observed between response-onset latency and verbal fluency is that persons who have a general propensity to retrieve alternative actions more quickly are generally more verbally fluent. That is, the correlations represent a general trait, rather than being representative of processing of the plans for specific issues. To test this alternative explanation, correlations were also computed between the response-onset latencies for the issue *not* argued 1 week later and verbal fluency displayed during the persuasion task. Within the Acquiescence condition, the correlation between response latency and fluency was .19 (ns.), whereas the same correlation within the Dissent condition was −.11 (ns.). The correlation for the two conditions combined was .04 (ns.). Thus, persons who showed longer response latencies on the issue not argued 1 week later were no less fluent than those who showed shorter latencies. These findings indicate that the availability of alternative actions is specific to issues and is not a general response tendency.

This study also provided indirect support for the hypothesis that high levels of goal desire may be a prerequisite for complex planning. Although desire to reach the persuasion goal was not directly indexed, attitude extremity, as measured by degree of polarization on a Likert-type item that tapped participants' attitudes toward the issue for which they planned, was found to be modestly related to: (a) the number of units contained in their persuasion plan ($r = .40$, $p < .001$), (b) the latency in responding to questions about their persuasion plans ($r = -.22$, $p < .04$), and (c) their fluency in making their arguments during their interactions ($r = .26$, $p < .02$). However, the attitude-extremity measure was not significantly related to the number of specific arguments contained in the persuasion plans ($r = .12$, $p > .15$). If attitude extremity can be taken as an indicator of involvement with the attitude issue then elevated levels of issue involvement apparently produce (a) more extensive planning, (b) faster access to alternative actions in the event of goal blockage, and (c) increased verbal fluency when performing. However, issue involvement does not seem to influence the sheer number of arguments produced. The relatively low ceiling on the number of different arguments that can be generated to support a position on an issue may explain this latter finding. Generally, these findings provide some evidence that a factor akin to goal desire is related to the complexity with which persons plan and to their actual performance of plans in social interaction.

Taken as a whole, the verbal-fluency studies just discussed provide little support for the notion articulated earlier—that when planners' goal-directed actions are thwarted, up to a point those planners with more alternative actions are more likely to exhibit greater action fluidity than those with few or no alternative actions. However, before disgarding this hypothesis, it is necessary to consider that, in the experiments just described, the persuasive interactions lasted for only 5 minutes. This period of time may have been insufficient to reveal the potential differences in action fluidity among persons with varying levels of plan complexity. Persons with relatively simple plans may have been able to maintain a reasonable degree of verbal fluency, even in the face of thwarting, because they had enough arguments to carry them through the limited time period of their interactions. Increasing the length of the interactions might serve to bring out the differences between planners with varying complexity levels.

In addition to the studies linking plan attributes such as complexity and the availability of action alternatives to verbal fluency are studies that have examined the relationship between the judged effectiveness of plans for reaching social goals and measures of social functioning such as loneliness and shyness. The general rationale underlying this work is that, all other things equal, including levels of communication skills, persons who develop more effective plans for reaching social goals are more likely to experience greater success in reaching those goals. This success, in turn, should reduce persons' levels of shyness and loneliness. Of course, it is possible that persons who are less shy and lonely may gain the social experiences that make them better planners for social goals. These relationships were examined in a study in which undergraduates wrote plans for reaching the social goals of asking another person out for a date and ingratiating themselves to a new roommate (Berger & Bell, 1988). In addition, under the guise of another study, subjects completed shyness and loneliness scales.

Students' plans for each goal were subsequently judged for their potential effectiveness by panels of judges. The effectiveness judgments were then correlated with the shyness and loneliness measures. These analyses revealed that, for the ingratiation goal, correlations between the effectiveness judgments and the shyness and loneliness measures for both males and females were all significant and inverse: Persons whose ingratiation plans were judged to be more effective were less shy and lonely. Correlations ranged from $-.24$ to $-.42$ across measures and genders. By contrast, effectiveness ratings of the date-requesting plans showed significant inverse relationships with shyness and loneliness measures for males only ($-.26$ and $-.37$, respectively). The same correlations for females were nonsignificant ($-.12$ and $-.03$). The pattern of gender differences observed for date-requesting plans is explicable in terms of the frequency with which persons in the samples studied requested dates from others. Generally, males were those who requested dates, whereas females were those who were asked out. As a result, one would expect males' social competence to be tied to their plan effectiveness in date requesting because their feelings of social worth would be determined partially by success and failures in this domain. Because females generally do not pursue date-requesting goals, their plan effectiveness in this domain should be irrelevant to their feelings of social competence. This pattern of differences between males and females was generally replicated by Berger and diBattista (1992a).

As was noted previously, these correlational findings cannot settle the issue of the direction of the causal relationship between plan effectiveness and social functioning. Most likely, plan effectiveness and social effectiveness are reciprocally related. Persons who are shy and lonely may be caught in a spiral, in which their shyness and loneliness deprives them of the experiences necessary for developing effective plans. When they try to reach social goals, their relatively ineffective plans fail to bring about desired outcomes. These failures then induce them to be more shy and lonely, or to cease pursuing certain social goals because of failure fears. The important point is that plan effectiveness appears to be related to social functioning.

CONCLUSION

This chapter began by pointing to the lack of concern shown by communication researchers and social psychologists for theoretical explanation in their quest to understand the strategies that persons use to reach social goals. The theory and research presented in this chapter suggests that a plan-based approach to the study of strategic communication is likely to be more heuristically provocative than are these descriptive approaches. A plan-based approach raises important questions about how plans are developed and how extant plans are retrieved and translated into social action. Moreover, this approach seeks to understand how attributes of plans are reflected in the fluency with which social action is generated. Finally, the plan-based approach asks questions about relationships between the quality of plans and the quality of social life. Thus, this approach is ultimately concerned with social efficacy.

The accretive nature of on-line planning and the hierarchy hypothesis raises questions about the utility of descriptive taxonomies of communication strategies cited earlier. Apparently, when persons pursue social goals, they may add parts of other plans to the main plan they are using at the time. Research needs to be done to see how these unique combinations are formed during interactions. Finding that highly complex plans may reduce the fluidity with which plans are performed, and that speed of access to alternative actions is also related to performance fluency, suggest processing models that go far beyond previous descriptive work. These findings may have important practical implications for those involved in communication situations where extensive preinteraction planning is possible. Moreover, the fact that some plans for reaching social goals are judged to be more effective than others, and that persons who devise less effective plans may suffer from feelings of shyness and loneliness, suggest the necessity of determining what characteristics differentiate between effective and ineffective plans. This order of question goes beyond the simple description of plans or strategies and asks, what differentiates between novice and expert social interactors? Although some work has already addressed this question (Cantor & Kihlstrom, 1987), contrasts between the attributes of effective and ineffective plans are few (Berger & Bell, 1988; Berger & diBattista, 1992a).

This plan-based approach's emphasis on social efficacy stands in marked contrast to theories of social cognition that focus on cognitive structures and processes but stop explaining at the point of judgment rather than at the point of social action. Such theories cast social actors in the role of passive observers who calculate for the sake of achieving an understanding of the social situation. As Enzle, Harvey, and Wright (1980) have shown, predicating theories on the idea that persons are detached observers of the social scene can yield misleading predictions about the behavior of persons who are actively involved in social-interaction episodes. The plan-based approach advocated here allows persons to be detached planners. However, it also recognizes that when persons involve themselves in social episodes, plans may be altered opportunistically as on-line contingencies arise. In support of this latter possibility, Waldron (1990) found that, of 2,273 thoughts that his subjects reported having during interactions, 44% were concerned with the goals they were pursuing in the conversation and the plans they were using to attain them. These data may underestimate the amount of on-line planning in which individuals engage during conversations because not all of this activity is amenable to verbal access. Consequently, Waldron's data provide persuasive evidence in support of the idea that planning is not only accomplished before interactions begin, but while they progress as well. Ultimately, then, theories of cognition and interpersonal communication, and the research programs spawned by them, must capture the interplay between ongoing social action and cognitive processing if they are to be maximally useful in explaining strategic-communicative conduct in the social world.

REFERENCES

Abbott, V., & Black, J. B. (1986). Goal-related inferences in comprehension. In J. A. Galambos, R. P. Abelson, & J. B. Black (Eds.), *Knowledge structures* (pp. 123–142). Hillsdale, NJ: Lawrence Erlbaum Associates.

Abelson, R. P. (1976). Script processing in attitude formation and decision making. In J. S. Carroll & J. W. Payne (Eds.), *Cognition and social behavior* (pp. 33–45). Hillsdale, NJ: Lawrence Erlbaum Associates.

Abelson, R. P. (1981). The psychological status of the script concept. *American Psychologist, 36* 715–729.

Ajzen, I. (1985). From intentions to actions: A theory of planned behavior. In J. Kuhl & J. Beckmann (Eds.), *Action control: From cognition to behavior* (pp. 11–39). Berlin: Springer-Verlag.

Alterman, R. (1988). Adaptive planning. *Cognitive Science, 12,* 393–421.

Baxter, L. A., & Wilmot, W. W. (1984). Secret tests: Social strategies for acquiring information about the state of the relationship. *Human Communication Research, 11,* 171–201.

Bell, R. A., & Daly, J. A. (1984). The affinity-speaking function of communication. *Communication Monographs, 51,* 91–115.

Berger, C. R. (1987). Planning and scheming: Strategies for initiating relationships. In R. Burnett, P. McGhee, & D. D. Clarke (Eds.), *Accounting for relationships: Explanation, representation and knowledge* (pp. 158–174). London: Methuen.

Berger, C. R. (1988a). Planning, affect and social action generation. In R. L. Donohew, H. Sypher, & E. T. Higgins (Eds.), *Communication social cognition and affect* (pp. 93–116). Hillsdale, NJ: Lawrence Erlbaum Associates.

Berger, C. R. (1988b, May). *Communication plans and communicative performance.* Paper presented at the annual convention of the International Communication Association, New Orleans, LA.

Berger, C. R. (1993). *Planning, plan adaptation and cognitive load: An assessment of the hierarchy hypothesis.* Unpublished manuscript, University of California, Davis.

Berger, C. R., & Abrahams, M. F. (1993, May). *Altering communication plans in response to goal failure.* Paper presented at the annual convention of the International Communication Association, Washington, DC.

Berger, C. R., & Bell, R. A. (1988). Plans and the initiation of social relationships. *Human Communication Research, 15,* 217–235.

Berger, C. R., & diBattista, P. (1992a). Information seeking and plan elaboration: What do you need to know to know what to do? *Communication Monographs, 59,* 368–387.

Berger, C. R., & diBattista, P. (1992b, October). *Adapting plans to failed communication goals.* Paper presented at the annual convention of the Speech Communication Association, Chicago, IL.

Berger, C. R., & diBattista, P. (1993). Communication failure and plan adaptation: If at first you don't succeed, say it louder and slower. *Communication Monographs, 60,* 220–238.

Berger, C. R., & Jordan, J. M. (1992). Planning sources, planning difficulty, and verbal fluency. *Communication Monographs, 59,* 130–149.

Berger, C. R., Karol, S. H., & Jordan, J. M. (1989). When a lot of knowledge is a dangerous thing: The debilitating effects of plan complexity on verbal fluency. *Human Communication Research, 16,* 91–119.

Berger, C. R., & Kellermann, K. A. (1983). To ask or not to ask: Is that a question? In R. Bostrom (Ed.), *Communication Yearbook 7* (pp. 342–368). Newbury Park, CA: Sage.

Berger, C. R., & Kellermann, K. A. (1986, May). *Goal incompatibility and social action: The best laid plans of mice and men often go astray.* Paper presented at the annual convention of the International Communication Association, San Francisco, CA.

Berger, C. R., & Kellermann, K. A. (1994). Acquiring social information. In J. A. Daly & J. M. Wiemann (Eds.), *Strategic interpersonal communication* (pp. 1–31). Hillsdale, NJ: Lawrence Erlbaum Associates.

Berscheid, E. (1983). Emotion. In H. H. Kelley, E. Berscheid, A. Christensen, J. H. Harvey, T. L. Huston, G. Levinger, E. McLintock, L. A. Peplau, & D. R. Peterson (Eds.), *Close relationships* (pp. 110–168). San Francisco: Freeman.

Black, J. B., & Bower, G. H. (1979). Episodes as chunks in narrative memory. *Journal of Verbal Learning and Verbal Behavior, 18,* 309–318.

Boster, F., & Stiff, J. B. (1984). Compliance-gaining message selection behavior. *Human Communication Research, 10,* 539–556.

Brand, M. (1984). *Intending and acting: Toward a naturalized theory of action.* Cambridge, MA: MIT Press.

Bratman, M. E. (1987). *Intention, plans, and practical reason.* Cambridge, MA: Harvard University Press.

Bratman, M. E. (1990). What is intention? In P. R. Cohen, J. Morgan, & M. E. Pollack (Eds.), *Intentions in communication* (pp. 15–31). Cambridge, MA: MIT Press.

Brewer, W. F., & Nakamura, G. V. (1984). The nature and functions of schemas. In R. S. Wyer, Jr., & T. K. Srull (Eds.), *Handbook of social cognition* (Vol. 1, pp. 119–160). Hillsdale, NJ: Lawrence Erlbaum Associates.

Brown, P., & Levinson, S. C. (1978). Universals in language usage: Politeness phenomena. In E. N. Goody (Ed.), *Questions and politeness* (pp. 56–289). Cambridge, England: Cambridge University Press.

Burns, R. (1819). To a mouse: On turning up her nest with a plough. In J. Currie (Ed.), *The works of Robert Burns* (Vol. 3, pp. 132–134). London: William Allason & J. Maynard. (Original work published 1785).

Butterworth, B., & Goldman-Eisler, F. (1979). Recent studies in cognitive rhythm. In A. W. Siegman & S. Feldstein (Eds.), *Of speech and time: Temporal speech patterns in interpersonal contexts* (pp. 211–224). Hillsdale, NJ: Lawrence Erlbaum Associates.

Cantor, N., & Kihlstrom, J. F. (1987). *Personality and social intelligence.* Englewood Cliffs, NJ: Prentice-Hall.

Cantor, N., Norem, J. K., Niedenthal, P. M., Langston, C. A., & Brower, A. M. (1987). Life tasks, self-concept ideals, and cognitive strategies in a life transition. *Journal of Personality and Social Psychology, 53,* 1178–1191.

Cappella, J. N., & Folger, J. P. (1980). An information-processing explanation of attitude-behavior inconsistency. In D. P. Cushman & R. D. McPhee (Eds.), *Message-attitude-behavior relationship: Theory, methodology, and application* (pp. 149–193). New York: Academic Press.

Cody, M. J., & McLaughlin, M. L. (Eds.). (1990). *Psychology of tactical communication.* London: Multilingual Matters.

Cody, M. J., McLaughlin, M. L., & Jordan, W. J. (1980). A multidimensional scaling of three sets of compliance-gaining strategies. *Communication Quarterly, 28,* 34–46.

Cody, M. J., McLaughlin, M. L., & Schneider, M. J. (1981). The impact of relational consequences and intimacy on the selection of interpersonal persuasion tactics: A reanalysis. *Communication Quarterly, 29,* 91–106.

Daly, J. A., & Wiemann, J. M. (Eds.). (1994). *Strategic interpersonal communication.* Hillsdale, NJ: Lawrence Erlbaum Associates.

De Lisi, R. (1987). A cognitive-developmental model of planning. In S. L. Friedman, E. K. Scholnick, & R. R. Cocking (Eds.), *Blueprints for thinking: The role of planning in cognitive development* (pp. 79–109). Cambridge, England: Cambridge University Press.

deTurck, M. A. (1985). A transactional analysis of compliance-gaining behavior: Effects of noncompliance, relational contexts, and actors' gender. *Human Communication Research, 12,* 54–78.

Dillard, J. P., & Burgoon, M. (1985). Situational influences on the selection of compliance-gaining messages: Two tests of the Cody–McLaughlin typology. *Communication Monographs, 52,* 289–304.

Donohue, W. A. (1978). An empirical framework for examining negotiation process and outcomes. *Communication Monographs, 45,* 247–257.

Donohue, W. A. (1981). Analyzing negotiation tactics: Development of a negotiation interact system. *Human Communication Research, 7,* 272–287.

Dorner, D. (1985). Thinking and the organization of action. In J. Kuhl & J. Beckmann (Eds.), *Action control: From cognitions to behavior* (pp. 219–235). Berlin: Springer-Verlag.

Douglas, W. (1987). Affinity-testing in initial interactions. *Journal of Social and Personal Relationships, 4,* 3–15.

Edwards, R., Honeycutt, J. M., & Zagacki, K. S. (1988). Imagined interaction as an element of social cognition. *Western Journal of Speech Communication, 52,* 23–45.

Enzle, M. E., Harvey, J. H., & Wright, E. F. (1980). Personalism and distinctiveness. *Journal of Personality and Social Psychology, 39,* 542–552.

Ericsson, K. A., & Simon, H. (1984). *Protocol analysis: Verbal reports as data.* Cambridge, MA: MIT Press.

Falbo, T. (1977). Multidimensional scaling of power strategies. *Journal of Personality and Social Psychology, 35,* 537–547.

Falbo, T., & Peplau, L. A. (1980). Power strategies in intimate relationships. *Journal of Personality and Social Psychology, 38,* 618–628.

Frijda, N. H. (1986). *The emotions.* London: Cambridge University Press.

Galambos, J. A., Abelson, R. P., & Black, J. B. (1986). Goals and plans. In J. A. Galambos, R. P. Abelson, & J. B. Black (Eds.), *Knowledge structures* (pp. 101–102). Hillsdale, NJ: Lawrence Erlbaum Associates.

Goffman, E. (1959). *The presentation of self in everyday life.* Garden City, NY: Doubleday Anchor.

Goffman, E. (1969). *Strategic interaction.* Philadelphia: University of Pennsylvania Press.

Goodstadt, B. E., & Kipnis, D. (1970). Situational differences in the use of power. *Journal of Applied Psychology, 54,* 201–207.

Green, G. M. (1989). *Pragmatics and natural language understanding.* Hillsdale, NJ: Lawrence Erlbaum Associates.

Greene, J. O. (1984). Speech preparation processes and verbal fluency. *Human Communication Research, 11,* 61–84.

Hammond, K. J. (1989). *Case-based planning: Viewing planning as a memory task.* New York: Academic Press.

Hayes-Roth, B., & Hayes-Roth, F. (1979). A cognitive model of planning. *Cognitive Science, 3,* 275–310.

Heider, F. (1958). *The psychology of interpersonal relations.* New York: Wiley.

Hewes, D. E. (1979). The sequential analysis of social interaction. *Quarterly Journal of Speech, 65,* 56–73.

Hewes, D. E. (1986). A socio-egocentric model of group decision-making. In R. Y. Hirokawa & M. S. Poole (Eds.), *Communication and group decision-making* (pp. 265–291). Newbury Park, CA: Sage.

Hewes, D. E., & Planalp, S. (1982). There is nothing as useful as a good theory . . . The influence of social knowledge on interpersonal communication. In M. E. Roloff & C. R. Berger (Eds.), *Social cognition and communication* (pp. 107–150). Newbury Park, CA: Sage.

Hewes, D. E., & Planalp, S. (1987). The individual's place in communication science. In C. R. Berger & S. H. Chaffee (Ed.), *Handbook of communication science* (pp. 146–183). Newbury Park: CA: Sage.

Hirokawa, R. Y. (1982). Group communication and problem-solving effectiveness: A critical review of inconsistent findings. *Communication Quarterly, 30,* 134–141.

Hirokawa, R. Y. (1983). Group communication and problem-solving effectiveness: II. An exploratory investigation of procedural functions. *Western Journal of Speech Communication, 47,* 59–74.

Hirokawa, R. Y. (1985). Discussion procedures and decision-making performance. *Human Communication Research, 12,* 203–224.

Hirokawa, R. Y., & Pace, R. (1983). A descriptive investigation of the possible communication-based reasons for effective and ineffective group decision making. *Communication Monographs, 50,* 363–379.

Hjelmquist, E. (1991). Planning and execution of discourse in conversation. *Communication and Cognition, 24,* 1–17.

Hjelmquist, E., & Gidlund, A. (1984). Planned ideas versus expressed ideas in conversation. *Journal of Pragmatics, 8,* 329–343.

Janis, I. L., & Mann, L. (1977). *Decision making: A psychological analysis of conflict, choice, and commitment.* New York: Free Press.

Jones, E. E. (1964). *Ingratiation: A social psychological analysis.* New York: Appelton-Century-Crofts.

Jones, E. E., & Nisbett, R. E. (1972). The actor and the observer: Divergent perceptions of the causes of behavior. In E. E. Jones, D. E. Kanouse, H. H. Kelley, R. E. Nisbett, S. Valins, & B. Weiner (Eds.), *Attribution: Perceiving the causes of behavior* (pp. 79–94). Morristown, NJ: General Learning Press.

Jones, E. E., & Wortman, C. (1973). *Ingratiation: An attributional approach.* Morristown, NJ: General Learning Press.

Kellermann, K. (1988, March). *Understanding tactical choice: Metagoals in conversation.* Paper presented at the Temple University conference on goals in discourse, Philadelphia, PA.

Kellermann, K., & Berger, C. R. (1984). Affect and the acquisition of social information: Sit back, relax, and tell me about yourself. In R. Bostrom (Ed.), *Communication Yearbook 8* (pp. 412–445). Newbury Park, CA: Sage.

Kipnis, D., & Consentino, J. (1969). Use of leadership powers in industry. *Journal of Applied Psychology, 53,* 460–466.

Kluwe, R. H., & Friedrichsen, G. (1985). Mechanisms of control and regulation in problem solving. In J. Kuhl & J. Beckmann (Eds.), *Action control: From cognitions to behavior* (pp. 183–218). Berlin: Springer-Verlag.

Kreitler, S., & Kreitler, H. (1987). Plans and planning: Their motivational and cognitive antecedents. In S. L. Friedman, E. K. Skolnick, & R. R. Cocking (Eds.), *Blueprints for thinking: The role of planning in cognitive development* (pp. 110–178). New York: Cambridge University Press.

Kuhl, J. (1986). Motivation and information processing: A new look at decision making, dynamic change, and action control. In R. M. Sorrentino & E. T. Higgins (Eds.), *Handbook of motivation and cognition* (pp. 404–434). New York: Guilford.

Lichtenstein, E. H., & Brewer, W. F. (1980). Memory for goal-directed events. *Cognitive Psychology, 12,* 412–445.

Mandler, G. (1975). *Mind and emotion.* New York: Wiley.

McLaughlin, M. L., Cody, M. J., & Robey, C. S. (1980). Situational influences on the selection of strategies to resist compliance-gaining attempts. *Human Communication Research, 7,* 14–36.

Miller, G. A., Galanter, E., & Pribram, K. H. (1960). *Plans and the structure of behavior.* New York: Holt, Rinehart & Winston.

Miller, G. R. (1987). Persuasion. In C. R. Berger & S. H. Chaffee (Eds.), *Handbook of communication science* (pp. 446–483). Newbury Park, CA: Sage.

Miller, G. R., Boster, F., Roloff, M. E., & Seibold, D. (1977). Compliance-gaining message strategies: A typology and some findings concerning the effects of situational differences. *Communication Monographs, 44,* 37–51.

Miller, G. R., Boster, F., Roloff, M. E., & Seibold, D. (1987). MBRS rekindled: Some thoughts on compliance-gaining in interpersonal settings. In M. E. Roloff & G. R. Miller (Eds.), *Interpersonal processes: New directions in communication research* (pp. 89–116). Newbury Park, CA: Sage.

Norman, D. A. (1981). Categorization of action slips. *Psychological Review, 88,* 1–15.

Nuttin, J. (1984). *Motivation, planning and action.* Louvain: Leuven University Press; Hillsdale, NJ: Lawrence Erlbaum Associates.

O'Keefe, B. J., & Delia, J. G. (1982). Impression formation and message production. In M. E. Roloff & C. R. Berger (Eds.), *Social cognition and communication* (pp. 33–72). Newbury Park, CA: Sage.

O'Keefe, B. J., & McCornack, S. A. (1987). Message design logic and message goal structure: Effects on perceptions of messages. *Human Communication Research, 14,* 68–92.

O'Keefe, B. J., & Shepard, G. J. (1987). The pursuit of multiple objectives in face-to-face persuasive interaction: Effects of construct differentiation on message organization. *Communication Monographs, 54,* 396–419.

Ortony, A., Clore, G. L., & Collins, A. (1988). *The cognitive structure of emotions.* Cambridge, England: Cambridge University Press.

Planalp, S., & Hewes, D. E. (1982). A cognitive approach to communication theory: *Cogito ergo dico?* In M. Burgoon (Ed.), *Communication Yearbook 5* (pp. 49–77). New Brunswick, NJ: Transaction Press.

Read, S. J., & Miller, L. C. (1989). Inter-personalism: Toward a goal-based theory of persons in relationships. In L. A. Pervin (Ed.), *Goal concepts in personality and social psychology* (pp. 413–479). Hillsdale, NJ: Lawrence Erlbaum Associates.

Reason, J. T. (1990). *Human error.* New York: Cambridge University Press.

Riesbeck, C. K., & Schank, R. C. (1989). *Inside case-based reasoning.* Hillsdale, NJ: Lawrence Erlbaum Associates.

Rogoff, B., Gauvain, M., & Gardner, W. (1987). The development of children's skills in adjusting to plans to circumstances. In S. L. Friedman, E. K. Scholnick, & R. R. Cocking (Eds.), *Blueprints for thinking: The role of plans in cognitive development* (pp. 303–320). Cambridge, England: Cambridge University Press.

Rosenfeld, H. M. (1966). Approval-seeking and approval-inducing functions of verbal and nonverbal behavior. *Journal of Personality and Social Psychology, 4,* 597–605.

Rule, B. G., & Bisanz, G. L. (1987). Goals and strategies of persuasion: A cognitive schema for understanding social events. In M. P. Zanna, J. M. Olson, & C. P. Herman (Eds.), *Social influence: The Ontario Symposium* (Vol. 5, pp. 185–206). Hillsdale, NJ: Lawrence Erlbaum Associates.

Rule, B. G., Bisanz, G. L., & Kohn, M. (1985). Anatomy of a persuasion schema: Targets, goals, and strategies. *Journal of Personality and Social Psychology, 48,* 1127–1140.

Sacerdoti, E. D. (1977). *A structure for plans and behavior.* Amsterdam: Elsevier North-Holland.

Schank, R. C. (1982). *Dynamic memory: A theory of reminding and learning in computers and people.* Cambridge, England: Cambridge University Press.

Schank, R. C., & Abelson, R. F. (1977). *Scripts, plans, goals and understanding.* Hillsdale, NJ: Lawrence Erlbaum Associates.

Schenk-Hamlin, W. J., Wiseman, R. L., & Georgacarakos, G. N. (1982). A model of properties of compliance-gaining strategies. *Communication Quarterly, 30,* 92–99.

Schmidt, C. F. (1976). Understanding human action: Recognizing the plans and motives of other persons. In J. S. Carroll & J. W. Payne (Eds.), *Cognition and social behavior* (pp. 47–67). Hillsdale, NJ: Lawrence Erlbaum Associates.

Schroder, H. M., Driver, M. J., & Streufert, S. (1967). *Human information processing.* New York: Holt, Rinehart & Winston.

Seifert, C. M., Robertson, S. P., & Black, J. B. (1985). Types of inferences generated during reading. *Journal of Memory and Language, 24,* 405–422.

Siegman, A. W. (1979). Cognition and hesitation in speech. In A. W. Siegman & S. Feldstein (Eds.), *Of speech and time: Temporal speech patterns in interpersonal contexts* (pp. 151–178). Hillsdale, NJ: Lawrence Erlbaum Associates.

Sillars, A. L. (1980). The stranger and the spouse as target persons for compliance-gaining strategies: A subjective expected utility model. *Human Communication Research, 6,* 265–279.

Snyder, M. (1981). Seek, and ye shall find: Testing hypotheses about other people. In C. T. Higgins, C. P. Herman, & M. P. Zanna (Eds.), *Social cognition: The Ontario Symposium* (Vol. 1, pp. 277–303). Hillsdale, NJ: Lawrence Erlbaum Associates.

Spitzberg, S., & Cupach, W. R. (1984). *Interpersonal communication competence.* Newbury Park, CA: Sage.

Srull, T. K., & Wyer, R. S., Jr. (1986). The role of chronic and temporary goals in social information processing. In R. Sorrentino & E. T. Higgins (Eds.), *Handbook of motivation and cognition* (pp. 503–549). New York: Guilford.

Sternberg, R. J. (1986). A triangular theory of love. *Psychological Review, 93,* 119–135.

Tracy, K., Craig, R. T., Smith, M., & Spisak, F. (1984). The discourse of requests: Assessment of a compliance-gaining approach. *Human Communication Research, 10,* 513–538.

Tracy, K., & Eisenberg, E. M. (1989, May). *Multiple goals: Unpacking a commonplace.* Paper presented at the annual convention of the International Communication Association, San Francisco, CA.

Trope, Y., & Bassok, M. (1982). Confirmatory and diagnosing strategies in social information gathering. *Journal of Personality and Social Psychology, 43,* 22–34.

Vallacher, R. R., & Wegner, D. M. (1985). *A theory of action identification.* Hillsdale, NJ: Lawrence Erlbaum Associates.

Vallacher, R. R., Wegner, D. M., & Somoza, M. (1989). That's easy for you to say: Action identification and speech fluency. *Journal of Personality and Social Psychology, 56,* 199–208.

von Cranach, M., Kalbermatten, U., Indermuhle, K., & Gugler, B. (1982). *Goal-directed action.* London: Academic Press.

Waldron, V. R. (1990). Constrained rationality: Situational influences on information acquisition plans and tactics. *Communication Monographs, 57,* 184–201.

Wegner, D. M., & Vallacher, R. R. (1986). Action identification. In R. M. Sorrentino & E. T. Higgins (Eds.), *Handbook of motivation and cognition* (pp. 550–582). New York: Guilford.

Wheeless, L. R., Barraclough, R., & Stewart, R. (1983). Compliance-gaining and power in persuasion. In R. N. Bostrom (Ed.), *Communication Yearbook 7* (pp. 105–145). Newbury Park, CA: Sage.

Wilensky, R. (1983). *Planning and understanding: A computational approach to human reasoning.* Reading, MA: Addison-Wesley.

6 The Conversation MOP: A Model of Patterned and Pliable Behavior

Kathy Kellermann
University of California, Santa Barbara

Conversational behavior is a study in seeming contradiction. On the one hand, conversation is an intricate interplay between interlocutors; on the other, it is the conveyance of common conventions. Conversation is adjustable and adaptive; it is regular and routine. Routines are available for everything from greetings to goodbyes, turn taking to topic sequencing, linguistically fixed expressions to sequentially dependent acts, and local to global coherence (see, for review, Clarke & Argyle, 1982; Coulmas, 1981; Craig & Tracy, 1983; Levinson, 1983; McLaughlin, 1984; Nofsinger, 1991; Wardbaugh, 1985). Yet, despite such routinization, conversations are not interchangeable events; they reflect a great deal of situationally adaptive and flexible behavior. Persons influence, adapt to, and accommodate the conversational behavior or others; they alter what they say to adjust to different hearers and to achieve different goals (see, for review, Cappella, 1981; Clark, 1992; Giles, Mulac, Bradac, & Johnson, 1987; Levinson, 1983). Conversational behavior is both fixed and flexible, methodical and malleable. Conversation is invention and it is convention, enacted without contradiction.

How can this be? How can conversational behavior be both ordered and changing, routinized and adapted, regular and adjustable? This seeming contradiction of conversational behavior lies not in its enactment, but rather in its study; not in its practice, but instead in its explanation. It is the study of conversation that expects routinization and is surprised by adaptation (or that expects accommodation and is surprised by convention). Inquiry tends to focus on either the fixed or the fashioned part of conversation, ignoring the simultaneity of stability and change in that behavior. Persons' ability to be simultaneously routine and yet flexible and adaptive poses a decided challenge to scholars attempting to describe, predict, and explain conversational interaction.

It is this fundamental aspect of conversational behavior—that is simultaneously patterned and pliable, fixed and flexible, routine and readjustable—that stimulates the theory and research reported in this chapter from a perspective called the conversation memory organization packet (MOP). The MOP perspective offers a cognitive account for patterned but pliable conversational behavior and is the theoretical successor of script theory (Abelson, 1976, 1981; Schank & Abelson, 1977). The MOP perspective offers a heuristically provocative and conceptually compelling cognitive explanation for the simultaneous occurrence of convention and invention in conversational behavior. Although it is not the only account (nor even the only cognitive account) of stability and change in conversational behavior, relatively few other perspectives can predict and/or explain the range of findings encompassed by the MOP perspective. The issue is not whether some perspective somewhere can account for some particular aspect of conversational behavior sometimes, but whether the range of conversational behaviors—conventional *and* inventional, as generated *and* as understood—can be predicted and explained from the point of view of one unified framework. In a cognitive account of conversational behavior, the MOP perspective offers this possibility.

As with any cognitive account, the MOP perspective makes assumptions about the nature of memory, the structures contained therein, and the means by which those structures develop and change. The first section of this chapter sketches the theory of dynamic memory, in which the MOP perspective is grounded. Following sections (a) outline the nature and principles of the perspective for conversational behavior, (b) explore the means by which generated behavior can be simultaneously routine and flexible, and (c) consider implications of the perspective for processing conversations and guiding competent performances.

FOUNDATIONS: A SKETCH OF DYNAMIC MEMORY THEORY

Dynamic memory theory is an outgrowth of the Yale Artificial Intelligence Project headed by Roger Schank (for a history of the project, see Johnson, 1986). Different aspects of the theory have been addressed by various researchers related to the project (Cullingford & Kolodner, 1986; Dyer, 1983; Hovy & Schank, 1984; Kolodner, 1983a, 1983b, 1984a, 1984b, 1989; Kolodner & Barsalou, 1982; Kolodner & Cullingford, 1986; Kolodner & Simpson, 1986; Leake, 1989; Lebowitz, 1980; Martin, 1989; Pazzani, 1985; Reiser, 1986a, 1986b; Riesbeck, 1982, 1986; Riesbeck & Martin, 1986; Riesbeck & Schank, 1989; Schank 1980, 1981, 1982a, 1982b, 1990; Schank, Collins, & Hunter, 1986; Schank & Leake,

1990; E. Turner, 1990, 1991a, 1991b; R. M. Turner, 1989; Turner & Cullingford, 1989a, 1989b, 1992). Because each researcher is guided by different interests and goals, consistency is not always maintained with the complete collection of writings or with Schank's (1982b) foundational treatise. Schank's own thinking has also undergone change, reflected in differences between the foundational treatise and pretreatise works (1980, 1982a). The sketch of dynamic memory theory that follows (and that grounds the research on the conversation MOP) is based on Schank's (1982b) foundational treatise, although ideas from the larger body of work are used when appropriate.

Perhaps the most fundamental idea of dynamic memory theory is that memory is constantly changing in response to experience; that is, memory is dynamic rather than static. Changes in memory occur by creating, altering, and updating *scenes,* the building blocks of memory. A scene is a grouping of generalized actions with a shared instrumental goal; it is a collection of events whose common features have been abstracted. For example, experiences involving conversations between persons who are unacquainted generally lead to the development of an "introduction" scene, with the most common generalized action being the stating of names. Scenes store memories of specific encounters as well as the general abstractions derived from those events. Memories are indexed in terms of how they differ from the generalized actions in the scene, leading to incorporation of scene-congruent experiences and tagging of scene-incongruent experiences. Scenes are developed based on the similarities of specific events and are updated (i.e., changed) based on repeated deviation (i.e., tagging) of actual experience from what is expected by the scene. For example, it is possible that people experience behaviors in some introductions that run counter to what they expect (e.g., refusal to provide one's name, a thrice kissing of alternate cheeks, etc.). These unexpected behaviors are tagged and, if repeated, serve to stimulate change in the representation of the scene.

Scripts are sequences of actions that take place within scenes, involving very specific behavioral variations that provide added detail to the general actions contained in a scene. Each script can be viewed as representing one specific method or set of tactics for helping to accomplish the goal of a scene. For example, an introduction scene might contain one script representing specific actions related to shaking hands, whereas another script might represent specific actions related to revealing the relationship between oneself and a partner (e.g., saying that you are a student in the person's class, saying that you have met before, etc.). Scripts are bounded by the scenes in which they are embedded, and they encode situation-specific possibilities for "coloring" the more general actions in the scene. Multiple scripts can be (and often are) attached to one scene. Scenes hold what is general about scripts, whereas scripts hold specific actions that detail the general actions of scenes. The independent memory unit in dynamic memory is a scene: a grouping a cross-situational (general) and situation-specific (scripted) actions.

A MOP describes how scenes are linked together in order to accomplish a higher order goal. MOPs record similarities in episodes much as scenes record similarities in events. In other words, MOPs describe combinations of scenes that frequently co-occur in persons' experiences. The function of a MOP is to prescribe what combination of a series of instrumental goals (in the scenes) can facilitate achievement of some more complex goal. Scenes are the basic building blocks of MOPs and are limited in number. Any given scene can be organized by many different MOPs as long as the instrumental goal facilitated by the general actions in the scene is useful for the accomplishment of different higher order goals. For example, an initial-interaction MOP and an interview MOP could both command use of the same introduction scene (presuming, of course, that introductions were instrumental to the goal of those interactions). Thus, rather than storing information about introductions in a number of different memory structures, the scene is the repository of that knowledge and is commanded by various MOPs as needed for higher order goals. As a result, scenes are not only updated dynamically based on experience, but contingent sequences of scenes (i.e., routines) can be generated dynamically. Based on experience, MOPs choose and sequence scenes so that higher level goals can be accomplished.

Three general classes of MOPs can be distinguished in terms of the nature of the scenes they organize. *Physical MOPs* sequence physical scenes (i.e., scenes that have physical settings [visual snapshots so to speak] as their common feature). A visit with a professor could be experienced as driving to the professor's office building, taking the elevator to the right floor, knocking on the professor's door, sitting down in the office, standing up to leave, and so on. *Societal MOPs* sequence societal scenes (i.e., scenes with social settings [generalizations of how people interact in defined situations] as their common feature). A societal scene "has a social setting that involves two people each pursuing a goal that the other person is a necessary participant in, at a common time, with a communication link between them. The actions comprising the interaction between the participants defines the scene" (Schank, 1982b, p. 96). Scenes change as different low-level (instrumental) goals are pursued. For example, the visit to the professor could be experienced as introducing oneself, asking for help on coursework, and saying goodbye. *Personal MOPs* sequence personal scenes (i.e., scenes with personal goals as their common feature). Personal scenes are idiosyncratic, representing repeatedly experienced private means for achieving goals. For example, people may have their own way of visiting a professor that is unrelated to the manner anyone else would use.

Physical and societal MOPs are culturally shared knowledge structures, whereas personal MOPs are idiosyncratic in their development. All MOPs are developed based on the identification of similarities and differences in episodes (sequences of scenes) in persons' experiences. Personal MOPs are frequently variations of physical and societal MOPS, where particular physical or societal scenes are replaced by personal scenes. Typically, people start their knowledge representation by defining scenes physically. These representations evolve over time, taking on societal and personal aspects. Multiple MOPs often co-occur and can be said to "overlay" each other. Physical, societal, and personal MOPs can all simultaneously be used for representing and guiding experience. A romantic interlude might generate expectations about the physical setting (e.g., dim the lights, turn on the music, stand close, etc.), the social setting (discussions about religion and politics do not seem high on the agenda), as well as one's personal plans (no elaboration needed here). All three types of scenes can also be used to store memories of the episode. People could remember the romantic interlude because of its physical setting (at MacDonald's), its social focus (discussed religion and politics), or some idiosyncratic behavior.

Although it is not a comprehensive account of dynamic memory theory, this sketch offers a glimpse of the theory in which the perspective of the conversation MOP is grounded. In essence, MOPs are composed of scenes (generalizations of events) that are organized to represent the common features of episodes that satisfy higher level goals. The next section details the nature and principles of conversation MOPs.

THE NATURE OF CONVERSATION MOPS

To refer to a conversation MOP minimally presupposes: (a) a definable type of episode so that generalization may occur due to similarities across experienced episodes, and (b) an associated higher order goal to be achieved through sequencing instrumental goals of scenes. In other words, many conversation MOPs probably exist, each representing the co-occurring scenes in frequently experienced episodes in persons' lives. Although an abstract archetypal conversation MOP may exist in memory, a starting point must be located by specification of an episode type. The perspective and research reported in this chapter focuses on an informal, initial conversation MOP (i.e., the representation of conversations between persons meeting informally for the first time).

Informal, initial interactions were chosen as the context of interest for a number of reasons, not least of which is that they facilitate testing of the MOP perspective. First, informal, initial interactions happen sufficiently frequently (Wheeler & Nezlek, 1977), such that episode generalization could be detected if it occurred. Generalization requires that similarities in and between events be noticed across episodes—in other words, that regularities are identified. Considerable literature on informal, initial interactions has focused on such conversational regularities of greetings, partings, turn taking, topic sequencing, linguistically fixed expressions, and sequentially dependent acts (for review, see Coulmas, 1981; Craig & Tracy, 1983; Levinson, 1983; McLaughlin, 1984).

Second, informal, initial interactions also provide a context in which a societal MOP is likely to operate. MOPs that relate to conversational behavior of marital couples, although theoretically and pragmatically interesting, have no necessary requirement of ritualized behavior across couples, making identification of scenes difficult. Variance in conversational structure across marital couples could obscure the real routines in marital couples' encounters. Many of the scenes expected to be in an informal, initial conversation MOP are likely to be commanded by different conversation MOPs for conversations in more developed relationships, as well as for other types of initial encounters (e.g., interviews). For example, greetings are used in task and social encounters as well as in conversations between strangers and friends. Certainly some scenes might be expected to vary as the relational stage (initial, developing, developed, decaying), purpose (social, task, etc.), and setting (formal, informal, etc.) vary. However, if the scenes used in informal, initial conversations are identified, such variation can then be usefully explored. The means would be at hand to make comparisons of relational stages, interaction purposes, and physical settings in terms of the representation of conversational behavior.

Third, informal, initial interactions offer a readily identifiable goal to be achieved through the sequencing of scenes in the MOP. People typically view initial interactions as a means of getting to know others (Douglas, 1983, 1984; Kellermann, Broetzmann, Lim, & Kitao, 1989; Kellermann & Lim, 1989). When meeting others informally for the first time, persons display this acquaintanceship goal by seeking out information about others as well as revealing personal information about themselves (Berger & Kellermann, 1994). Consequently, the minimal requirements for a conversation MOP to even exist (definable type of episode with an associated higher order goal) are met in the context of informal, initial encounters.

Not only were initial interactions chosen as a context because they facilitate testing of the MOP perspective, but they are important episodes in their own right. Informal, initial encounters are the basis of the development of our permanent relationships. Without an initial interaction, future interactions cannot occur. Persons who are lonely frequently report not knowing how to meet others (see, e.g., Rook & Peplau, 1982; Young, 1982). When they are faced with an initial interaction, they tend to engage in nonnormative behavior for which they are judged negatively (for review, see Bell, 1987; Jones, 1982; Solano, 1986). Informal, initial encounters have important relational implications. Consequently, for theoretical and pragmatic reasons, the fashioning of an understanding of routine but flexible conversational behavior centered on an investigation of an informal, initial conversation MOP.

Scenes in the MOP

The verification and description of the conversation MOP for informal, initial encounters was undertaken by Kellermann et al. (1989). Through examinations of self-reports of memory organization for casual first meetings between strangers as well as analysis of actual conversations, a conversation MOP was identified that did have the goal of becoming acquainted. As anticipated, the scenes in the MOP were found to be topic centered, each topic (scene) consisting of a set of utterances having a single, overarching content objective. The scenes comprising the MOP include: greeting, introduction, health (e.g., "how are you?"), present situation, reason for presence, weather, where one lives, hometowns, persons known in common, what one does, education, occupation, social relations, compliments, interests, family, sports, near-future activities, evaluation of the encounter, planning a future meeting, positive evaluation of the cointeractant, saying until laters, providing a reason to terminate the conversation, and goodbyes. Each scene has an associated instrumental goal. For example, greetings serve the goal of recognizing the other, introductions provide identifying information, and other topics facilitate extraction of cultural, social, and psychological information.

The scenes in this conversation MOP are mainly societal scenes, rather than personal or physical scenes. Personal scenes were reported as part of cognitive representations and produced in actual conversations, although with relatively low frequency. Of 3,292 scenes reported by 158 persons in their cognitive representations of initial interactions, only 13 were not duplicated by any other participant. However, personal variations did arise in terms of the relative frequency with which scenes existed as part of the MOP. A number of scenes such as age, recent life events, fashion, music, politics, and religion were included in the conversation MOP of less than 20% of the participants, reflecting personal variations on the culturally shared societal MOP. By contrast, scenes such as greetings, introduction, talk about the present situation, persons known in common, hometowns, and goodbyes were reported and produced by most participants. The only scene that makes direct reference to a physical setting is the present situation scene, which is a very stable element of the representation of initial encounters. As is discussed later, this physical scene of the present situation plays a critical role in generating flexible but routine behavior in initial encounters.

Scripts Attached to Scenes

Although not the focus of the initial investigation, some rather striking findings occurred in terms of the linguistic reporting of scenes contained in memory. In essence, scenes were referenced and reported with marked linguistic invariance. For example, when discussing a future meeting (a scene occurring near the end of initial encounters), persons provided two general actions: offering and responding to the offer. Offers of future meetings were reported in only five ways: (a) discussing, (b) suggesting, or (c) requesting to meet again; and (d) inviting or (e) requesting the other person to do a specific activity. Similarly, responses were reported in only two ways: (a) evaluation and (b) acceptance/rejection. It was

exciting and provocative that every scene was marked by this linguistic invariance in its reporting and referencing.

Although this linguistic invariance was initially interpreted as the result of the
reporting of scripts that color each scene, further examination suggests two
sources of the invariance. Some of the linguistic invariance in referencing and
reporting of conversational topics seems to stem from persons describing general
action(s) of each scene, whereas other parts of the invariance appear to be due to
the delineation of scripts that color the general actions. For example, consider the
introduction scene. Although the general action of exchanging names is frequently used in reports of the introduction scene, various scripts for coloring how
this exchange occurs also seem to be offered (e.g., asking for a person's name
and telling one's own). By contrast, the reports on the health scene tend to outline
the general actions involved in the scene, rather than scripts used to color them
("how are you?", answers, reciprocations).

Although suggestive only, the linguistic invariance detected in the reporting of
scenes in the MOP hint that tactics creating variations on general actions in each
scene are relatively few in number. Such a finding corresponds well with research that consistently reports a limited (and often small) set of distinguishable
tactics and strategies for a variety of communicative purposes (for review, see
Daly & Weimann, 1994). Clearly, further research would be useful to uncover
the various scripts attached to each of the scenes in the conversation MOP.

Sequencing of the Scenes

The purpose of any MOP is to represent the ordering of co-occurring scenes in
given types of episodes. At the most general level, it was found (as expected;
Kellermann et al., 1989) that the scenes follow the linear sequencing of (a)
initiation, (b) maintenance, and (c) termination phases (Douglas, 1984). A clear
change in focus of the scenes was noticeable through the maintenance phase and
in comparison with the initiation phase. In contrast with the initiation phase,
scenes in the maintenance phase focused on the individual as a psychological and
unique entity. The maintenance phase progressed from factual information
(where one lives, hometown, persons known in common, etc.) to opin-
ion/attitude/value information (social relations, compliments, personal interests,
family, etc.). However, the maintenance phase terminated when a decrease in
personal information occurred, as seen by a shift in focus to such topics as sports.
This decrease in intimacy serves as a preparatory cue for wanting to initiate
movement into the termination phase and winding down the conversation.

It was also expected and verified that individual scenes (topics) are weakly
ordered, but that groups of scenes (topics) are strongly ordered. In other words,
at any particular point in time, multiple scenes (topics) are likely, although the
nature of scenes that are appropriate at different points in time in the conversation

varies. For example, when persons are meeting for the first time, it is common to discuss: (a) the situation where the conversation is occurring, (b) the reason each is present, (c) the weather, (d) where each lives, (e) where each is from, and (f) persons known in common. Although these scenes tend to occur near the beginning of initial interactions, any of these six topics is appropriate at that point; no one of these topics must "come before" the others. However, these scenes tend to be discussed prior to topics such as family and social relations. In other words, scenes are organized into subsets of scenes, such that any of the scenes in a given subset is a candidate for the next action in the conversational encounter as long as that subset is currently "where the conversation is at." The idea here is that the subsets are linearly ordered, such that scenes in Subset 1 come before those in Subset 2, which come before those in Subset 3, and so on. However, no particular order is required for scenes contained in any given subset. Figure 6.1 diagrams the grouping of scenes into subsets and the ordering of those subsets.

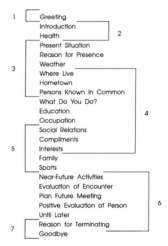

FIG. 6.1.   The informal, initial conversation MOP.

As can be seen in Fig. 6.1, certain scenes (topics) bridge subsets; that is, certain scenes are members of more than one subset. These bridge scenes serve a linking function to permit the conversation to maintain at its current state (within the present subset) or progress to another state (the next subset). From this perspective, the two conversations that follow are equally "routine" and equally "ordered" as both follow the linear progression of the subsets while enacting somewhat different scenes:

Conversation 1:	Hi. (greeting)
	How are you? (health)
	Isn't the Bay Area expensive? (present situation)
	Where do you live? (where live)
	What do you do? (what do you do)
	What do you like to do for fun? (interests)
	Do you have any brothers and sisters? (family)
	You sound like you are doing well. (compliments)
	Well, I've got to go. (reason for terminating)
	Bye. (goodbyes)
Conversation 2:	Hi. (greeting)
	My name is Kathy. (introduction)
	How are you? (health)
	Where are you from? (hometown)
	Do you know John Doe? (persons known in common)
	What are you majoring in? (education)
	Do you like to play tennis? (sports)
	Maybe we could get together sometime. (future activity)
	It was nice to meet you. (positive evaluation)
	Catch you later. (until later)
	Bye. (goodbyes)

Although these two conversations are different in some respects, they are nevertheless quite similar in their structure, (i.e., in terms of the sequential progression through subsets of scenes). Both conversations move from scenes in Subset 1 to those in Subset 2, and so on; that is, both conversations exhibit sequential progression through sets of appropriate topics relative to the point each conversation is at.

The sequencing of scenes in the conversation MOP corresponds to the sequencing of actual conversational behavior. A correlation of .80 was found in the initial investigation between the ordering of scenes in the MOP and scenes produced in 43 conversations between persons meeting for the first time. A second investigation (Kellermann, 1991) extended this analysis to include dyads that varied in the degree they wished to become acquainted, again finding consistently high correlations between the ordering of scenes in the conversation MOP and the ordering of scenes in actual discourse. This research also examined transition probabilities between scenes, finding that persons transit (as expected) to scenes in the same or next subset of scenes. Across dyads conversing under 10 different acquaintanceship desires, this same transition pattern was uncovered with virtually no variation. This research also suggests that a mechanism of conversational control exists in the form of a "one subset backward jump" after the initiation of a new subset as a means of regulating the pace of conversational interactions. This jump back to a scene in an immediately preceding subset is a means of refusing forward progression of the conversation. Acceptance of forward movement makes backward movement significantly more difficult, to the point where it is exceedingly rare and usually linguistically marked (e.g., "Oh, I forgot to mention that. . ."). Ninety-five percent of all topic transitions involved initiating talk on topics in the same or next subset, or refusing talk on scenes from a newly initiated subset by returning to the previous subset. A third investigation (Kellermann & Lim, 1990) examined the likelihood of each subset occurring over time in initial interactions. As expected, movement was from scenes in early subsets to scenes in later subsets as conversations progressed. These research studies suggest that the conversation MOP sequentially organizes scenes in a manner corresponding to how people organize their topical talk in conversational encounters.

Conversation Meta-MOPs

The informal, initial conversation MOP is likely to be a specialization of a more general conversation MOP, a structure Schank (1982b) referred to as a *meta-MOP*. Meta-MOPs do not have direct memories in them as MOPs do, because they are more general structures from which MOPs can be constructed. A conversation meta-MOP would contain very general and abstract scenes that describe the ordered progression of conversations, regardless of whether they are interviews, initial interactions, or negotiations. Although the main focus of the research conducted to date has been on informal, initial interactions, at times participants have generated responses that offer inklings of what the conversation meta-MOPs might look like. In the initial investigation (Kellermann et al., 1989), some participants provided descriptions of their cognitive structures that could apply to virtually any conversation. Three different structures were reported: centered on (a) goal sequencing, (b) topic sequencing, and (c) form sequencing. The goal-sequencing structure represents conversations in terms of the goal of identifying commonalities with actions of search–find commonalities, discuss commonalities, exchange opinions, find another commonality, and then eventually winding down the conversation and making parting remarks. The topic-sequencing structure follows a similar pattern, but focuses on topic exchange as the central defining feature of the actions in a conversation. This topic-sequencing structure has general actions of suggesting a topic, discussing the topic, changing topics, and then returning to an earlier, more general topic to end the conversation. The form-sequencing structure represents conversation as an ordered progression of linguistic acts, containing actions of interrogation (many question–answer sequences), discussion, agreement, back channeling, obtaining opinions, debating, telling stories, and then shortening responses to end the conversation.

The sequencing found for each of these three structures was similar, regardless of whether conversation was being viewed as a search for commonalities, an exercise in topic exchanges, or a development of form. Question–answer periods co-occur with and guide the search for commonalities through the suggestion of topics. The discussion of commonalities parallels the discussion of topics, which occurs through linguistic forms of discussion, agreement, and back channeling. The exchange of opinions on commonalities co-occurs with the exchange of opinions on form, which also includes debating and storytelling. It is interesting to note the iterative process assumed by the actions of finding another commonality and changing topics. Winding down the conversation appears to occur by returning to an earlier, more general topic, with shortened responses. These structures provide evidence for: (a) a goal of conversations of searching for commonalities, (b) a method of conducting the search through topic sequencing, and (c) a means of following the method through specification of linguistic components.

These three co-occurring meta-MOPs provide an example of overlapping memory structures being able to simultaneously guide and represent conversation. The meta-MOPs offer a means of constructing contextualized conversation MOPs where the very general, abstract actions are transformed into the more familiar scenes on which the mainstay of the research has focused to this point. However, these results must be considered exploratory and tentative because the sample sizes on which they were based were relatively small. Nevertheless, the results provide clues to the possibilities of more general structures that help guide conversational encounters. Moreover, these structures provide a means of understanding how conversation could be represented and remembered in terms of the quantity of question asking or how much someone has in common with another.

A particularly interesting test of the overlaying of the conversation MOP with meta-MOPs can be seen in work conducted by Turner (1990, 1991a), in which she implemented an advice-giving system (for meal planning) on a computer with a conversational interface. To provide an effective conversational interface, Turner found the need to provide meta-MOP capabilities to the advice-giving system in the form of what she called *procedural C-MOPs*. Turner found that an effective conversational interface required distinguishing between procedural and declarative C-MOPs, with procedural C-MOPs being similar in nature to what are referred to here as meta-MOPs, and the declarative C-MOP being a particular conversation MOP (one involving topically defined conversational scenes related to meal planning). Turner's advice-giving system, called *JUDIS,* relies on the overlaying of procedural and declarative C-MOPs for its ability to flexibly generate and understand conversational utterances. Thus, Turner found it both necessary and possible to model routine adaptation in conversational behavior through the use of meta-MOPs being overlaid on a conversation MOP. These meta-MOPs serve the same purpose as those reported by participants in the Kellermann et al. (1989) research; that is, they are general structures that describe the ordered progression of conversations and can be used to simultaneously guide and represent ongoing conversational interactions.

Summary

The informal, initial conversation MOP is a memory structure that primarily contains societal scenes grouped into subsets that represent the topical develop-

ment people tend to follow when they meet for the first time. Scripts that color
the scenes and meta-MOPs, that overlay the representation of casual first encounters, are also part and parcel of the memory structures used to generate and
process conversational interactions. The means by which this perspective of the
conversation MOP accounts for simultaneously flexible and routine behavior is
taken up in the next section.

ACCOUNTING FOR ROUTINE AND FLEXIBLE BEHAVIOR

The perspective of the conversation MOP tells a simple but multifaceted story of
how conversational behavior can be simultaneously flexible and routine. This
story makes the point that, for the most part, variance in conversational behavior
might simply be called *routine variance*. Although responsive to situational
features and varying goals, the behavior that is guided by the conversation MOP
is still routine. In other words, the routines are flexibly deployed to meet the
demands of varying circumstances, goals, and conversational partners. In essence, the conversation MOP "provides a method for combining intention and
convention to generate flexible discourse and a means to sequence . . .
conversational activities" (Turner & Cullingford, 1989b, p. 938).

MOP Overlays

One method by which the conversation MOP generates routine adaptation is in
terms of which other MOPs are overlaid on it. The societally defined initial
interaction MOP might be combined with various physical MOPs that jointly
determine conversational behavior. Indeed, the physical MOP that gets associated with the generation of behavior in any particular episode is likely to directly
specify the topic of talk of the present-situation scene in the conversation MOP.
The present-situation scene appears to be a pivotal scene in the MOP for adapting
conversational behavior (Kellermann, 1991). Specifically, the present-situation
scene allows for the importing of topics that would normally not occur until later
(if at all) in initial encounters. For example, at a political rally, it would not be
unusual for two people to discuss politics very early on in a first meeting, despite
this typically not being a topic of discussion in most initial encounters. In such a
case, the present-situation scene imports the politics scene based on the activation of a physically defined political-convention MOP; that is, politics defines
the present situation so it becomes a topic for talk in the early stages of initial
interactions.

The present-situation scene offers a means for routinely introducing what
might otherwise be considered unlikely topics into the conversational stream for
the purpose of situational adaptation. The importation role of the present-
situation scene would predict that people meeting in grocery stores might talk

about food (normally a low-frequency scene that, if it occurs at all, typically occurs in the more advanced stages of initial interactions), or that people meeting after a church service might talk about religion (another low-frequency scene normally, but part of the present church setting). Such importance of other low-frequency scenes retains the systematic sequencing represented in the MOP while permitting situational adaptation based on activation of memory structures that define the physical setting. It would be worthwhile to explore whether various defining features of different situations were reflected in conversations at the point where talk on the present situation is anticipated by the informal, initial interaction MOP.

Scene Selection

Scene selection occurs dynamically as the conversation unfolds in order to meet the goals of initial interaction, as well as the constraints and expectations introduced by other meta-MOPs or MOPs overlaying the conversation MOP. At any point, a decision can be made to abandon the current topic (scene) and pursue a different topic (Hovy & Schank, 1984), although which topics tend to come next are constrained by the conversation MOP. However, certain scenes tend to occur almost out of habit, rather than being a result of on-line adjustment (e.g., greetings, introductions, goodbyes). Turner and Cullingford (1989a, 1989b) referred to scenes that are almost always included in actual conversations as *mandatory scenes*. These researchers differentiated mandatory from optional scenes based on frequency of selection, noting that the on-line ability to activate certain scenes (i.e., optional scenes) is part of what gives rise to flexibility in the generation of conversational behavior. On-line scene selection permits flexible adaptation of both the number and the nature of topics in a conversation while maintaining the routines of talk on each topic and across the conversation as an episode.

Number of Scenes Selected.   One means of adapting routine conversational behavior is to activate varying numbers of scenes from the MOP, ranging from activating almost all scenes in each subset or, contrarily, selecting only a few from each subset. A very short conversation could be held by selecting one scene per subset (and not developing talk on any of the topics). By contrast, conversational length could be increased dramatically by talking on almost every scene in every subset. Most likely many different factors influence the number of scenes selected for use in a conversation. Although speculative, it is likely that a person's expectation about the length of a particular initial interaction will be one determinant of the number of scenes selected. The idea here is that more or fewer scenes will be selected to make a conversation "fit" the expected time interval. Cues to such expectations often occur directly in the conversational stream, as witnessed in such utterances as "I don't have much time to talk," "I have to go soon," "I was on my way out the door," "I'm not doing anything much," and "I need a break." These expectations could also be generated without linguistic directioning based on aspects of the physical setting (e.g., waiting for a bus to come) or the social setting (e.g., one of many persons waiting in line for help). The point is that persons can adapt their conversational behavior as a function of their expectations of the amount of time they think the conversations can or should last by selecting more or fewer scenes from the subsets of the conversation MOP.

The number of scenes selected are also influenced by persons' goals for an encounter. For example, it was found that when people desire to become acquainted, less attention is paid to scenes in the earlier subsets of the conversation MOP and more attention is directed to scenes in later subsets of the MOP. By contrast, persons without strong acquaintanceship desires tend to focus more on scenes from earlier subsets of the MOP than on scenes from later subsets (Kellermann & Lim, 1990). Such a finding is consistent with the nature of the subsets in the MOP. Early subsets contain scenes that are relatively impersonal (present situation, education), whereas later subsets contain scenes that are more personal (interests, family, social relations). The early subsets focus on cultural and sociological information, whereas the later subsets tend to focus on psychological information (i.e., information that uniquely defines the person—that makes the person different from others). Persons wanting to get to know each other speed their progression through the earlier subsets containing less psychologically useful, nonpersonal information while slowing their progression through the MOP in the later subsets, where information that will more readily help them become acquainted can be obtained. Despite variations in the number of scenes selected in early and later stages of the MOP for persons of differing desires to become acquainted, the sequential progression of subsets of scenes expected by the MOP occurred in the conversations. In many ways, this result can be considered surprising: Elevated acquaintance desires could as easily encourage people to jump to the more personal information in scenes in the later subsets of the MOP, rather than initiating conversation and *progressing* it up to those later points in an adaptive and flexible way related to the quantity of scenes selected. However, the findings of this study comport well with evidence from other research, which suggests that people delay utterances until they fit more "naturally" into the conversation (Schegloff & Sacks, 1973). Therefore, the number of scenes selected in each subset can permit flexible adaptation of conversational routines as a function of the nature of persons' goals.

The number of scenes selected can also reflect judgments about the conversational participant. In the initial investigation (Kellermann et al., 1989), participants frequently reported that, is they liked the person they were talking to, then they would engage in almost all of the scenes in Subset 6 (near-future activities, planning a future meeting, evaluation of the encounter and the other person, etc.), scenes that reflect persons' desire to meet again. By contrast, neutral to negative affect reduced the number of scenes that participants reported would occur in this subset, typically resulting in the selection of only the scene related to the reason for terminating the conversation. Indeed, when people want to retreat from a conversation, they rarely do so by initiating talk about future meetings and typically do so by making excuses (Kellermann, Reynolds, & Chen, 1991).

The Nature of Scenes Selected.   Not only can the quantity of scenes selected in each subset result in flexible adaptation of routine conversational behavior, but the conversation MOP perspective also suggests that the nature of the scenes selected on-line permits adjustment of these routines. For example, bridge scenes can be selected or avoided in order to progress or maintain a conversation at its current place. Persons not wanting a conversation to end, and/or wanting to prolong a conversation might attempt to do so by avoiding all bridge scenes, thus making it more difficult for their partners to progress the conversation forward in a smooth manner. By contrast, persons wanting to have a short conversation, or needing to end one quickly when in the middle of a conversation, might start initiating bridge scenes to complete the conversation in a manner perhaps best defined as "skipping through the subsets." Of course, these maneuverings can be accepted or rejected. For example, forward progression can be refused by jumping back to a scene in the previous subset when movement to a new subset is attempted (Kellermann, 1991). Certainly there are times when one person initiates a scene in a new subset when the other person in the conversation wants to hold the talk at its current place. For example, people offer explanations of their failure to seek or provide some particular bit of information because the "moment passed them by" or they had "trouble getting back to what they wanted to talk about." It is also not uncommon to hear comments that sometimes people "move too fast" in conversation. Given these occurrences of perceived timing difficulties, it would make sense that a routine tool would exist for regulating the development of the conversation, not only suggesting the nature that forward movement should take (to the next subset) but also offering a means for cueing one's desire not to progress forward at that particular point. The interactive ability to manage forward progression is a powerful tool for flexibly adapting the routines of conversational behavior.

The nature of scenes that are selected can also vary as a function of persons' goals. The choice of optional scenes is goal directed; these scenes are selected when speakers want to do so (Turner & Cullingford, 1989a) for reasons related to their own or another person's benefit. For example, topics might be initiated because a belief or expectation is generated that the topics would be of interest to the other person (Hovy & Schank, 1984). Optional scenes might also be initiated because they permit the pursuit of personal goals (Turner & Cullingford, 1989a). For example, meeting a neighbor for the first time might not only involve an acquaintance goal, but also a personal goal of wanting to ask a favor (borrowing a lawn mower, or whatever). In such an instance, particular scenes might be selected to further one's personal goals. However, these scenes are selected at the appropriate time vis-à-vis the sequential progression envisioned by the conversation MOP. Consider work by McLaughlin and her colleagues concerning how people insert brags about themselves into informal, initial conversations with others (McLaughlin, Baaske, Cashion, Louden, Smith, & Smith-Altendorf, 1984; McLaughlin, Louden, Cashion, Altendorf, Baaske, & Smith, 1985). People used one of three approaches to inserting brags: (a) waiting for the right moment to arise because the needed topic was naturally bound to come up, (b) exploiting topical pathways that happened to arise in the conversation, and (c) actively manipulating topics in the conversation to provide the opportunity to make the brag. These three approaches, although differing in how brags are inserted, uniformly rely on scene (topic) selection within an expected get-acquainted topical progression to accomplish the goal of bragging. The nature of the optional scenes that are selected permits the pursuit of personal goals within the context of informal, initial interactions. "People seem to be quite good at manipulating a conversation to discuss a subject that they find interesting" (Turner, 1990, p. 118). The conversation MOP indicates where these various optional scenes are likely to arise while also permitting observers and partners to gain insight into participants' personal goals by the simple fact that these scenes were selected. "Optional scenes are important because they can indicate intention while using convention to guide the conversation" (Turner & Cullingford, 1989a, p. 70). Consequently, scene selection is one relatively simple mechanism by which conversational behavior can be simultaneously flexible and routine.

Script Activation

Another means by which the perspective of the conversation MOP accounts for pliable but patterned conversational behavior is through the activation of different scripts to color the enactment of general actions of a scene. As multiple scripts are attached to a given scene, routinized behavior sequences might vary somewhat in employment of the scene, dependent on the specific script instantiated for the scene. Some of these scripts are likely to be activated so as to meet expectations generated by other MOPs and meta-MOPs that are overlaying the conversation MOP. For example, a physical MOP co-occurring with the conversation MOP might generate assessments of the formality of the situation in which a conversation is occurring. When engaged in the introduction scene, formal settings might activate the shaking of hands, whereas informal ones may not. The point is simply that variation in script instantiation results in flexible adaptation of the generalized actions of the scene. Accounting for such variation is important. Research probably overlooks, and even relegates to random error, various scripts that are used to color general conversational actions of a scene. Scenes exhibit "routine variance" dependent on the use of specific scripts to color the more general actions of the scenes.

The Universal Scene

Flexible adaptation of routines can also occur through a mechanism called the *universal scene* (Kellermann et al., 1989; Kellermann & Lim, 1989). Universal scenes are defined as generalized action sequences that are role related but context-free (Schank, 1982b). A universal scene applies to some general role domain (such as "interlocutor"), but can be used in any particular context related to that role. A universal scene related to the conversation MOP would provide a means of developing talk on any MOP-related scene (topic).

Suggestive evidence of a universal scene for developing talk on a topic was obtained in the first investigation on the conversation MOP (Kellermann et al., 1989) and is being pursued in follow-up work (Kellermann, in preparation). Based on the findings of the first investigation (which need to be considered somewhat tentatively), the universal scene contains six generalized acts: (a) get facts, (b) discuss facts, (c) evaluate, (d) explain, (e) discuss goals/intentions, and (f) discuss enabling conditions for the goals/intentions. For example, when applied to the hometown scene, talk might proceed as follows: "Where are you from?" (get facts), "What is there to do there?" (discuss facts), "Do you like it there?" (evaluate), "Why do or don't you like it?" (explain), "Do you want to go back there?" (goals/intentions), and "Could you get a job there?" (enabling conditions). This same structure was found for each of the six scenes in which multiple actions were generated by participants (hometown, where one lives, persons known in common, what do you do, education, and occupation).

The first general action of getting facts tends to be question driven, centering around the "where are, do you, how" questions that Robinson and Rackstraw (1972) have found to be important in discourse. For example, getting facts about hometowns involves asking "Where are you from?", "Do you know it?", and "How long have you lived there?" Although the next general action of the universal scene of discussing facts was often not described by the participants, it seems to be related to the "what, when, who" questions isolated by Robinson and Rackstraw. For example, discussing facts about hometowns seems to involve such questions as, "What do you do there?", "When is a good time to go there?", and "Who lives there?" Unlike the first two general actions, which are based on question–answer exchanges, the actions of evaluation, explanation, goals, and enabling conditions tend to occur more in the form of statement-statement exchanges.

Evidence consistent with the structure of the universal scene is available in research on initial interactions that reports cyclicity in various conversational behaviors (Berger & Kellermann, 1983, 1989; Kellermann, 1984; Kellermann &

Berger, 1984). For example, this research finds that question asking cycles over the course of conversations, as do explanations for behavior and information about goals/intentions, rising up in frequency and then dropping in frequency and then rising and dropping again and again. Use of the universal scene to develop talk on topics provides one account of how and why this cyclicity in conversational behavior occurs. As each scene in the conversation is initiated, question asking would be expected to be high as per the question-driven nature of the first "get facts" action. However, as persons move toward the discussion-based stages of the universal scene (i.e., evaluation, explanation, goals/intentions, enabling conditions), interrogation sequences diminish and statement-based linguistic forms increase. As new scenes are selected, question asking should increase again; when it is decided to develop talk on a topic, question asking should decline. Thus, the existence and use of a universal scene is consistent with the cyclicity results found in other research.

The existence of this universal scene does not imply that persons pursue such detailed talk on all topics that arise during initial interactions. Rather, to the extent that a topic (scene) is pursued, talk would be structured according to the universal scene. Persons might simply "get facts" on a number of scenes ("What is your name?", "What is your major?", "Where are you from?", etc.), or they might decide, out of interest or other motivation, to elaborate on particular scenes. Even a decision to elaborate on some particular scene does not require use of the entire universal scene. Rather, talk on a topic can be exhausted at any stage, be it getting facts, discussing them, evaluating, explaining, or whatever. Another study was designed to assess the extent to which topical talk did, indeed, follow the general actions of the universal scene (Kellermann, in preparation). Although still underway, preliminary results find support for this structure across topics ranging in how much people know about, are interested in, and talk about them. Similar structures emerge for topics as diverse as stamp collecting, personal faults, education, hometowns, weather, persons known in common, getting together again in the future, health, required volunteer service in order to graduate, drug abuse on campus, social life, and the campus food service. The extent to which the universal scene is deployed for talk on some specific scene also offers flexibility in the use of routines; that is, a routine manner seems to exist for developing talk on a topic.

Having a routine means of developing talk on a topic provides a needed flexibility for engaging in conversation, because only rarely is one interlocutor completely able to control the direction a conversation will take. If a topic is initiated about which someone has virtually no information (such as stamp collecting), the conversation does not need to come to a screeching halt while persons try to comprehend and plan their behavior on-line. Rather, people can access the universal scene to guide their behavior and the conversation in a routine manner (Schank, 1982b). In other words, the universal scene permits adaptation to novel topics in conversations. It provides a needed comprehension skill for such situations as well. "The ability of MOPs to make useful predictions in somewhat novel situations for which there are no specific expectations but for which there are relevant experiences from which generalized information is available is crucial to our ability to understand" (Schank, 1982a, p. 470).

Structural Flexibility

The account offered for simultaneously flexible and routine conversational behavior by the perspective of the conversation MOP is centered around on-line adaptations of routines. In other words, the conversation MOP perspective suggests that conversational behavior is routinely different, rather than uniquely different. Through (a) overlays of different MOPs, (b) selection of different scenes, (c) activation of different scripts, and (d) deployment of the universal scene on different topics and to different degrees, conversational behavior is continuously routine although adapted to varying situations, goals, circumstances, and conversational partners. Indeed, it is possible to speculate that conversational behavior, even in novel or unfamiliar situations, is routine even if different than the behavior of other people. People typically wish to see new situations in familiar ways and strive to do so (Schank, 1982b). The variation in behavior in seemingly novel situations might be more a function of different MOPs being overlaid, different scenes being selected, different scripts being activated, and so on. Each individual's behavior may still be basically routine, just differently routine than others. In other words, idiosyncratic routines are being organized to handle these novel situations. Given sufficient experience and feedback, shared routines can emerge (Turner & Cullingford, 1989a).

IMPLICATIONS OF THE CONVERSATION MOP PERSPECTIVE

To this point, the focus of the discussion has centered around accounting for the generation of pliable but patterned conversational behavior. The perspective of the conversation MOP is not limited to examining production of talk. The dynamic-memory structures used to generate and guide conversational behavior are able to do so precisely because they encode persons' experiences with conversations. In other words, these dynamic-memory structures are used to process and understand conversations as well as to generate and guide them. This section focuses on processing of conversations by examining three subareas: focusing on (a) conversational memory, (b) updating knowledge, and (c) generating understanding. The goal of this section is not to argue that the MOP perspective is the only one that could account for each of these findings, but rather that it is able to explain what is known about a wide variety of conversational behaviors. In other words, this section demonstrates that the MOP perspective has a great deal of explanatory power as evidenced by its ability not only to account for routine but flexible behavior, but also by its ability to account for the wider base of research findings about conversational interaction (e.g., conversational memory, updating knowledge, and generating understanding).

Conversational Memory

The conversation MOP (and other overlaid physical, societal, personal, and meta-MOPs) not only guides the generation of conversational behavior, but also serves to process conversations as they occur. Just as multiple MOPs may be overlaid in the production of behavior, specific episodes can be remembered as instances of many different frames or perspectives. Thus, it is possible to remember aspects of meeting another person for the first time in terms of where you met (physical MOP), what you talked about (societally based conversation MOP), whether your own personal goals were achieved (personal MOP), whether the person asked too few or too many questions (form MOP), whether you talked about few or many different things (topic MOP), and whether you had anything in common (goal MOP).

Conversations are processed by being broken down into appropriate aspects and then stored in the structure to which they are relevant. In other words, different aspects of conversations will be remembered and stored in different memory structures. The breaking down and storing of episodes in a variety of knowledge structures provide some insight into why people can remember what they were talking about but not who they were talking to, or they can remember talking to someone in a given location but not what they were talking about, and so on. Different memory structures are being used to store these various aspects of the conversational interaction. As Schank (1990) noted: "Collecting events from the various MOPs in which they were stored is a sloppy process at best. You might find something different each time. You would certainly lose information or at least fail to find it some of the time" (p. 139).

Having multiple memory structures being used to store conversational episodes suggests that recall of particular episodes will depend on which memory structures are accessed at the time of recall. Cueing people to focus on and recall specific details related to conversational content would lead persons to access the actual scenes of the conversation MOP and attempt to tap memories from the particular episode in question. By contrast, cueing people to focus on broader aspects of the encounter, by suggesting they form an impression of the conversation, is more likely to encourage them to access the MOPs (form, topic, goal, etc.) that yield these types of descriptions and evaluations. Indeed, Stafford and Daly (1984) reported these results of memory for conversations when comparing a recall-instruction set to an impression-instruction set. Persons told to recall the specifics of a conversation made fewer inferences and evaluations and generated more content specifics than persons told to form an impression of a conversation.

Another implication of the MOP perspective for conversational memory concerns the way in which such memories would be stored. In the MOP perspective, memories are stored within scenes, indicating that episodes are remembered as pieces and not as wholes. This piecemeal storage is why, for example, we can remember talking about a particular topic but not necessarily what else was talked about before or after. Although whole conversations may be viewed as meaningful cognitive units (Hurtig, 1977; Kintsch, 1972; Stafford, Burggraf, & Sharkey, 1987; Stafford & Daly, 1984; Stafford, Waldron & Infield, 1989; Winograd, 1977), this does not mean that the conversations are stored as such. Conversations are stored piecemeal, with aspects relevant to each activated scene being stored in that scene. Recall of a given episode requires that the scenes initially used to process the episode be relocated. Consequently, even if people are trying only to recall the specific content of a conversation, thereby needing only to access scenes in the conversation MOP, it may not always be possible to remember exactly which scenes were produced in any given conversation. Rather, these memories are typically reconstructed based on sequential or causal dependencies between scenes (Schank, 1982b). The weaker these dependencies between scenes, the more difficult it will be to recall particular aspects of the episode. Indeed, researchers interested in conversational memory (Stafford & Daly, 1984; Stafford et al., 1987, 1989) have noted that the more variable structure of dialogues makes it more difficult to recall than text whose structure exhibits little to no variability.

The conversation MOP perspective provides insight into why recall of conversational episodes is so incredibly poor and oriented toward nonnormative behaviors. Studies very consistently find that people recall only 10% or so of their conversations with others only 5–10 minutes after completing them (Benoit & Benoit, 1987; Stafford & Daly, 1984; Stafford et al., 1987, 1989). This recall level reduces even further as time passes, going down to 4% within a week after the conversation first occurred (Stafford et al., 1987; Woodall & Folger, 1985). However, despite this loss of conversational detail, the gist and broader themes of conversational episodes are likely to be remembered (Keenan, MacWhinney, & Mayhew, 1977; Stafford & Daly, 1984; Stafford et al., 1987, 1989), as are highly salient speech acts such as personal criticism, sarcasm, and witty remarks (Keenan et al., 1977; MacWhinney, Keenan, & Reinke, 1982). Indeed, speech acts that are considered socially inappropriate are better remembered than those that are normative (Kemper & Thissen, 1981).

An understanding of these results starts from how scenes are developed. Scenes are generalizations of the similar features found in stored memories of episodes. As new experiences occur, scene-congruent behaviors are processed and incorporated into the general actions of the scene, with the scene-incongruent behaviors being indexed and retained as individual memory traces. Consequently, "events are remembered as they happen, but not for long. After awhile, the less salient aspects of an event fade away. What is left are generalized events plus the unusual or interesting parts of the original event from event memory" (Schank, 1980, p. 260). Because memories of events are based on differences, the aspects most likely to be recalled are those where the person, situation, topic, or other behaviors deviated in some way from expectations of the activated MOPs. By this definition, memorable conversations would be ones that were quite different in many respects from other conversations. For example, Stafford and Daly (1984) noted that conversations about medical instructions, safety warnings, and directions are more memorable than other types of conversations. The MOP perspective suggests that these types of conversations are more memorable than others because they deviate in more ways from what is expected by the MOPs being used to process them. On the other hand, these very same types of conversations might be quite forgettable if comprehended by memory structures that anticipated their occurrence. Perhaps this is why medical instructions from doctors, warnings from our parents, and directions from professors seem to be routinely ignored and forgotten.

Finally, the MOP perspective also provides insight into the occurrence of memory confusions. The source of memory confusions, within this perspective, is the sharing of scenes by different MOPs. Scenes organized by one MOP can also be organized by others. Memory confusions take place when it is forgotten to which MOP a particular scene-based memory was connected. As the motivation for engaging in a scene is specified by the goal of the MOP that organizes it, knowing a given scene occurred provides no help in understanding why it occurred. In other words, you might know that a given topic was discussed but be unable to recall why it came up. The inability to access the explanation for a scene occurring stems from being unable to remember which MOP organized the scene initially. Clearly, the conversation MOP perspective suggests many interesting implications in terms of conversational memory and provides an account of results reported to date.

Updating Knowledge

Dynamic memory theory includes the word *dynamic* because memory is envisioned as changing in response to persons' experiences. Scenes, MOPs, meta-MOPs, and other dynamic-memory structures initially arise due to identification of similarities or regularities encountered in experiences. When subsequently activated in other episodes, these abstracted memory structures give rise to a variety of expectations about the people, setting, and course of events. To the extent that correspondence exists between expectations and events, the abstracted memory structures incorporate the individual episodes into their more general knowledge base. However, anomalies are bound to arise, and expectations are bound to be incorrect. These incorrect expectations provide the impetus for updating knowledge. As Schank (1986) noted, little can be learned from success other than that one's knowledge works as is. Although success can increase faith in one's knowledge, failure permits learning by activating change in one's knowledge. In other words, updating occurs when sufficient reason exists to modify, replace, and/or reorganize parts of memory, and failure (rather than success) provides this sufficient reason (Schank, 1982b).

Failure occurs when current knowledge generates predictions that are wrong, which can happen because expected events do not materialize or because events materialize that are not expected. Failed expectations are recognized because basic believability checks (e.g., expectations about sequence, temporal separation, roles, and limits) are applied to all input to detect anomalies and are combined with fine-grained tests (e.g., action decomposition, action consistency, plan choice) to identify inaccurate and/or inadequate expectations (Leake, 1989; Schank & Leake, 1990). Expectation failures are then stored with the knowledge structure(s) that generated them. An index is created between the memory of an individual event and the MOPs, scenes, scripts, and other structures active when the failure occurred. Individual events conforming to expectations are incorporated into the general actions represented in the activated scenes, whereas those that fail to conform are stored not as general actions, but in terms of the way(s) they deviate from expectations about those general actions.

Such indexing of events to violated expectations provides both the ability to recognize whether repeated violations of particular expectations occur and the capability to generate explanations for the failure (Schank, 1986). The source of the expectation failure is traced, and change, if it is to occur, is based on the explanation that is generated for the failure. Explanation is at the heart of the workings of dynamic memory. It is through explanation that (a) memory changes, (b) knowledge is updated, (c) learning occurs, and, as is seen in the next section, (d) understanding ensues. For example, consider the first time you expected you would shake hands with another person when meeting him or her and this handshake did not occur or occurred awkwardly. This episode was indexed by this (and any other) expectation violation in terms of the reason generated for the failure. Possible reasons for the failure of this expectation about handshaking are many, ranging from a misunderstanding of the situation (e.g., not as formal as you thought it was) to dispositional inferences about the other's character, values, and/or beliefs (e.g., the other person dislikes being touched, the other person is angry, etc.) to relational assessments (e.g., not on friendly or cordial terms) to the occurrence of an anomaly (e.g., this is truly an exception; Schank, 1982b, 1986; Schank et al., 1986). If the explanation for violation of the handshaking expectation is traced to a misunderstanding of the situation, then knowledge contained in the relevant physical scenes will be updated, whereas if the explanation is traced to it being a true anomaly, then memory structures will not change other than to retain the indexed failure. The point is that knowledge updating is an explanation-based process.

If an explanation for the expectation failure has not been generated on the basis of its first occurrence, when a subsequent failure is encountered within the same structure, the previous case of failure is accessible (through is indices). Generalizations drawn between cases of repeated failures specify what is "missing" in knowledge, and thereby guide the dynamic updating of knowledge structures (Schank & Leake, 1990). *ALFRED* is a computer-simulated model concerned with understanding articles in the domain of economics that illustrates how failure-driven reminding leads to updating of knowledge structures (Riesbeck, 1981):

> The system uses rules that reflect everyday knowledge. If one of those rules of thumb fails, an *exception* episode describing the failure and the recovery procedure is indexed under the faulty rule. When the next failure of the rule is encountered, the original failure is remembered. The previous case provides information to aid in revision of the problematic rule: if it is possible to group the failure episodes into a single class, the rule can be modified to deal correctly with that class. (Schank & Leake, 1990, p. 357)

The explanation generated for the expectation failure is the identification of similarities in the "failure episodes." As with the stimulus for dynamic-memory structures to initially arise, these similarities give rise to new structures and determine how and in what ways old knowledge is changed and updated.

Recently, Planalp and her colleagues (Planalp, 1985, 1987, 1989; Planalp & Honeycutt, 1985; Planalp & Rivers, 1988; Planalp, Rutherford, & Honeycutt, 1988) focused on changes in relational knowledge with findings that are remarkably consistent with the MOP perspective and dynamic memory theory. First, relational knowledge has been found to involve multiple-knowledge structures, rather than be contained in a relational schema. Moreover, these relational-knowledge structures have been found to exist at different levels of abstraction, and evidence suggests that these structures overlay each other when interpreting particular events, traced through linkages between knowledge about generic relationship types (e.g., friends, marriages, etc.), specific relationships (e.g., our marriage), specific people (e.g., self, partner), and so on (Planalp & Rivers, 1988). These findings are completely consistent with the script, scene, MOP, and meta-MOP perspective of dynamic memory theory, where multiple-knowledge structures are commonly activated to guide and process ongoing interaction. In fact, related research (Cantor, Mischel, & Schwarz, 1982; Reiser, 1986b) emphasizes that the utility of person and relational information is its connection with event-knowledge structures.

A second finding of Planalp's research on updating relational knowledge concerns the nature of the events that generated the change. Without fail, these events (e.g., engaging in deception, betraying a confidence) are described as unexpected, unpredictable (except in hindsight), unusual, hard to assimilate into existing knowledge, and coming like bolts from the blue. In other words, violations of expectations (i.e., failures) are stimulating the updating of relational knowledge. Interestingly, this research also notes that relational knowledge can be separated, to some degree, from the certainty with which it is held. As noted previously, successful prediction generates increased certainty, whereas failure generates change.

A third finding of Planalp's research is that the explanations found for the expectation violations, rather than the quantity of such violations, determined the updating of relational knowledge. Changes in relational knowledge were based on the reasons that individuals generated for these unexpected events occurring. Explanation was pervasive in the accounts of relational-knowledge updating, although in the relatively few instances in which it did not occur, the events were "less unexpected" (Planalp & Rivers, 1988). Dynamic memory theory sees this explanation process as the way of identifying features to change so that increased certainty can ensue. "In order to modify our knowledge structures in useful ways, it is crucial that we determine the conditions that caused any expectation failure" (Schank et al., 1986, p. 649). Uncertainty did increase when these events that violated expectations occurred, but then it decreased again as time passed by (Planalp & Honeycutt, 1985; Planalp et al., 1988). This trajectory is directly derivable from dynamic memory theory: Expectation violations increase uncertainty; once explanations for the events are found, more certainty should ensue. Successful prediction then reinforces the certainty with which the revised knowledge is held in the future, whereas further expectation violations would reduce certainty once again. Interpretation and integration of knowledge is, as Planalp and Rivers noted, a very important focus in understanding communication and interpersonal relationships.

A fourth finding of interest in Planalp's research focuses on the way in which relational knowledge is updated. Dynamic memory theory allows for (a) adding new structures (scripts, scenes, MOPs, meta-MOPs, etc.), (b) eliminating old structures, and (c) modifying existing structures. New structures are added when new functions need to be performed (a new or different goal is being pursued) or when an event is unrelated to present structures. Old structures are eliminated when they no longer serve a useful purpose, often determined by repeated failures of expectations generated by the structures. Modification occurs when performance is suboptimal, although what structure(s) are modified depends on which ones generated the violated expectation (Schank et al., 1986). All of these methods of updating knowledge hinge on the exact explanation generated for the expectation failure, implying that different explanations for failure will result in differences in how knowledge is updated. Planalp and her colleagues (Planalp & Honeycutt, 1985; Planalp & Rivers, 1988) reported significant differences in the exact relational beliefs and knowledge structures that are altered, as well as in how these beliefs are then related to each other. These differences can be accounted for in dynamic-memory theory by tracking how the failed predictions were accounted for. Wrong assumptions, insufficient/incomplete information, misinterpreting cues, and the relational partner changing were among reasons offered for unanticipated relational events (Planalp et al., 1988). These reasons were based on (a) evidence of recurrent patterns of behavior (noticed in hindsight), (b) co-occurrences of events, and (c) new information (Planalp & Rivers, 1988). Given the varying reasons generated for updating relational knowledge, it is unlikely that a consistent updating pattern will be found, and that changes in one particular structural component would be related to changes in some other structural component. Dynamic memory theory would predict that changes in one structural component will affect changes in others only to the degree that both structures were instrumental in generating the violated expectation. Explanations are found to focus on events central to the making of the prediction that failed, as well as being responsive to the point in sequential order where failure occurs (Leddo & Abelson, 1986).

Finally, Planalp's research also offers insight into the content of various relational-knowledge structures. Among the more significant results is the finding that persons had somewhat different contents that were patterned in substantially different ways in their relational-knowledge structures (Planalp & Rivers, 1988). In other words, scripts and scenes in relational-knowledge structures differed, as did the grouping of those scenes into various relational-knowledge structures. Because experience is the determiner of memory structures—failure in predictions guiding learning and success serving as a reinforcer of what has been learned—some differences in knowledge structures are highly likely to occur. Personal experiences in relationships are likely to be highly varied across people and, as a result, lead to more varied memory representations than personal experiences which are more societally or culturally constrained (i.e., less idiosyncratically responsive). Nonetheless, both the personal and the societal aspects of the scenes are worth pursuing and investigating in future research. The role of explanation in creating and modifying those knowledge structures is exciting for helping gain purchase on how idiosyncratic relational knowledge is developed.

Understanding

Explanation is not only critical to updating knowledge, but it is the very essence of understanding. In dynamic memory theory, understanding entails finding the knowledge structures where an experience fits; if these structures are located, then understanding transpires. "We feel we have understood when we know where a new input belongs in memory" (Schank, 1986, p. 8). Finding the right knowledge structures means de facto that an explanation for the behavior has been identified. People often account for such "understood" behavior by implying it makes sense to them because it is a known regularity (i.e., a regularity noticed and abstracted into scripts, scenes, MOPs, etc. in memory). For example, consider a married couple that divided household tasks, such that the husband regularly took out the garbage. If the couple was asked why he did so, an automatic explanation would tend to be generated that simply references that it is a known convention for this couple (e.g., "he's always done it," "he takes out the garbage, I mow the lawn," or "I don't know, that is just the way it is"). This type of explanation does not really account for why these duties were split as they were; rather, it is a way to respond that "makes sense" (Schank, 1986). Nonetheless, understanding occurs because an explanation is automatically available; the knowledge structure where the experience fits is known. In other words, in the MOP perspective, understanding is not a function of choosing which hypothesis might best explain some event, but rather one of verifying expectations (Martin, 1989).

Sillars's work on spouses' understanding of each other (Sillars, 1985, 1989; Sillars, Pike, Jones, & Murphy, 1984; Sillars & Scott, 1983; Sillars & Weisberg, 1987; Sillars, Weisberg, Burggraf, & Zietlow, 1987) is consistent with dynamic memory theory's stance on understanding. As discussed in the previous section, in dynamic memory theory, relational knowledge is acquired and updated based on relational experiences and the violation of expectations. Consequently, common experiences that require representation along with the opportunity they provide to test expectations should, over time, lead to increases in mutual understanding (the accuracy of spouses' perceptions). A robust finding in research on spousal understanding is that common experience does increase accuracy in understanding (Sillars & Scott, 1983). Zietlow (1986) reported consistent gains in accuracy of spouses' understanding of each other as relationships progress from beginning to latter stages across the life span. Changes in relational knowledge (decreased use of social and cultural stereotypes, increased use of acquired and specialized communication codes) are accompanied by improved attributional accuracy (Sillars, 1985). In the words of dynamic memory theory, explanations become increasingly accurate over time, which is reflected in the development of more individuated knowledge structures.

Despite these gains in mutual understanding, married couples do overestimate the degree to which each person accurately understands and is understood by the other (see Sillars, 1985, 1989; Sillars et al., 1984; Sillars & Scott, 1983). Increased mutual understanding does not mean that couples understand each other perfectly or, for that matter, even very well. However, understanding of a spouse is higher for various instrumental attitudes (money, cleaning/caring for the house, leisure activities, career and work pressures) than for more abstract relational and companionate aspects of marriage (e.g., affection, communication, irritability, criticism; Sillars et al., 1987). Dynamic memory theory accounts for these findings in terms of how knowledge is updated, predicting that accurate understanding will be less likely when relational experiences do not permit sufficient grounds for acquiring knowledge or testing the knowledge that was previously learned. As Sillars (1985) noted, expectations of instrumental attitudes are more likely to be tested in ongoing experience because they are closely tied to everyday activities, occurring more frequently and being more readily observable. By contrast, the relational and companionate aspects of marriage are cloaked in ambiguity; they are rarely directly addressed verbally, being read from cues whose features are coded with less consistency and consensus across people. In the perspective of dynamic memory theory, lower relational understanding is virtually assured, given that violations of expectations are less likely to be noticed and explained accurately. In addition, spouses simply may not have much opportunity to test particular perceptions. Much of marital interaction is of a routine nature, where stereotypic knowledge is sufficient for understanding (Sillars, 1985). These routine interactions leave less room for locating inaccurate knowledge about a spouse simply because it will be activated less frequently. Because knowledge structures are commonly found that match experience, marital partners think they understand each other more than they actually do. This understanding is based on the ability of their knowledge structures to explain each other's behavior, even though those explanations may not be accurate.

Understanding occurs by finding where an experience belongs in memory. A handy explanation for that experience is available if knowledge structures that fit the experience can be located. The experience is understood because it can be accounted for by existing knowledge structures. However, experiences also happen that seem incomprehensible. In dynamic memory theory, this incomprehensibility is a direct indicator that insufficient knowledge structures are available for processing the experience and, as a result, the experience is not well understood. Unusual or out-of-the-ordinary experiences will not be understood until they are explained. Through explanation, knowledge is updated and memory is reorganized. In other words, dynamic memory theory would predict that understanding of a spouse could become more accurate only when the spouse acted in unusual (i.e., unexpected) ways, which Sillars (1989) referred to as a "deviance monitoring" or "autistic" system. The detection of anomalies (i.e., the tracking of deviations from expectations) is a routine part of understanding within dynamic memory theory (Leake, 1989). Sillars et al. (1984) found that spouses who communicate in a more negative manner (e.g., by faulting, rejecting, or hostilely questioning the partner) are more accurately understood than spouses who communicate in more positive or ambiguous ways. Sillars (1989) argued that positive messages are "more conventional and expected" (p. 315) and that they "do not increase understanding much; they confirm prior impressions" (p. 319). Dynamic memory theory suggests why these unexpected messages may function in this manner: Explanation generated more accurate understanding.

A number of points need clarification concerning increased accuracy of understanding. First, more accurate understanding of a spouse need not come about through the use of negative messages; unexpected messages, whether negative or not, should have more impact on the how accurately a spouse is perceived. Of course, this statement presumes that an unexpected message can be accounted for and that the explanation is accurate. Not all explanations for unexpected events will be correct, despite a spouse believing he or she has achieved improved understanding of the partner by having generated a new explanation. Repeated violations of expectations may be necessary for more accurate understanding to occur. Finally, understanding that is achieved through an initially inaccurate explanation may eventually become accurate because it alters the interaction behavior or one or both of the spouses. Because explanation alters the content and/or structure of memory, and because this updated knowledge is then used to guide one's own behavior as well as generate expectations about another's, an inaccurate explanation might be corroborated in future interactions. For example,

> When intimate couples and members of other dyads attribute relationship problems to the negative traits of each other, they are then likely to communicate in a negative, verbally competitive or ambiguous manner that often provides the other person with additional confirmation for his or her attributions about the source of these communications. . . . Therefore, over time, communication patterns generate increasingly greater (self-confirming) evidence for the validity of attributions about the partner. In long-standing conflicts it may be extremely difficult to break this cycle. . . . (Sillars, 1985, p. 285).

From the perspective of dynamic memory theory, these self-confirming spirals are difficult to break because neither partner has any substantive reason for updating his or her knowledge structures.

Admittedly, dynamic memory theory paints a somewhat pessimistic picture about the ability of any two people to ever fully (i.e., accurately) understand each other. All understanding is based on each person's experiences and explanations generated for them. These explanations are dependent on the various goals and plans being pursued, as well as related beliefs and expectations. Intentions can be misread: Scenes are attached to many MOPs, and each MOP is one possible reason a cointeractant produced the scene. Intentions can be misread if the "explanation" for the scene is attributed to different MOPs. Sillars (1989) noted that any given speech act can be construed in a number of ways (e.g., advising, needling, explaining, lecturing, requesting information, requesting action). Dynamic memory theory suggests that the way messages will be construed hinges greatly on the memory structures activated to understand them. Clearly, people can provide signals (direct and indirect) that incorrect construals have been made. However, different goals for an interaction will activate different memory structures, and these signals may not always be found acceptable. Relational conflict is a context where differences occur in terms of persons' goals and where disagreement over construals are common. The issue underlying a conflict is frequently perceived differently between husbands and wives: The interpretation of what each spouse has said is a common point of disagreement, and personal agendas of spouses differ greatly (Sillars, 1989; Sillars & Scott, 1983; Sillars & Weisberg, 1987). Simply put, "people who have different goals, beliefs, expectations, and general lifestyles will understand identical episodes quite differently" (Schank, 1986, p. 3). Schank argued that full understanding can only occur when people have sufficient shared experiences that create similar memory structures and when their goals for any given episode are the same.

Despite the pessimistic assessment that dynamic memory theory offers for full understanding, improved understanding is fundamental to the perspective. Dynamic memory is meant to be functional, changing when it cannot perform adequately. Consequently, despite detours and blockages, the trajectory in updating knowledge is aimed in the direction of more accurate understanding. This improvement in understanding is dependent on experience, in terms of both generating knowledge structures and changing them. To the extent that experiences are predictable and relatively unvarying, memory will not change significantly in content and/or structure. To the extent that experiences are unpredictable, memory will change significantly in content as these episodes are tagged and in structure to the extent that these episodes can be explained. Future episodes are then understood (i.e., explained) because where they belong in memory is known.

CONCLUSION

The conversation MOP perspective offers exciting possibilities for understanding conversational behavior. Not only is this perspective able to provide a unified account of the flexible production of talk, but it is also simultaneously able to broadly account for such related phenomena as (a) conversational recall, (b) relational knowledge updating, and (c) relational understanding. Although the MOP perspective is certainly not the only account that could be offered for these phenomena, it is a particularly useful one: (a) It is consistent with what is known about cognition, (b) it accounts for cross-contextual application of knowledge, (c) it provides on unified explanation for flexible adaptation of routines, and (d) (as is discussed) it can be applied across almost any type of communicative episode (e.g., conversations, newspaper story reading, small-group interactions, computerized advice-giving systems, relational growth–decay trajectories, etc.).

First, unlike its theoretical ancestor of script theory, the MOP perspective does not conflict with basic principles of cognitive processing. The concept of a *script* was based on the presumption that whole sequences of events were stored together for each type of social sequence having a given situational context. "Because scripts are inherently specific to particular experiences, slightly different experiences would require different scripts. Yet most of those thousands of scripts would be partially redundant, with actions and combinations of actions appearing in many scripts" (Smith, 1991, p. 391). Schank (1982b) noted that the seemingly endless number of scripts such a presumption requires would make storing, retrieving, and updating these knowledge structures virtually impossible. Moreover, Bower, Black, and Turner (1979) found that memory confusions occurred between stories that called on different, albeit similar, scripts (e.g., visits to the doctor and the dentist). If different scripts were stored as separate memory structures, these confusions should not have occurred.

In contrast with scripts, MOPs are not situation-specific, prepackaged, action sequences. MOPs contain "smaller, more flexible structures" that are "computationally more tractable and better model the processes by which people explicate discourse" (Smith, 1991, p. 391). Rather than storing an introduction or a waiting room scene inside each script, any MOP that needs those general actions taps into the needed scene stored in one location in memory. In dynamic memory theory, scenes are shared by different MOPs rather than replicated in each knowledge structure where they are needed (Schank & Leake, 1990; Turner, 1990). Scenes are accessed via pointers from whatever MOPs might require accomplishment of the instrumental goal of the scene (Smith, 1991). Updating of knowledge to alter how introductions occur or how behavior unfolds in waiting rooms requires only updating one shared scene rather than countless scripts. Because scenes are used and re-used, knowledge is stored more efficiently (Smith, 1991; Turner, 1990). "Most of the redundancies in scripts are wrung out of the representations" (Smith, 1991, p. 392). This more efficient and shared use of knowledge, which is flexibly deployed to perform many different tasks, better conforms to what is known about human cognition (Smith, 1991).

Equally important to the MOP perspective conforming to basic principles of cognitive processing is that it also promotes and accounts for cross-contextual learning (Schank & Leake, 1990). Scenes speak to what is general across contexts where a set of actions having the same instrumental goal might be useful. Because scenes are shared between MOPs, what is learned in introductions in an interview setting would be available for use in meeting a president. What is learned in ending conversations with friends would be available for use in ending meetings with employees. Script theory (and other theoretical ancestors) has difficulty accounting for such cross-contextual learning. Dynamic memory theory focuses on precisely this process of change and learning, generalization and differentiation, and applying what one knows to new and/or novel episodes.

The conformity to cognitive principles and accounting of cross-contextual learning is what makes the MOP perspective able to account for the flexible adaptation of behavior: to explain the seeming contradiction of invention and convention in conversation as well as other behavior. Scripts (and similar knowledge structures) cannot respond to the unexpected; only an adaptive representation such as a MOP is capable of flexibly responding to novel events (Smith, 1991). "Scenes can be borrowed from familiar episodes in order to understand episodes that are entirely unfamiliar or contain novel variations" (Smith, 1991, p. 392). This perspective removes from the study of conversation the expectation of routinization followed by the surprise of adaptation (or, conversely, the expectation of accommodation and the surprise of convention). The MOP perspective expects the flexible adaptation of routines.

Applied to conversational interaction, these inherent features of the perspective are quite useful. "One advantage of conversation MOPs is their ability to capture both the conventions found in natural language and the goals that these conventions serve" (Turner, 1990, p. 19). Dynamic-memory theory and MOPs suggest: (a) how "segments" of conversations occurring in widely varying contexts and for widely varying overall goals could appear similar in structure, (b) how conversational structures can be embedded hierarchically and sequenced linearly, and (c) how understanding is related to production of conversational behavior. Perhaps most exciting is that the MOP perspective as a theory of human cognition generates expectations consistent with empirical research on conversational behavior.

However, the ultimate test of the perspective will come in its ability to: (a) generate new research, (b) adapt to new principles of cognition and communication, and (c) incorporate future research findings. The first of these three tests is currently underway: The MOP perspective has been found by many to be heuristically provocative across a variety of domains of communicative behavior. For example, Lebowitz (1980) designed a computer program called *IPP* to read newspaper stories about terrorist attacks and used MOPs to provide expectations and make inductive generalizations about what was read. From reading newspaper stories about Italy when the Red Brigades were active, IPP formed the generalization that the usual victims of kidnapping in Italy were businessmen. IPP built new knowledge structures on the basis of generalizations and used them to organize episodes in memory. Thus, IPP could recognize a story as commonplace, and could also notice novel aspects of a story.

Pavitt (1993) recently used the MOP perspective to understand small-group interaction, arguing the group discussion process is best represented by a type of conversation MOP called a *recursive MOP*. Pavitt argued that group discussion is both linear (progressing through stages) and cyclical (involving "reach testing"), but that decision-making routines are also adapted to task demands and the social structure of the group. As a result, Pavitt argued that "group discussion procedure is best approached as a top-down process, and well represented by a model known as the 'conversation MOP'" (Pavitt, 1993, p. 150). Pavitt examined the sequencing of scenes in small-group decision making and concluded that: "The findings of this study suggest that belief about ideal group discussion procedure may be structured hierarchically in a manner reminiscent of the integration of linear and reach-testing models and well represented by a recursive MOP" (p. 166). Pavitt's research suggests the reach that the MOP perspective may have across types of communication episodes. As Pavitt noted, his results are "consistent with claim that the basic sequence may generalize across any type of face-to face communicative encounter" (p. 166).

Also indicative of the possibilities offered by the MOP perspective is research conducted by Turner and Cullingford (Turner, 1990, 1991a; Turner & Cullingford, 1989a, 1989b), which relies on the perspective of the conversation MOP for the development and successful implementation of an interactive, advice-giving system called *JUDIS* on a computer. Propelling these researchers' interest in the conversation MOP as a basis for their work is the MOP's ability to account for both convention and invention, flexibility and routine, pattern and pliability. These artificial-intelligence (AI) researchers are interested in modeling a skilled advice giver (i.e., a competent communicator). Communication competence is, in part, dependent on knowledge to guide the communicative performance. Unlike other theories of conversational behavior, the MOP perspective specifies the type of knowledge needed and offers general structures that could be taught to persons to help them improve their communication skills.

As a final example, Honeycutt and colleagues (Honeycutt, in press; Honeycutt & Cantrill, 1991; Honeycutt, Cantrill, & Allen, 1992; Honeycutt, Cantrill, & Greene, 1989) used the MOP perspective to understand the growth and decay of interpersonal relationships. These researchers have focused on relational meta-MOPs that might "call on" an informal-conversation MOP during relational initiation. Not only does Honeycutt's research extend the conversation MOP focus, but it does so by incorporating it: It moves the focus from one conversation at the start of a relationship to a series of conversations comprising a relationship. Moreover, this change in focus from MOP to meta-MOP at a theoretical level is found to be consistent with assumptions and knowledge of developmental models of relationships at an empirical level. Results from Honeycutt's research have identified prototypical memory structures for the general actions involved in both the process of relational escalation and the process of deescalation. Relational experience was also found to help shape these escalation and deescalation memory structures in terms of both the number and nature of relational actions comprising them.

These four applications of the MOP perspective to communicative phenomena other than conversational interaction suggest that the perspective is heuristically provocative and has broad explanatory power. However, further tests both within these domains and in other communicative domains will be needed to ultimately know the true viability of the perspective. McPhee (chapter 7, this volume) argues that cognitive theories of communication will never be viable because they ignore the inherent social nature of interaction. However, rather than divorcing the cognitive system from the social system, dynamic memory theory and the MOP perspective integrate these (and other) systems together. Dynamic memory theory explains (a) the process by which individuals come to recognize and understand social norms, (b) how individuals come to represent and construct the social world in which they interact, and (c) how their experiences influence their understandings and their understandings influence their experiences. The MOP perspective merges social experiences and cognitive representation. In this perspective, memory is far more than a recall instrument; it is a living understanding and explanation of one's experiences and life. Although primarily a cognitive theory, the MOP perspective offers an account of intrapersonal (cognitive), interpersonal (social), and even cultural (conventions) experience. The perspective is consistent with our general knowledge as well as our conversational knowledge. In other words, the cognitive system envisioned by dynamic memory theory has integrity in its own right, but it also interfaces particularly well with other human systems (intra- and interindividual). I believe it is a mistake to presume primarily cognitive theories must (or even should) be divorced from social theory, or to presume that a memory-based explanation must sort out what is cognitive and what is social. Cognitive and social systems are interrelated; a theory of memory that is ultimately found to be viable will have to bridge these arbitrarily defined domains. One of the strengths of dynamic-memory theory is that it can account for intrapersonal, interpersonal (social), and cultural outcomes, and that the memory structures are responsive to one's social experiences. In my mind, it is necessary that dynamic memory structures be "built from social materials, according to a social blueprint" (McPhee, chapter 7, this volume. I would want nothing else to be the case.

However, many alternative explanations, some cognitive and some not, exist to explain (a) the sequencing of conversational topics, (b) the timing of the topics, (c) the development of talk on the topics, (d) the influence of goals and context on topical selection, (e) the recall of conversations, (f) the updating of relational knowledge, or (g) the ability to talk in routine ways in novel situations. The issue is not whether alternative explanations for these individual phenomena exist—they do. The issue is whether these explanations can account for the wide range of conversational and communicative behavior, rather than offer only piecemeal accounts for a few limited regularities. Dynamic memory theory and the conversation MOP perspective provide one unified, parsimonious answer to these questions. Alternative explanations that can simultaneously account for the full range of these phenomena are harder to come by. Taken as a group, the body of research findings makes alternative explanations more difficult to generate. So, yes this chapter focuses on "social patterns of initial interaction about which individuals are knowledgeable, due to experienced routines, norms, and bases for self-interpreting action" (McPhee, chapter 7). The issue is how these phenomena are to be explained: How do individuals become knowledgeable? How are these social patterns learned? Where does that knowledge reside and how is it organized? How is it that people can access it and use it? How are experiences recognized and enacted as routines or norms? And how are these routines and norms flexibly adapted and used? McPhee begs the question by assigning all this knowledge to the "social" realm, with no explanation of how the individual bridges between the social and the cognitive. Dynamic memory theory and the MOP perspective offers one account for how social experiences interface with intrapersonal understanding, and thereby account for fixed yet flexible conversational behavior.

The MOP perspective is not without problems, however. First, further specification of the theory would be useful (for debate, see Schank et al., 1986, and following responses). For example, clarification is needed concerning how

MOPs are overlaid and how scenes are selected. Wilensky (1983) formulated one account of how actions participate in scenes and scenes participate in episodes in his work on planning. However, more work needs to be done on how instrumental goals (of scenes) are organized for the attainment of higher level goals (of MOPSs). Similarly, intact MOPs are "fossilized plans" (Schank & Leake, 1990, p. 359) and must be interfaced with other principles of on-line adaptation that are also simultaneously guiding behavior.

Second, clearer principles that permit the perspective to be more easily put to the test must be developed. Although it is possible to derive tests that permit the theory to be determined to be false, some of the theory's claims are sufficiently unclear so that any reported finding could be explained. For example, the perspective permits variations in the ambiguity of topical content in the pursuit of various goals (e.g., evasiveness, deception, privacy, etc.), although it is silent about how that variation is achieved. Similarly, although presumptions of local and global coherence are hinted at in the perspective, mechanisms by which such outcomes are achieved within the framework of the conversation MOP are not at all clear. Nonetheless, the perspective is heuristically provocative and potentially powerful in its ability to account for a wide range of communication behavior. Further exploration of its possibilities will certainly alter the perspective and even, perhaps, ultimately lead to its rejection. The outcome of this exploration is bound to be positive, however, regardless of the final judgment of the MOP perspective and dynamic memory theory; what emerges will be a more accurate explanation of conversational behavior.

REFERENCES

Abelson, R. P. (1976). Script processing in attitude formation and decision-making. In J. S. Carroll & J. W. Payne (Eds.), *Cognition and social behavior* (pp. 33–45). Hillsdale, NJ: Lawrence Erlbaum Associates.

Abelson, R. P. (1981). Psychological status of the script concept. *American Psychologist, 36,* 715–729.

Bell, R. A. (1987). Social involvement. In J. C. McCroskey & J. A. Daly (Eds.), *Personality and interpersonal communication* (pp. 195–242). Newbury Park, CA: Sage.

Benoit, W., & Benoit, P. (1987, May). *Conversational memory employing cued and free recall.* Paper presented at the annual meeting of the International Communication Association, Montreal, Canada.

Berger, C. R., & Kellermann, K. (1983). To ask or not to ask: Is that a question? In R. Bostrom (Eds.), *Communication Yearbook 7* (pp. 342–368). Newbury Park, CA: Sage.

Berger, C. R., & Kellermann, K. (1989). Personal opacity and social information gathering: Explorations in strategic communication. *Communication Research, 16,* 314–351.

Berger, C. R., & Kellermann, K. (1994). Acquiring social information. In J. Daly & J. Weimann (Eds.), *Strategic interpersonal communication* (pp. 1–31). Hillsdale, NJ: Lawrence Erlbaum Associates.

Bower, G. H., Black, J. B., & Turner, J. T. (1979). Scripts in text comprehension and memory. *Cognitive Psychology, 11,* 177–200.

Cantor, N., Mischel, W., & Schwarz, J. C. (1982). A prototype analysis of psychological situations. *Cognitive Psychology, 14,* 45–77.

Cappella, J. N. (1981). Mutual influence in expressive behavior: Adult-adult and infant-adult dyadic interaction. *Psychological Bulletin, 89,* 101–132.

Clark, H. H. (1992). *Arenas of language use.* Chicago, IL: University of Chicago Press.

Clarke, D. D., & Argyle, M. (1982). Conversation sequences. In C. Fraser & K. R. Scherer (Eds.), *Advances in the social psychology of language* (pp. 159–204). Cambridge, England: Cambridge University Press.

Coulmas, F. (Ed.). (1981). *Conversational routine: Explorations in standardized communication situations and prepatterned speech.* The Hague: Mouton.

Craig, R. T., & Tracy, K. (Eds.). (1983). *Conversational coherence: Form, structure, and strategy.* Newbury Park, CA: Sage.

Cullingford, R. E., & Kolodner, J. L. (1986). Interactive advice giving. In *Proceedings of the 1986 IEEE International Conference on Systems, Man and Cybernetics* (pp. 709–714). Atlanta, GA.

Daly, J., & Weimann, J. (Eds.). (1994). *Strategic interpersonal communication.* Hillsdale, NJ: Lawrence Erlbaum Associates.

Douglas, W. (1983). Scripts and self-monitoring: When does being a high self-monitor really make a difference? *Human Communication Research, 10,* 81–96.

Douglas, W. (1984). Initial interaction scripts: When knowing is behaving. *Human Communication Research, 11,* 203–220.

Dyer, M. G. (1983). *In-depth understanding: A computer model of integrated processing for narrative comprehension.* Cambridge, MA: MIT Press.

Giles, H., Mulac, A., Bradac, J. J., & Johnson, P. (1987). Speech accommodation theory: The first decade and beyond. In M. L. McLaughlin (Ed.), *Communication yearbook 10* (pp. 13–48). Newbury Park, CA: Sage.

Honeycutt, J. M. (in press). Memory structures for the rise and fall of personal relationships. In S. Duck (Ed.), *Individuals in relationships.* Newbury Park, CA: Sage.

Honeycutt, J. M., & Cantrill, J. G. (1991). Using expectations of relational actions to predict number of intimate relationships: Don Juan and Romeo unmasked. *Communication Reports, 4,* 14–21.

Honeycutt, J. M., Cantrill, J. G., & Allen, T. (1992). Memory structures for relational decay: A cognitive test of sequencing of de-escalating actions and stages. *Human Communication Research, 18,* 528–562.

Honeycutt, J. M., Cantrill, J. G., & Greene, R. W. (1989). Memory structures for relational escalation: A cognitive test of the sequencing of relational actions and stages. *Human Communication Research, 16,* 62–90.

Hovy, E. H., & Schank, R. C. (1984). Language generation by computer. In B. G. Bara & G. Guida (Eds.), *Computational models of natural language processing* (pp. 165–195). Amsterdam: North-Holland.

Hurtig, R. (1977). Toward a functional theory of discourse. In R. O. Freedle (Ed.), *Discourse production and comprehension* (pp. 89–106). Norwood: Ablex.

Johnson, G. (1986). *Machinery of the mind: Inside the new science of artificial intelligence.* Redmond, WA: Microsoft Press.

Jones, W. (1982). Loneliness and social behavior. In L. Peplau & D. Perlman (Eds.), *Loneliness: A sourcebook of current theory, research, and therapy* (pp. 238–252). New York: Wiley-Interscience.

Keenan, J. M., MacWhinney, B., & Mayhew, D. (1977). Pragmatics in memory: A study of natural conversations. *Journal of Verbal Learning and Verbal Behavior, 16,* 549–560.

Kellermann, K. (1984). *A formal model of information exchange in social interaction.* Unpublished doctoral dissertation, Northwestern University, Evanston, IL.

Kellermann, K. (1991). The conversation MOP: II. Progression through scenes in discourse. *Human Communication Research, 17,* 385–414.

Kellermann, K. (in preparation). The conversation MOP: IV. Using the universal scene in discourse.

Kellermann, K., & Berger, C. R. (1984). Affect and the acquisition of social information: Sit back, relax, and tell me about yourself. In R. Bostrom (Ed.), *Communication yearbook 8* (pp. 412–445). Newbury Park, CA: Sage.

Kellermann, K., Broetzmann, S., Lim, T., & Kitao, K. (1989). The conversation MOP: Scenes in the stream of discourse. *Discourse Processes, 12,* 27–62.

Kellermann, K., & Lim, T. (1989). Conversational acquaintance: The flexibility of routinized behavior. In B. Dervin, L. Grossberg, B. J. O'Keefe, & E. Wartella (Eds.), *Rethinking communication: Vol. 2. Paradigm exemplars* (pp. 172–187). Newbury Park, CA: Sage.

Kellermann, K., & Lim, T. (1990). The conversation MOP: III. Timing of scenes in discourse. *Journal of Personality and Social Psychology, 59,* 1163–1179.

Kellermann, K., Reynolds, R., & Chen, J. (1991). Strategies of conversational retreat: When parting is not sweet sorrow. *Communication Monographs, 58,* 362–383.

Kemper, S., & Thissen, D. (1981). Memory for the dimension of requests. *Journal of Verbal Learning and Verbal Behavior, 20,* 552–563.

Kintsch, W. (1972). Notes on the structure of semantic memory. In E. Tulving & W. Donaldson (Eds.), *Organization of memory* (pp. 247–308). New York: Academic.

Kolodner, J. L. (1983a). Maintaining organization in a dynamic long-term memory. *Cognitive Science, 7,* 243–280.

Kolodner, J. L. (1983b). Reconstructive memory: A computer model. *Cognitive Science, 7,* 281–328.

Kolodner, J. L. (1984a). *Retrieval and organization strategies in conceptual memory: A computer model.* Hillsdale, NJ: Lawrence Erlbaum Associates.

Kolodner, J. L. (1984b). Knowledge-based self-organizing memory for events. In A. Elithorn & R. Banerji (Eds.), *Artificial and human intelligence: Edited review papers presented at the International NATO Symposium on artificial and human intelligence sponsored by the Special Programme Panel held in Lyon, France, October, 1981* (pp. 57–66). Amsterdam: North-Holland.

Kolodner, J. L. (1989). Selecting the best case for a case-based reasoner. In *Program of the eleventh annual conference of the Cognitive Science Society, 16–19 August 1989, Ann Arbor, Michigan* (pp. 155–162). Hillsdale, NJ: Lawrence Erlbaum Associates.

Kolodner, J. L., & Barsalou, L. W. (1982). Psychological issues raised by an AI model of reconstructive memory. In *Proceedings of the Fourth Annual Conference of the Cognitive Science Society* (pp. 118–120). Ann Arbor, MI.

Kolodner, J. L., & Cullingford, R. E. (1986). Towards a memory architecture that supports reminding. In *Program of the eight annual conference of the Cognitive Science Society* (pp. 467–477). Hillsdale, NJ: Lawrence Erlbaum Associates.

Kolodner, J. L., & Simpson, R. L. (1986). Problem solving and dynamic memory. In J. L. Kolodner & C. K. Riesbeck (Eds.), *Experience, memory, and reasoning* (pp. 99–114). Hillsdale, NJ: Lawrence Erlbaum Associates.

Leake, D. B. (1989). Anomaly detection strategies for schema-based story understanding. In *Program of the eleventh annual conference of the Cognitive Science Society, 16–19 August 1989, Ann Arbor, Michigan* (pp. 490–497). Hillsdale, NJ: Lawrence Erlbaum Associates.

Lebowitz, M. (1980). *Generalization and memory in an integrated understanding system.* Unpublished doctoral dissertation, Yale University, New Haven, CT.

Leddo, J., & Abelson, R. P. (1986). The nature of explanations. In J. A. Galambos, R. P. Abelson, & J. B. Black (Eds.), *Knowledge structures* (pp. 103–122). Hillsdale, NJ: Lawrence Erlbaum Associates.

Levinson, S. C. (1983). *Pragmatics.* Cambridge, England: Cambridge University Press.

MacWhinney, B., Keenan, J. M., & Reinke, P. (1982). The role of arousal in memory for conversation. *Memory and Cognition, 10,* 308–317.

Martin, C. E. (1989). Pragmatic interpretation and ambiguity. In *Program of the eleventh annual conference of the Cognitive Science Society, 16–19 August 1989, Ann Arbor, Michigan* (pp. 474–481). Hillsdale, NJ: Lawrence Erlbaum Associates.

McLaughlin, M. L. (1984). *Conversation: How talk is organized.* Newbury Park, CA: Sage.

McLaughlin, M. L., Baaske, K., Cashion, J., Louden, A., Smith, S., & Smith-Altendorf, D. (1984, May). *Conversational planning and self-serving utterances: The manipulation of topical and functional structure in dyadic interaction.* Paper presented at the annual meeting of the International Communication Association, San Francisco, CA.

McLaughlin, M. L., Louden, A. D., Cashion, J. L., Altendorf, D. M., Baaske, K. T., & Smith, S. W. (1985). Conversational planning and self-serving utterances: The manipulation of topical and functional structures in dyadic interaction. *Journal of Language and Social Psychology, 4,* 233–251.

Nofsinger, R. E. (1991). *Everyday conversation.* Newbury Park, CA: Sage.

Pavitt, C. (1993). Describing know-how about group discussion procedure: Must the representation be recursive? *Communication Studies, 43,* 150–170.

Pazzani, M. J. (1985). Explanation and generalization based memory. In *Program of the seventh annual conference of the Cognitive Science Society* (pp. 323–328). Irvine, CA.

Planalp, S. (1985). Relational schemata: A test of alternative forms of relational knowledge as guides to communication. *Human Communication Research, 12,* 3–29.

Planalp, S. (1987). Interplay between relational knowledge and events. In R. Burnett, P. McGhee, & D. D. Clarke (Eds.), *Accounting for relationships: Social representation of interpersonal links* (pp. 173–191). London: Meuthen.

Planalp, S. (1989). Relational communication and cognition. In B. Dervin, L. Grossberg, B. J. O'Keefe, & E. Wartella (Eds.), *Rethinking communication: Vol. 2. Paradigm exemplars* (pp. 269–279). Newbury Park, CA: Sage.

Planalp, S., & Honeycutt, J. M. (1985). Events that increase uncertainty in personal relationships. *Human Communication Research, 11,* 593–604.

Planalp, S., & Rivers, M. (1988, May). *Changes in knowledge of relationships.* Paper presented at the annual meeting of the International Communication Association, New Orleans, LA.

Planalp, S., Rutherford, D. K., & Honeycutt, J. M. (1988). Events that increase uncertainty in personal relationships: II. Replication and extension. *Human Communication Research, 14,* 516–547.

Reiser, B. J. (1986a). Knowledge-directed retrieval of autobiographical memories. In J. L. Kolodner & C. K. Riesbeck (Eds.), *Experience, memory, and reasoning* (pp. 75–93). Hillsdale, NJ: Lawrence Erlbaum Association.

Reiser, B. J. (1986b). The encoding and retrieval of memories of real-world experiences. In J. A. Galambos, R. P. Abelson, & J. B. Black (Eds.), *Knowledge structures* (pp. 71–99). Hillsdale, NJ: Lawrence Erlbaum Associates.

Riesbeck, C. K. (1981). Failure-driven reminding for incremental learning. In *Proceedings of the IJCAI-81* (pp. 115–120). Vancouver, BC.

Riesbeck, C. K. (1982). Realistic language comprehension. In W. G. Lehnert & M. H. Ringle (Eds.), *Strategies for natural language processing* (pp. 37–54). Hillsdale, NJ: Lawrence Erlbaum Associates.

Riesbeck, C. K. (1986). From conceptual analyzer to direct memory access parsing: An overview. In N. E. Sharkey (Ed.), *Advances in cognitive science 1* (pp. 236–258). Chicester: Ellis Horwood.

Riesbeck, C. K., & Martin, C. E. (1986). Direct memory access parsing. In J. L. Kolodner & C. K. Riesbeck (Eds.), *Experience, memory, and reasoning* (pp. 209–226). Hillsdale, NJ: Lawrence Erlbaum Associates.

Riesbeck, C. K., & Schank, R. C. (1989). *Inside case-based reasoning.* Hillsdale, NJ: Lawrence Erlbaum Associates.

Robinson, W. P., & Rackstraw, S. J. (1972). *A question of answers* (2 vols.). London: Routledge & Kegan Paul.

Rook, K. S., & Peplau, L. A. (1982). Perspectives on helping the lonely. In L. Peplau & D. Perlman (Eds.), *Loneliness: A sourcebook of current theory, research, and therapy* (pp. 351–378). New York: Wiley-Interscience.

Schank, R. C. (1980). Language and memory. *Cognitive Science, 4,* 243–284.

Schank, R. C. (1981). MOPs and learning. In *Proceedings of the third annual conference of the Cognitive Science Society* (pp. 166–169). Berkeley, CA.

Schank, R. C. (1982a). Reminding and memory organization: An introduction to MOPs. In W. G. Lehnert & M. H. Ringle (Eds.), *Strategies for natural language processing* (pp. 455–493). Hillsdale, NJ: Lawrence Erlbaum Associates.

Schank, R. C. (1982b). *Dynamic memory: A theory of reminding and learning in computers and people.* Cambridge, England: Cambridge University Press.

Schank, R. C. (1986). *Explanation patterns: Understanding mechanically and creatively.* Hillsdale, NJ: Lawrence Erlbaum Associates.

Schank, R. C. (1990). *Tell me a story: A new look at real and artificial memory.* New York: Charles Scribner's Sons.

Schank, R. C., & Abelson, R. P. (1977). *Scripts, plans, goals, and understanding: An inquiry into human knowledge structures.* Hillsdale, NJ: Lawrence Erlbaum Associates.

Schank, R. C., Collins, G. C., & Hunter, L. E. (1986). Transcending inductive category formation in learning. *Behavioral and Brain Sciences, 9,* 639–686.

Schank, R. C., & Leake, D. B. (1990). Creativity and learning in a case-based explainer. In J. Carbonell (Ed.), *Machine learning: Paradigms and methods* (pp. 353–385). Cambridge, MA: MIT Press.

Schegloff, E. A., & Sacks, H. (1973). Opening up closings. *Semiotica, 7,* 289–327.

Sillars, A. L. (1985). Interpersonal perception in relationships. In W. J. Ickes (Ed.), *Compatible and incompatible relationships* (pp. 277–305). New York: Springer-Verlag.

Sillars, A. L. (1989). Communication, uncertainty, and understanding in marriage. In B. Dervin, L. Grossberg, B. J. O'Keefe, & E. Wartella (Eds.), *Rethinking communication: Vol. 2. Paradigm exemplars* (pp. 307–328). Newbury Park, CA: Sage.

Sillars, A. L., Pike, G. R., Jones, T. J., & Murphy, M. A. (1984). Communication and understanding in marriage. *Human Communication Research, 10,* 317–350.

Sillars, A. L., & Scott, M. D. (1983). Interpersonal perception between intimates: An integrative review. *Human Communication Research, 10,* 153–176.

Sillars, A. L., & Weisberg, J. (1987). Conflict as a social skill. In M. E. Roloff & G. R. Miller (Eds.), *Interpersonal processes: New directions in communication research* (pp. 140–171). Newbury Park, CA: Sage.

Sillars, A. L., Weisberg, J., Burggraf, C. S., & Zietlow, P. H. (1987). Content themes in marital conversations. *Human Communication Research, 13,* 495–528.

Smith, G. W. (1991). *Computers and human language.* New York: Oxford University Press.

Solano, C. H. (1986). People without friends: Loneliness and its alternatives. In V. J. Derlega & B. A. Winstead (Eds.), *Friendship and social interaction* (pp. 227–246). New York: Springer-Verlag.

Stafford, L., Burggraf, C. S., & Sharkey, W. F. (1987). Conversational memory: The effects of time, recall mode, and memory expectations on remembrances of natural conversations. *Human Communication Research, 14,* 203–229.

Stafford, L., & Daly, J. A. (1984). Conversational memory: The effects of recall mode and memory expectancies on remembrances of natural conversations. *Human Communication Research, 10,* 379–402.

Stafford, L., Waldron, V. R., & Infield, L. L. (1989). Actor–observer differences in conversational memory. *Human Communication Research, 15,* 590–611.

Turner, E. H. (1990). *Integrating intention and convention to organize problem-solving dialogues.* Technical Report GIT-ICS-90/02, School of Information and Computer Science, Georgia Institute of Technology, Atlanta, GA.

Turner, E. H. (1991a). Discourse structure as predictions to organize discourse. In *Working notes of the AAAI fall symposium series on discourse structure in natural language understanding* (pp. 120–121). Asilomar, CA.

Turner, E. H. (1991b). *Organizing dialogue from an incoherent stream of goals.* Unpublished manuscript, University of New Hampshire, Durham.

Turner, E. H., & Cullingford, R. E. (1989a). Using conversation MOPs in natural language interfaces. *Discourse Processes, 12,* 63–90.

Turner, E. H., & Cullingford, R. E. (1989b). Making conversation flexible. In *Proceedings of the eleventh annual conference of the Cognitive Science Society* (pp. 932–939). Ann Arbor, MI.

Turner, E. H., & Cullingford, R. E. (1992). *Exploiting knowledge of convention to organize communication goals.* Unpublished manuscript, University of New Hampshire, Durham.

Turner, R. M. (1989). When reactive planning is not enough: Using contextual schemas to react appropriately to environmental change. In *Program of the eleventh annual conference of the Cognitive Science Society, 16–19 August 1989, Ann Arbor, Michigan* (pp. 940–947). Hillsdale, NJ: Lawrence Erlbaum Associates.

Wardbaugh, R. (1985). *How conversation works.* Cambridge, MA: Basil Blackwell.

Wheeler, L., & Nezlek, J. (1977). Sex differences in social participation. *Journal of Personality and Social Psychology, 35,* 742–754.

Wilensky, R. (1983). *Planning and understanding: A computational approach to human reasoning.* Reading, MA: Addison-Wesley.

Winograd, T. (1977). A framework for understanding discourse. In M. Just & P. Carpenter (Eds.), *Cognitive processes in comprehension* (pp. 63–88). New York: Wiley.

Woodall, W. G., & Folger, J. P. (1985). Nonverbal cue context and episodic memory: On the availability and endurance of nonverbal behavior as retrieval cues. *Communication Monographs, 52,* 319–333.

Young, J. E. (1982). Loneliness, depression and cognitive therapy: Theory and application. In L. Peplau & D. Perlman (Eds.), *Loneliness: A sourcebook of current theory, research, and therapy* (pp. 379–405). New York: Wiley-Interscience.

Zietlow, P. H. (1986). *An analysis of the communication behaviors, understanding, self-disclosure, sex roles, and marital satisfaction of elderly couples and couples in earlier life stages.* Unpublished doctoral dissertation, Ohio State University, Columbus.

IV

THE COGNITIVE APPROACH
TO INTERPERSONAL
COMMUNICATION:
A PHILOSOPHICAL CRITIQUE

7 Cognitive Perspectives on Communication: Interpretive and Critical Responses

Robert D. McPhee
University of Wisconsin-Milwaukee

The field of cognitive science is vast. It encompasses most of psychology, plus sizable chunks of other disciplines, and includes a growing segment of communication. By comparison, the number of interpretive scholars who have done work relevant to cognitive communication research is small indeed. But I think it is important to note the range of complementary work, too extensive to be cited here, from other disciplines, including philosophy (e.g., Searle, 1984), neurophysiology (Edelman, 1989, 1992), linguistics (Lakoff, 1987), physics (Penrose, 1989), general postmodern studies (Coward & Ellis, 1977; Henriques, Holloway, Urwin, Venn, & Walkerdine, 1984), and psychology (e.g., Bruner, 1990; Harre, 1984). Hence, this chapter does not represent the "opposition view" to the cognitive perspective, but a few rival streams of theory and research criticism. I have tried to formulate these in a way that has maximum pragmatic significance for cognitive communication research as well as theorizing. I not only believe that the cognitive perspective is founded on dubitable philosophical assumptions, but that those assumptions have also led to blind spots in the formulation of research questions and procedures.

Before beginning the substantive argument of this chapter, I need to explain what I mean by *cognitive communication theory or research*. The most common-sense meaning would be those theories that assume that people think about the interactions they are involved in, and that their thoughts lead to interactional differences. Frankly, I have no problems with that kind of theory involving thought, and I doubt that anyone else does. The "cognitive positions" I argue against in this chapter go farther than traditional common sense, to make three assumptions. First, they assume that "the cognitive system" has *integrity* as a distinct system with its own structure and processes, which should be studied as processing-input information in relatively stable ways. Often they assume that cognitive processes are emergent—on a different level of analysis from the neurophysiological. The clearest example is Dennett's theory (1978). Second, they assume that cognition is a *casual* system at the cognitive level of analysis. They seek lawlike process regularities, involving cognitive constructs like plan or speed of recall, that depend only on the state of the cognitive system being focused on, not on a broader interpretive frame or social process. This assumption may be abetted by the computer metaphor that underlies much cognitive theory—the tacit (and often explicit) equation set up between cognitive structures/processes and the structure/processing of a computer program. Based on that metaphor, I label cognitive models that involve information processing whose causal organization is established by a program-like structure as *programmed processes*. Third, they assume that the cognitive system is *central* in interaction and its explanation—that programmed processes are the most important mediators of the past and shapers of the future.

I start out this counterstatement by praising cognitive-communication theories and research on three counts in particular. First, cognitivist research aims at *realist* scientific theories (Harre & Secord, 1973)—theories that attribute observed regularities to presumed underlying powers and properties, in this case of the mind. Second, cognitive research, especially in communication, has taken seriously the *interpretive* and *choice-making* powers of human beings and has tried to explain them and to use them in explaining interaction. The substance of a cognitive theory, involving complex structures and processes, thus allows for greater sensitivity and flexibility in relations among variables than can more typical propositional theories. Third, cognitive studies have made, and will continue to make, real contributions to our knowledge of social interaction by revealing ways in which our specific cognitive apparatus enables, and especially constrains, our interactions. All of these are valuable and important tendencies. They are among the valid reasons that communication researchers choose to do cognitive communication research.

However, I claim that these valuable tendencies are undercut by the extremity and single-mindedness with which they are typically applied. The assumptions that distinguish the cognitive perspective tempt cognitive-communication researchers to reduce all processes to cognitively grounded processes, and to derogate chains of events in which cognitive processes have little explanatory relevance. Other theoretical positions are treated as unduly ignoring cognitive processing, without regard for the specific explanatory importance of cognitive processes relative to others. I can do no better here than refer to critiques of structuration theory, including some of my own work, by cognitive theorists. Greene (1984) argued that "from a cognitive perspective behavior is to be explained by reference to the mental operations which produced it . . . any [communicative] behavior must have arisen purely as a result of the information processing system; there simply are no other inputs to the efferent system" (p. 243). I think there is widespread acceptance, among cognitive theorists (cf.

Fodor, 1975) and others, that this reasoning is flawed because of its reductionism: Explanations should be cast at the level of analysis where qualitative differences match (and cause) important differences in the phenomena needing explanation. For instance, a gunshot death should not be accounted for as death by heart failure; regularities of the cultural and educational systems, not regularities of individual psychology, account for widespread consensus that Columbus discovered America. Indeed, if cognitive scientists took Greene's argument to its logical extreme, they would shift to studying muscle physiology because there is "no input" to communicative behavior except through muscle contractions. Our real concern is not Greene's argument, however, but the way cognitive assumptions may have led him to exclude social-explanatory patterns.

A second case is Hewes and Planalp's (1987) account of three approaches to studying communication. They presented the "cognitive/interpretive approach" as appealing "to differences in cognitive structures that lead to different interpretations . . ." (p. 156). They presented this approach as a cohesive alternative to "trait" and "transindividual" approaches, which "oversimplify individuals" by avoiding any analysis of cognition. This account overlooks the fact that at least some of their "transindividual" approaches make eager use of concepts describing human thought processes. For instance, Giddens' (1984) structuration theory depends on human knowledgeability, discursive and practical consciousness, reflexive monitoring, and so on. His examples show that differences in these respects are vital for explaining human action. But Giddens was also clear that these resources of agency are usually dependent on social structure, and thus not *foundational* for social explanation. The point of this chapter is to push cognitive theorists to be as open to social and noncognitive sorts of explanation as Giddens was to cognitive explanation.

To that end, this chapter is composed of three distinct sections. The first reviews some relatively well-known arguments made by interpretive and critical theorists against the cognitive position as defined previously. The second section summarizes and extends the implications of these arguments as a list of revised assumptions that might initiate a shift from the cognitive position as currently conceived to a more defensible synthetic position, with room for cognitive explanation and research. The third section uses this list of assumptions to analyze two recent pieces of cognitive-communication research. I try to illustrate how a synthetic position—allowing for cognitive, more globally interpretive, and social processes and explanation—leads to sounder analysis and research and new questions worth exploring.

INTERPRETIVE AND CRITICAL ARGUMENTS AGAINST THE COGNITIVE POSITION

I start this section with an apology. Both *interpretive theory* and *critical theory* (broadly conceived) are umbrella terms referring to family-resemblance groupings with debatable boundaries, important internal rifts, and no common properties that I can find. Many theorists, such as Heidegger (1962) and Wittgenstein (1958), have developed critiques of the whole social-scientific endeavor of which cognitive theory is part, therefore they are not covered in this chapter. A descriptive exposition encompassing the range and debates within either school is also beyond the scope of this chapter. But prominent advocates, especially of interpretive theory, have developed their own critiques of cognitive social science. I present some of those arguments here, and describe their foundations in passing.

The first set of arguments is drawn from a school—analytic philosophy—whose work is on the borders of interpretive theory generally. However, it is of special interest to us because many of its current leaders have devoted extensive attention to the philosophy of cognitive science, and some arguments developed by scholars like Putnam (1988) and Stich (1983) illustrate and advance the interpretive position well. (I note that these arguments are the work of a few analytic scholars, not the dominant position among many adopted by analytic philosophers about cognition.)

Putnam, Stich, and others used conceptual analysis to attack the idea that programmed processes can adequately represent cognitive phenomena like thinking, believing, understanding, or planning. The main problem they focused on was the standard cognitive-science practice of describing a programmed process and saying it represents how humans understand word meanings, or plan and execute activities. These analytic philosophers argued that, in general, programmed processes and cognitive phenomena like belief do not match up. The basic problem is that an unbelievably wide range of specific mental states can work as adequate versions of belief.

For instance, take a belief like "There is a cat in this room." Standard practice in cognitive science would be to describe a programmed process that would function in the way that belief functions for us in general, that is, it would be caused by certain things (seeing a cat, hearing the words "My cat is behind the couch," or hearing meows) and would cause, in appropriate situations, specified behaviors (calling "Kitty, kitty," or looking for the cat). But Stich brought up the example of Helen Keller. She could have "the same" belief as I that a cat is here, but it could not be caused by any of those same inputs, or have the same consequences. Indeed, the belief I might have that would most closely resemble Keller's belief, in cause-and-consequence terms, might be the belief that "There is a ghost-cat in the room" (i.e., I might feel the cat, but would see and hear nothing). This is only an extreme example. My neural system, at the time I believe a cat is in the room, might be very different from yours in inputs, processes, and outputs, yet we could, for all practical purposes, have the same belief.

Putnam (1988) offered an example with even broader consequences. I believe my wedding ring is made of silver, yet I know nothing of the makers of my ring, who supplied them with silver, or even the tests that might be done to determine whether it is silver. My belief is based on a "linguistic division of labor"—on believing that my wife dealt with people who do know these things. Many, perhaps most, of our beliefs rest on "knowing" our place in an elaborate social structure of knowledge differences. Despite very different programs and processes, the silversmith who made my ring and I have the same belief: that for all practical purposes, it is silver.

Of course, the tricky terms are *for all practical purposes*. Putnam argued that very different neural causes and consequences, and very different experiences and ideas, can function as "the same" belief, plan, or memory because a variety of interpretive practices, which he called *ethnomethods* or *discounting differences,* are constantly in play in social experience. We adjust to differences so well that I can speak with a silversmith about silver, or know that we both believe there is a cat in the room even as I call it while you recoil in dislike. No theory should assume that identity or functioning of beliefs are well described by identity or the functioning of programmed-process representations. Stich introduced the term *folk psychology* for the ideas about cognition and cognitive processes like memory, amounting to a sort of theory, that are widely shared in Western culture. His philosophic analysis concludes that there is an unbridgeable divide between folk psychological ideas of cognition and any theory using programmed processes to represent cognition. The latter just cannot match the diversity and flexibility of the former.

At the very least, the arguments of Putnam and Stich lead us to challenge the centrality, and even the integrity, assumptions of the cognitive position. In analyzing laboratory studies of memory, we should remember that remembering is not just internal and individual—it has its character partly as a result of ethnomethods that let us use memory in interacting despite the wide differences involved in the linguistic division of labor (cf. Shotter, 1990). So a study of memory structure might find a response lag that seems to reveal structure, but has no interactional significance because it is actually glossed by social-interpretive work in interaction. Some delays in processing may even be habitual adaptations to routinely invoked ethnomethods. As another example, the organization of a planned interaction may be generated not by a plan "cognitively represented," but by a social distribution of planning labor to which any one individual contributes in varied, mostly spontaneous, socially supplemented, and often redundant ways. In short, a systematic, cognitive representation that constitutes an understood meaning, plan, or belief may neither exist not be central to the explanation of communication. Wegner, Erber, and Raymond's (1991) study, which demonstrated recollection differences due to different interaction rules imposed on remembering couples, described not peculiar relations but the normal way memory works.

A further implication of this argument, and an assumption underlying much interpretive theory, is that cognitive work plays on a vicious equivocation, almost analogously to Skinner in dealing with human behavior (Chomsky, 1959). On the one hand, *cognitive* refers to the sort of thinking people do in everyday life, with all the social support and discounted differences mentioned previously—thinking as described and practically dealt with in folk psychology. I often refer to this domain of study as "folk psychology," although nearly all social science draws on or focuses on this domain. For instance, nearly all attitude theory and research uses and extends our ordinary ideas of what an attitude is and how it works. On the other hand, cognitive theory uses *cognitive* to refer to the parts or the versions of the folk-psychological domain that can be expressed as causal or programmed systems or processes (i.e., what cognitive theories describe *is* thinking, memory *is* activation of stored information, etc.). This equivocation may be as mystifying and misleading as Skinner's to cognitive researchers as well as to readers. If computer programmers knew as little, and took as much on faith, of the processes involved in writing artificial-intelligence (AI) programs as human cognitive researchers do in designing and instructing subjects for their experiments, the programmers would never get started.

A second body of argument that reveals some fundamental interpretive objections to cognitive theories in general was developed by Taylor (1985). His work rests on his analysis of the importance of human self-understanding, which is a vital part of human nature and emotion. He drew the distinction between human and mechanism on the basis of *significance:* A machine's operation has no importance for it, whereas a human agent's activity and situation can be essentially significant for him or her, not relative to any designer or user. Of course, machines can register certain things about their states and react to them, but such feedback does not capture the idea of significance. The difference can be expressed by contrasting the feelings of *hotness* and *shame*. A machine can register temperature and react to it, and so can a human; such similarities lead to (misled) imputations of purposiveness to machines (when, said Taylor, the purpose is actually relative to an agent's use of the machine). But the case of shame is different—such an emotion involves the perceived relevance of our situation to our self-interpreted nature.

> Someone can only experience shame who has a sense of himself as an agent. For I feel ashamed of what I am like/how I appear as an *agent* among other agents, a subject of significance among others. It may seem sometimes that the immediate object of my shame is some physical property that a non-agent could bear. I may be ashamed of my small stature, or outsized hands. But these can only be objects of shame because of their significance: small stature means being overshadowed, failing to have a commanding presence among others; outsize hands embody indelicacy, lack of refinement, are proper to peasants. (1985, p. 198)

Notice that a program could be written to trigger an output sentence "I feel shame" when, say, the computer's input mechanisms register certain values—but that sentence, significant to the computer's users, would have no more significance to the computer than any other signal or internal state, no matter what effects it caused. Taylor argues that other human/machine distinctions resting on meaningfulness or consciousness are secondary to his—consciousness is distinctive because we can focus on things that are significant to us.

Taylor elaborates several other distinctions supporting the idea of a "significance feature," including chiefly the self-interpreting nature of human agents and the expressive nature of language.

Taylor begins his argument that humans are self-interpreting by considering emotions like shame. Such emotions are aroused by the *imports* of situations— properties of those situations which make them important or concernful. Imports may involve mere facts (hand size, or the objective danger that leads to fear), but an import leading to shame also involves a dimension of existence of the subject—what Taylor calls "subject-referring properties." A person is ashamed, not just because his hands are a certain size, but because he aspires to respect in a culture where big hands express ignoble personal attributes. Explaining such emotions requires seeing things from the viewpoint of a subject for whom things can have this distinctive, culturally grounded kind of meaning. Finally, having or understanding such emotions depends on the articulation of certain distinctions and threads of reasoning. The quality of the shame is different if we simply know of people's disapproval than if we understand the inference they draw (from big hands to lack of refinement) and agree with the value they put on refinement, or even with the logic of their inference.

Taylor's emphasis on expression of emotions ties in with his general theory of language. He called it an *expressive theory* as opposed to *designative theories,* which portray language as an instrument for representing reality. Expressive theories instead, cast language as a medium for the expression or realization/manifestation of meaning. This view emphasizes activity—the work of developing expressive powers (in general, language acquisition) and achieving expressive adequacy (about particular issues, for particular tasks). The basic distinction involved is between language as *reaction*—associative word choice following a percept or thought—and language as *recognition*—a reflective sense, usually tacit, that the word is "the *right* description." Recognition of this sort requires different words that might be chosen, and a sense that some are better than others. Choice and normativity are characteristic of language as a system. But then language is the vehicle or medium of this reflective recognition and awareness. It comes to exist through language, and indeed is given expression through language. Such recognition is a basic feature of human experience. Here Taylor's argument links back to his analysis of emotions as dependent on expression: "The expressive conception gives a view of language as a range of activities in which we express/realize a certain way of being in the world" (1985, p. 234). Taylor noted that this theory, although compatible with very subjective stances, is also compatible with the Heideggerian objective account of subjectivity, which he favored.

I have given some of the flavor of Taylor's general position in order to express the depth of his opposition to typical cognitive theories. The significance feature is not a simple point of anomaly. It is bound up with an emphasis on linguistic expression, development, holism and depth of reflection, and constitutive being in the human social world, which is far removed from the isolated formulation of structures and processes explaining isolated segments of cognitive and overt activity. For instance, from Taylor's viewpoint, an explanation of discourse based on stored plans would be deficient because it would not capture the significance of (a) planning, (b) the means and goals involved in the plan, and (c) the specific way they are expressed (to oneself or others). People intermittently monitor and judge their plans and activities based on their ultimate significance, and that larger interpretive level, rather than any localized program structure, is the source of ultimate direction and meaning. Thus, program-based explanations lose the substance of their explanandum and forego the realism that was such an advantage in the cognitive clash with behaviorism.

The third argument I review is offered by two philosophers who are fairly closely aligned to Taylor. Hubert Dreyfus is most famous for his book *What Computers Can't Do* (1973). In the more recent *Mind over Machines* (1986), he and Stuart Dreyfus presented some additional arguments that illustrate their basic objections to cognitivism.

Interestingly, their arguments attack programmed-process models not in general, but as applied specifically to explain human proficiency. They allow that such models are fairly good for cognition in the first few stages of adult development toward expertise, but that they fail, and must fail, in matching up to the later stages (including the communicative competence of most humans).

Dreyfus and Dreyfus distinguished five such "stages of skill acquisition." In the first two stages—*novice* and *advanced beginner*–people learn to apply particular rules to a situation. By the third stage, *competence,* people find an immense number of potentially relevant rules and aspects of a situation, and they develop the ability to (a) make an overall situational assessment, (b) formulate a plan, (c) focus on a few key situational factors, and (d) react to the *constellation* of such factors on the basis of experience. That is, on the basis of the plan, the person forms a perspective. For instance, using a plan of treatment for a patient, a competent nurse will decide "that if certain signs are present a number of days after surgery, say, the time has come to talk to the patient about his wound and its care outside the hospital. When discussing the matter, various medical aspects of the patient's condition will be ignored, and psychological aspects will become important" (Dreyfus & Dreyfus, 1986, p. 26). Cognitive decision-making models often include some aspects of this third stage, but they fail to capture the experience-based holism of the competent person's response or the way it leads to an involved interactive stance. Dreyfus and Dreyfus argued that these aspects become more important as the development of expertise continues.

Thus, in the fourth stage, *proficiency,* a person starts a task in a stance of involvement and ongoing perspective, without separate steps of analysis and key-factor focus. The key factors simply "stand out" and lead to analog changes in diagnosis, based on "holistic similarity recognition" of similar past cases. But this intuitive insight into situations is not yet matched by intuitive reaction to the situation. Instead, sequential, temporarily detached, and often conscious problem solving will guide action. In the fifth stage, *expertise,* intuitive insight into situations will be accompanied by involved, intuitive choice and action. Experience is sufficiently mastered so that the reaction is simply "what normally works" in this sort of situation. Dreyfus and Dreyfus used the analogy of a chess expert who can recognize and remember as many as 50,000 different whole-board positions, including, in many cases, the exact circumstances of the game in which they took place. They cited studies demonstrating that such experts do not use abstracted "chunks" or "schemata," and do not "plan" in an abstracted way. Rather, they use the resource of 50,000 understood past situations to forge a perspective, and they use it to react to salient issues in an intuitively right way. Just so, an expert nurse can diagnose and react to a situation without an abstracted stage of plan formation. Just so, they argued, people react to everyday situations like driving to work or making everyday decisions. Indeed, they argued that cognitivists' identification of biases and reasoning failures depend on forcing subjects into situations where the intuitions appropriate for everyday life are not apt. Finally, such intuitions seem to match up well to the "accomplishments" identified by conversational analysis.

Dreyfus and Dreyfus argued that cognitive approaches up through the 1980s emphasize sequential-symbol manipulation, and are not capable of modeling the holistic intuition involved in much of human thought. They were more impressed by the *kind* of models developed by connectionists, but these would have to be broad enough to allow for the kind of holistic intuition of their later stages. Like Taylor, Dreyfus and Dreyfus lead us to question models based on programmed rationality because they leave out involvement and understate human powers of holistic command of memory resources.

So far I have examined interpretive theories and neglected critical positions. This is partly because I have seen relatively few articles that develop a directly critical argument against cognitive science. Most focus more broadly on traditional psychology and social psychology generally. Also, it is hard to choose a single representative from three rather disparate critical perspectives. One is aligned with an enlightened dialectical materialism, with which I would group Vygotsky (1962; Wertsch, 1985) and Luria (1976). A second is aligned with ideology critique not far from the Frankfurt School (Leonard, 1984; Wexler, 1983). A third draws on structuralistic Marxism (Henriques et al., 1984). A relevant research line from the first group is labeled *critical psychology* (Tolman, 1991). Critical psychologists aim to develop a more relevant, less indeterminate psychology. Both these aims are important because ordinary psychology either ignores them or pursues them in a distorted way. A good illustration of their argument here is their analysis of the concept of *attitude* (Markard, 1991). The many incompatible definitions of attitude, and the difficulty of reconciling widely accepted affective, cognitive, and conative dimensions of it, are taken as evidence that it should be discarded. Critical psychologists argue that it works well only in situations where subjects are passive, controlled, or placed in forced-choice activities, and they stress that traditional psychology valorizes such situations because military-industrial funders like them. They might make the same charge against a number of concepts, such as *activation,* that seem especially relevant to experimental situations.

Critical psychologists argue that they can avoid the social irrelevance and indeterminacy of traditional psychological concepts by using an advantageous method of concept formation. For any proposed concept, they choose a definition that fits the way the phenomenon developed in sociocultural history (as traced by dialectical materialism). A good example here is their analysis of the concept of *need* (Tolman, 1991). They argue that typical conceptions of human needs fail to recognize the differences that have developed through history and through the life stages of individuals. Early stages, where unmet needs lead to individual search or frustration reactions, are replaced as humanity and humans mature by the essentially different situation of "societal mediatedness." The process of meeting needs is no longer direct, but is mediated by tools, language, and social organization. As this development takes place, the concept of *need* must change. The need of hunger no longer involves simply a lack of food, but a lack of resources to grow food or a societal defect that keeps food surpluses from needy people. Meeting a need must be seen not as a "handout," but as allowing a person an opportunity to earn a living. The concept that they present as preferable is *action potence,* which involves

> The individual's ability to do the things that he or she feels are necessary to satisfy his or her needs, that is, to ensure an acceptable quality of life. It has a subjective side, which is how one feels about oneself and one's relations with the world. It has an objective side in the actual possibilities for need satisfaction through cooperative effort with other members of society. Action potence is what mediates individual production and societal reproduction. (Tolman, 1991, pp. 16–17)

Notice that this replacement concept involves not an instantaneous state or stimulus, but an aspect of life processes over a relatively long time. It extends beyond the individual psyche because the psyche itself is transformed by the mediations (i.e., language, social relatedness) that we learn as we mature. This is the same sort of transformation that Vygotsky argued for in stressing the relational basis of learning and cognition (Bruner, 1986). Cognitive theories influenced by this critical view would emphasize the typical place of a thought phenomenon in social life, rather than purely the instantaneous structure or microprocess. For instance, *schema* might be replaced by a concept that includes the basis of a cognitive power and the social conditions to which it answers.

IMPLIED CORRECTIVE ASSUMPTIONS

I think all these arguments lead to a set of conclusions about the nature of human thought and the conceptual domain of cognitive communication research, which, if accepted, would dramatically change the way researchers now interpret and conduct their work. The rival set of assumptions is that most cognitive concepts involved in cognitive-communication research actually refer to phenomena that are:

1. Interpreted.   That is, they are meaningful and their meaning is essential to them. There are actually two senses of interpretation that are relevant here. The first is that the concepts are intrinsically related to a whole web of other interpretations, of other concepts on more or less the same level of analysis, but also of past experiences, current context, significance, and self. These relations are not causal, and cannot be validly reduced to a causal system such as a computer program. Instead, to quote Taylor (1985), they are "interpretive all the way down." Every activity, tacitly and often explicitly, reflexively implicates our most general senses of order and worth, and involves emotion-laden judgments about rightness, trustworthiness, competence, and pride. Every cognitive process involves such interpretation and rests on preinterpretation; theoretical and computer models that make other sorts of relations (i.e., causal) basic are flawed in the realism they attribute to their theories. Models that do not rest on such basic senses of agency and order (including very limited models of particular activities) are misdescriptions at their very heart.

The second sense of interpretation involves the application of conceptual or cognitive materials in a concrete case of situated action. The materials do not simply "apply themselves," and a model implying that they do is false. Rather, situational adaptations are always involved, based on but also creating the sense of meaning and significance discussed earlier. In routine cases, the adaptations are tacitly judged to be unimportant. In many cases, the process of interpretation involves strategic, aesthetic, political choice, or production. The process of adaptation inevitably involves a "duality of structuration," in Giddens' (1984) sense. The conceptual background supporting the interpretation has to be drawn on in processes of selection and stylization. But the process of interpretation also richens or challenges the conceptual background that has been used. This process seems to demand an agent with considerable powers of interpretation.

2. Essentially Social.   This claim means that typical concepts used by cognitive-communication researchers actually refer to patterns and forces that belong to the social domain, not the intrapersonal. In particular, their explanatory import is typically a reflection of content or processes that are arbitrary and learned, not on specifically psychological constraints on how it is learned, stored, or used. Four aspects of the sociality of purported "cognitive" constructs are worth distinguishing: (a) Social in origin: Purportedly cognitive constructs often refer to regularities derived from *socialization* within *organized social practices*. Indeed, often they are the results (both intended and unrecognized as such) of more-or-less explicit training. A useful example comes from mathematics: Ask people, "What is 2 + 2?" and they will regularly say (and think) "4"; ask them "what is 343 + 49?" and they will (less quickly and with more errors) say "392." But it is silly to call these regularities cognitive, for many reasons. The main one here is that "2 + 2" is repeated by rote over and over, and is *made* obvious by teachers and others using sets of four objects, so it is internalized or introjected as a routine. However, "343 + 49" is probably never learned; what is taught is a complex way of solving it. Just so, many so-called "cognitive regularities" can be found stated explicitly or practiced regularly out in the open, waiting to be added to the knowledge, or introjected into the "cognitive system" of the individual. Harre's (1984) analysis of the self as a public, collective concept, appropriated to guide private self-understanding and only thereafter given unique, individual import, is a good example.

(b) Social in character: Purportedly cognitive constructs are not only learned in organized social practices; they are often primarily social in their very nature. They are not primarily unseen, mysterious processes hidden in the cognitive system; they are things we do in the world, or features of those things. They can be found stated explicitly, practiced regularly out in the open, available to be learned, written up as a textbook or computer program, or "worked through" by a group. Take the mathematical answers mentioned previously: I claim that it is wrongheaded to take them as regularities of cognitive psychology. Mathematics is an organized social practice with its own norms and procedures. If agents know math, they will give the answers stated earlier no matter how their cognitive system works. No psychological theory would valorize the answer "4". On the other hand, a behaviorist theory could predict that people would say "4" as well as a cognitive theory. Now, the fact that people go more slowly and make more mistakes on the second question may seem to be more of a "cognitive" regularity, reflecting reaction time and processing load. But the interpretive position pushes us to see this sort of regularity also as social in character. Schools do not encourage memorization of the second answer, as mentioned previously. Because it is worked out by socially enactable mathematical procedures, it is more complex and there are more chances for mistakes (that is a property of the problem, not of the cognitive system, if any, used to represent and solve it). A computer or an organized social group that divided up the labor of the problems would analogously take more time on the second than the first and be mistaken more often. Its complexity is also partly dependent on the arbitrary social representation of the problem, which would be much simpler in Base 7. Western individualistic ideologies lead us to be tempted to reduce all these regularities to psychology. The authors cited previously are dedicated to having us avoid mistaking variable, subtly culturally inscribed structures for natural laws imposed by genetics or demanded by the requirements of rationality.

(c) They receive and practically require vital support from routine social-interaction processes. These include routines that maintain a sense of who and where we are, and a sense that the kind of challenges to reality described by Garfinkel (1967) and Goffman (1961) will not take place. For instance, Putnam (1988) mentioned the importance of "ethnomethods," "charity in interpretation," and "discounting differences" in maintaining a presumption of mutual understanding during communication (p. 13). Another example, highlighted by Giddens (1984), is the extent to which general-cognitive processes are changed and impeded by traumatic changes in social routines. He referred to Bettelheim's study of life in concentration camps. Interaction routines also help contextualize purportedly cognitive processes in more mundane ways. Other people's actions can inform or remind us of various important contextual features, their facework can help us control our own attention, and their remarks can spark (thereby creating) our memories (Wegner et al., 1991) or our reasoning (Doise & Mackie, 1981).

I use the term *social* broadly here to include several seemingly distinct domains. First and most obviously, it includes interpersonal processes like dialogue and education. Second, it also includes patterns that can be modeled by another or explicitly stated, and that are typically learned through consciousness of such manifestation. For instance, we learn to add multidigit numbers by "carrying" to later columns. I resist calling the explanation of this sort of behavior *cognitive* because its form is externally derived and the specific mechanisms of its learning are irrelevant. (Of course, the processes whereby we recall this routine, or learn it, might require cognitive explanation, but they might not, too, if we learned socially how to recall and learn such things.) Perhaps as part of the second category, I also call such socially generated and reinforced patterns as language, social norms, and so on *social* as well. The category roughly resembles Harre's (1984) *collective* pole.

The idea that thought processes can be social in their form, generation, and primary reinforcement processes is important for two reasons. First, it helps break the habit of equivocation mentioned earlier—the habit of assuming that thinking is purely cognitive, as psychologists used to claim that action is purely behavioral. It leads us to regard some thought processes as "of the same stuff" as remarks. Second, they remind us that the cognitive system is by no means self-sustaining, so that drawing system boundaries around it, as cognitivists are prone to do, is unjustified. That idea is emphasized even more in the next main point.

3. Essentially Open. Supposedly cognitive phenomena are open to transformation in the course of social interaction. For any cognitive structure used to explain interaction, there are interaction processes that can bring it to awareness, change its significance, lead us to reflexively limit its application, and so on. If there is a script for initial interactions, a sarcastic remark about predictability by an attractive other can easily lead us to be aware of it and leave it. But that means the explanatory power of the script is limited and conditional, dependent in myriad ways on social and self-interpreting routines. Moreover, structural transformations can happen a little more slowly than in a single interaction, as Dreyfus and Dreyfus' (1986) analysis indicated. One could even claim that a growing relationship is just the process of transforming an initial-interaction script, indexed to a specific pair, into something else.

4. Equifinal but Widely Varied. Cognitive phenomena are equifinal and widely varied both in structure and process, and in feature or variable meaning, at the cognitive level of neurophysiological molarity. The contrast that Stich (1983) drew between my cognitive system and Helen Keller's illustrates these variations, and the Dreyfus and Dreyfus analysis of different levels of chess mastery does even more. People at all levels can play chess, talk about it, and discuss their "plans" for victory, yet their thought about chess is astonishingly different in its organization, as in-depth cognitive study readily reveals. Our complaint is that the cognitive measures and correlations dealt with in most cognitive-communication studies depend on understating these variations and assuming that people's thought processes are essentially similar or different except in detailed content or in ways captured by particular cognitive variables. Now, this assumption might indeed be valid—but clear evidence of that is rare. The unexamined alternative is that it might play on exactly the kind of difference-concealing processes of glossing and discounting that people constantly use to achieve communication. The temptation to assume that programs or processes underlying communication are identical, at least in some ways, may be extra powerful due to the practical identity of overt actions (spoken/written words) and extremely high skill in overcoming differences during communication.

That completes our list of rival assumptions about the actual subject matter of cognitive research, suggested by interpretive critiques of that position. I believe that a middle position is possible between these assumptions and cognitive ones. One could argue for genuine cognitive regularities that constrain a basically interpretive social-cognitive realm. Rather than pursue that synthesis, I next indicate the implications and value of these interpretive assumptions for redirecting or reinterpreting cognitive research.

APPLICATION TO COGNITIVE COMMUNICATION RESEARCH

Let me illustrate these points using two examples that I consider to be strong, prototypically cognitive communication research. They are exemplary in focusing on interaction and reporting concrete details about procedures and interactions that permit my development of an alternative approach. The first is an article by Berger, Karol, and Jordan (1989) in the special issue of *Human Communication Research* devoted to cognitive studies, which examined effects of plan complexity on verbal fluency. Berger et al. had subjects (all but controls) write down a plan (i.e., the steps they would take to persuade someone toward their own view about alcohol consumption in student dormitories). Then subjects in a "Question" condition were asked what they would do if specific steps of their plan failed. Then all subjects had one-on-one discussions with confederates whom they tried to persuade but who expressed increasingly hostile views.

Berger et al. found that the Question-condition subjects had lowest fluency (i.e., they hesitated more, especially when their plans contained lots of arguments), and questioning led to more new, unplanned arguments expressed by subjects.

I do not want to criticize this article, but use it to illustrate the relevance of the critique stated in the last section, point by point. One strength of this study is that it involves issues (e.g., drinking, student rights) that were probably significant to student subjects, both intrinsically and because they were being hotly debated in the student newspaper and elsewhere. Due only partly to a legitimate limitation of scope, the meaning and significance of these issues to subjects is basically unexplored. The topic is treated as equivalent to asking subjects to plan to persuade someone that they live in the United States or not to commit suicide.

Probably more important is that a certain structure—regarded as cognitive in this study (a plan)—is practically interpreted by subjects in a variety of ways (e.g., used as a conversational resource, reflected on in response to questions, written down, etc.). Indeed, the study depends crucially on subjects' practical *interpretation* of the plan and the questions about it, not the structure of the plan written down. If subjects followed their plans step by step, fluency would probably not be affected. Instead, the questioning may affect what they do with the plan. One outcome is that they think of new arguments that are added to the plan and increase its complexity, but that alone might not necessarily decrease fluency. With regard to the Berger et al. interpretation, subjects then see the extra arguments as alternatives they must choose among, which slows them down. But this is the result of interpretation by subjects, not a necessary result of plan structure. Another possibility is that questioning makes subjects more committed to the plan, so that they try harder to carry it out despite opposition. (I know that my own fluency would be low because I would be trying to remember the blasted plan!) But this leads to the most interesting likelihood: Questioning leads to increased awareness of the opposed viewpoint (as Berger et al. indicated in passing), which leads to attempts to choose an *optimal* argument for persuading an opponent, which is a harder problem than simply following the steps of a plan.

But the subject matter of the study—both dorm-drinking issues and planning—should also be reframed as more fundamentally social than cognitive. Planning is an organized social practice that is shaped by learning and the need to account for one's activities. It depends on habits of mind socially demonstrated and internalized especially at school, as Vygotsky (1962) illustrated. In the Berger et al. study, it may also have depended on the protocol that imposed a specific communication goal (planning rather than open-minded joint decision), explicitly demanded "a plan," and suggested that such a thing had "steps" (based on the redescription in Berger et al.). The Berger et al. subjects knew how to plan, and they could see the implications of questions about their plan. But these are skills that are more dependent on learning from social practice than on cognitive constraints.

But planning is not merely socially learned—it is that because it is social in character. Both the output and the sequence of output-generating steps could easily appear in discourse within a planning group, and there the thought sequences of members would be quite different from those of the Berger et al. subjects. The main implication of this point follows from some previous remarks. If the last interpretation offered is correct, subjects take longer to choose their words because they see argument choice as a harder problem than before, and solving harder problems takes longer. Is this a cognitive explanation? I would say, "No, of course not! It's an explanation rooted in the nature of problems and problem solving!" A harder problem solution takes longer for a human mind, sure, but it also takes longer for a computer, for a group, for someone to write up or read in a text—it is not a specifically cognitive regularity.

At a cultural level, planning connects up with the issue of dorm drinking in a special way. As Berger et al. noted, the plans that subjects come up with are very different than plans to get someone to go out on a date. So this study rests for its design and interpretation on lots of tacit knowledge about dorm drinking, persuasion, and planning. Such knowledge is not the idiosyncratic inferences of individuals. It is mutual and mutually manifest in persuasive conversations, and so is part of social structure as Giddens (1984) defined it. It could be made explicit and systematic in an ethnographic study that documented the place of views and persuasion about dorm drinking in a broad system of social practice.

Another strength of this study, from our perspective, is that it makes the "openness" of purportedly cognitive phenomena to interaction very apparent. For one thing, the "stuff" of the plans that subjects made was "salient" on the campus where the study took place (i.e., discussed in the media and probably frequently discussed and argued about by students). Students' exposure to this material, and to its organization as arguments about a focused issue, is a sociostructural matter that a praxical position would lead us to examine. Even more clearly, in this study, planning is not treated as "inside the head," but as an open process. Berger et al. imposed interactive, not purely cognitive, planning on their subjects by asking them to write it down, to write down distinct steps, and to answer questions about it that might suggest modification or change. As Berger et al. recognized, this changes the nature and impact of plans.

Finally, this study treats variability among subjects in a symptomatic and revealing way. That differences exist is recognized, both in variables like complexity and in the selection of subjects who included explicit arguments in their plans for a Study 3. But in all sorts of ways, Berger et al. could and did gloss differences among the overt, and especially the cognitive, characteristics of the plans—whether they depend on scripts developed in past arguments, how much they depend on beliefs about possible opposed viewpoints, and so on. The study could rely on the fact that all its subjects "know how" to follow plans, how to construct them, and so on. Such assumptive moves, which are almost unavoidable in communication research, mean that Berger et al. must have taken a viewpoint that is essentially folk psychological. But then cognitivist, hard-science rhetoric (which they do not engage in too much) has the potential to be seriously misleading about the nature and assumptions of this study.

Indeed, our conclusion is that this study is quite informative about the phenomena of planning and communication problems and praxis at the level of folk sociopsychology. It is not a cognitive study as described in the assumptions at the beginning of this chapter, but those do not fit the sociopraxical essence of plans anyway. It does not really depend on a cognitive constraint, but rather one related to the nature of planning and problem solving in whatever medium they are implemented. The biggest problem with the study is that it ignores the social and interactive sources of the phenomena that it studies. It treats plans as varying but essentially similar cognitive resources, not as social-cognitive structurings.

The second example is Kellerman's chapter (chapter 6, this volume). She focused on memory-organization packets (MOPs), which store and provide information about social activities like initial interactions with strangers. MOPs are combinations of scenes that commonly co-occur and/or are linked by similar episodic features such as a common higher level goal (e.g., having an interview). The building blocks of MOPs are scenes (goal-related activities and experience groupings like greetings and introductions) and sometimes scripts (sequenced activities for specific goal accomplishment). Kellerman focused on memory structures and processes for initial encounters. She used the ideas of dynamic-memory theory to describe scenes, MOPs, and a meta-MOP containing only general information about sequencing of scenes. The theory's processing claims involve the flexible adaptation of memory: (a) MOPs can be overlaid, (b) any one scene can be selected within different MOPs, (c) addition of information to memory (as expectations generated by scenes are violated, then explanations of the violations allow understanding—assignment of the experience to a fitting memory location), and (d) change of knowledge structures including scenes and MOPs. She used the theory to explain (a) why the sequence of topics in initial interactions is so consistent and constraining (the MOP's structure constrains it), (b) why we often remember a conversational topic but forget how it arose (the memory is linked to a scene that is flexibly related to varying MOPs), or (c) how inaccurate understanding of a spouse can persist (expectation violations do not recur often enough).

The main impetus of dynamic-memory theory seems to be to come up with a conception of memory structure that would not be immediately excluded from viability due to excessive simplicity and rigidity. However, interpretive and critical theorists would still find problems in this version of human memory.

Of course, memory is a central concern of interpretive theorists such as Heidegger. Despite its flexibility and extreme emphasis on the explanatory power of memory structures, dynamic-memory theory still portrays memory as a recall instrument—as the use of storage chips or discs (to resort to the computer analogy). Instead, interpretive theory sees memory as co-involved with temporality, the mode of human being (i.e., as CPU architecture, or the overall form of the system). More to the point, it denies that any particular memory structure or program is instrumental or controlling. When we follow a sequence of topics in an initial conversation, we know what we are doing: Each topic and the sequence are interpreted, and the sequence of topics involves us; we may feel shame if the conversation seems boring, and so on. Dynamic-memory theory, implementable on a computer, does not include these vital facets of human interaction, and so from the interpretive perspective it is inadequate.

Dynamic-memory theory seems to confuse the flexibility of memory structures and explained processes with the flexible adaptiveness of the human agent acting in a particular context. For instance, Kellerman stated that, "One method by which the conversational MOP generates routine adaptation is in terms of which other MOPs are overlaid on it" (p. 193). This is analogous to saying that a ruler generates its routine adaptation for propping windows open by having a window-propability feature overlaid on it. Why not say that the agent, in routine interaction, draws on different parts/types of his or her knowledge? We would not see a need to build flexibility and overlay capability into our description of knowledge organization if we did not start from the image of a computer executing programs stored in various ways, rather than an agent drawing on knowledge in action in a specific-situational context.

Perhaps even more telling is the way Kellerman clearly represented social aspects of our powers as implications of a psychological theory. I am currently involved in teaching my son some procedures for minimally polite interaction (e.g., that if another person says, "Hello," he should say "Hello" in return, that he should ask them "How are you," etc.), and I have had him practice these routines with me. We do not interact as we do simply because we happen to have these MOPs and not others. A lot of time and work is taken by society to create agents who can and want to interact competently.

Kellerman presented memory structures as causing and explaining behavior structures: "The MOP perspective" offers the possibility "that the range of conversational behaviors . . . can be predicted and explained from the point of view of one unified framework." (p. 182) The interpretive perspective would suggest that a mechanistic psychological explanation might well be misplaced here, yet alternate explanations receive no consideration (perhaps due to space) in Kellerman's chapter. A number of explanations come to mind quickly: (a) Perhaps we simply copy an arbitrary sequence handed down in cultural or subcultural tradition, (b) plain social norms lead us to judge deviations from the typical sequence harshly, or (c) we choose topics seeking to balance risk (from intimate topics) with informativeness (by socially established criteria). The question of "why" initial interactions have the structure they do would seem to depend much more on the social logics of cultural-normative patterning, accountable calculation aimed at self-presentation or meeting third-party expectations, or conversational self-organization, than on constraints on possible cognitive systems. As Kellerman indicated in noting that MOPs depend on experienced similarities in episodes, experience with social regularities, implications, and judgments helps determine what scenes, MOPs, and meta-MOPs we formulate, and which type of structure is formulated. Neither the three MOPs she listed, not the universal scene, nor a possible meta-MOP are natural to human cognition. They are built from social materials, according to a social blueprint. Indeed, the flexibility of dynamic-memory theory makes it less able to explain conversational and other regularities by reference to psychological constraint. There seem to be no constraints at all at the level of the general theory. For instance, I found most interesting Kellerman's suggestion that we remember topics but forget how they arose because topic memory is attached to specific scenes that may be organized by different MOPs on different occasions. But we sometimes do remember how topics arose, and doubtless we could learn to remember such details very efficiently. Perhaps a richer explanation could account for why our scene-linked memories leave out transitions, and could refer to the fact that topic discussions in one conversation are dealt with in later conversations much more frequently than are transitions (i.e., we learn what it is important to remember, and our recall is patterned accordingly).

An interpretive approach would lead us to place special emphasis on situated interaction as an organizer of recall. Remarks or implications by the other person may lead us to (a) talk of a certain topic, (b) recall certain specialized information, or (c) remember certain conversational details. The physical context is also important. Kellerman's focus on a "present-situation scene" seemed to misdescribe the importance of the actually present context as an organizer of interaction and thought (including recall): The fact that people recall talk about context does not mean that a memory structure—past memories of the current context—guided the conversation in question.

It is certainly possible, or even commonplace, for our knowledge to be reconfigured as a result of interaction. My wife might refer to a pattern in recent conversations and lead me to reorganize my recall of past (and later) conversations around that pattern (cf. Wegner et al., 1991). A strength of dynamic-memory theory is that it allows for this possibility, although it seems very narrow in the range of events and motives that could lead to reorganization, compared, say, with Dreyfus and Dreyfus' (1986) portrayal of the chess expert's recall-based powers. Also, as mentioned earlier, a cognitive theory that allows for reorganization as a constant possibility loses a good deal of its predictive potential.

Dynamic-memory theory seems to confuse a regular disposition to sequence conversations in a certain way, with a uniformity of cognitive structure (in a functional sense) of the memory representation of such conversations. This is a little like inferring that all levels of expertise in chess involve a single structure of memory for chess rules, just because all people describe the rules in about the same way. The perspective developed here would urge Kellerman to extend her research to: (a) look for fundamental differences in people's knowledge about initial interactions, and (b) look for the ways that people generate coherent, and often boringly typical, dialogues despite such differences. Such ways could depend both on reportable (socially structurated) knowledge about how to do interaction, and on coordination routines found only in the dialogues.

My own conclusion is that much of Kellerman's chapter could be reconceptualized as focusing on social patterns of initial interaction about which individuals are knowledgeable, due to experienced routines, norms, and bases for self-interpreting action. In some ways, the findings she reviewed may depend on genuine cognitive constraints, but the description of everything in memory-theory terms makes it more difficult to determine what is cognitive and what demands another form of explanation.

As this last section illustrates, I do not think the interpretive and critical positions eliminate the possibility of cognitive research. Some of its findings they would explain by referring to social forces, including socially produced conformity to folk psychology; others they would call artifactual or ill conceived. I believe that room for genuine cognitive regularities remains, although it may be dwarfed by socially produced regularities. Even if cognitivist readers of this chapter disagree with this general conclusion, I hope some of the particular arguments and examples have force. A rigidly cognitive orientation has tended to blind us to salient aspects of phenomena and to potentially important explanatory factors. Building good theory about what folk psychologically called *cognition* requires that we shake off the blinders that are a large chunk of cognitive-communication theory.

ACKNOWLEDGMENTS

The author wishes to thank Dean Hewes, Scott Poole, and Kathryn Olson for comments on earlier versions of this chapter. A much earlier version was presented as background material for a panel presented at the International Communication Association Convention, Dublin, Ireland, June 1990.

REFERENCES

Berger, C., Karol, S., & Jordan, J. (1989). When a lot of knowledge is a dangerous thing: The debilitating effects of plan complexity on verbal fluency. *Human Communication Research, 16,* 91–119.

Bettelheim, B. (1960). *The informed heart.* Glencoe, IL: Free Press.

Bruner, J. (1986). *Actual minds, possible worlds.* Cambridge, MA: Harvard University Press.

Bruner, J. (1990). *Acts of meaning.* Cambridge, MA: Harvard University Press.

Chomsky, N. (1959). *Review of B. F. Skinner. Verbal behavior. Language, 35,* 26–57.

Coward, R., & Ellis, J. (1977). *Language and materialism.* London: Routledge & Kegan Paul.

Dennett, D. (1978). *Brainstorms: Philosophical essays on mind and psychology.* Cambridge, MA: Bradford.

Doise, W., & Mackie, D. (1981). On the social nature of cognition. In J. Forgas (Ed.), *Social cognition: Perspectives on everyday understanding.* New York: Academic Press.

Dreyfus, H. L. (1973). *What computers can't do: A critique of artificial intelligence.* New York: Harper & Row.

Dreyfus, H. L., & Dreyfus, S. E. (1986). *Mind over machine: The power of human intuition and expertise in the era of the computer.* New York: Free Press.

Edelman, G. M. (1989). *The remembered present: A biological theory of consciousness.* New York: Basic Books.

Edelman, G. M. (1992). *Bright air, brilliant fire: On the language of the mind.* New York: Basic Books.

Fodor, J. (1975). *The language of thought.* London: Crowell.

Garfinkel, H. (1967). *Studies in ethnomethodology.* Englewood Cliffs, NJ: Prentice-Hall.

Giddens, A. (1984). *The constitution of society.* Berkeley: University of California Press.

Goffman, E. (1961). *Asylums.* Garden City, NY: Anchor.

Greene, J. (1984). Evaluating cognitive explanations of communicative phenomena. *Quarterly Journal of Speech, 70,* 241–254.

Harre, R. (1984). *Personal being: A theory for individual psychology.* Cambridge, MA: Harvard University Press.

Harre, R., & Secord, P. (1973). *The explanation of social behavior.* Totowa, NJ: Littlefield, Adams.

Heidegger, M. (1962). *Being and time* (J. MacQuarrie & E. Robinson, Trans.). New York: Harper & Row.

Henriques, J., Holloway, W., Urwin, C., Venn, C., & Walkerdine, V. (1984). *Changing the subject: Psychology, social regulation, and subjectivity.* London: Methuen.

Hewes, D. E., & Planalp, S. (1987). The individual's place in communication science. In C. Berger & S. Chaffee (Eds.), *Handbook of communication science* (pp. 147–183). Newbury Park, CA: Sage.

Lakoff, G. (1987). *Women, fire, and dangerous things: What categories reveal about the mind.* Chicago: University of Chicago Press.

Leonard, P. (1984). *Personality and ideology: Towards a materialist understanding of the individual.* Atlantic Highlands, NJ: Humanities Press.

Luria, A. (1976). *Cognitive development: Its cultural and social foundations.* Cambridge, MA: Harvard University Press.

Markard, M. (1991). On the concept of attitude. In C. W. Tolman & W. Maiers (Eds.), *Critical psychology: Contributions to a historical science of the subject.* (pp. 197–224). New York: Cambridge University Press.

Penrose, R. (1989). *The emperor's new mind.* New York: Oxford University Press.

Putnam, H. (1988). *Representation and reality.* Cambridge, MA: MIT Press.

Shotter, J. (1990). The social construction of remembering and forgetting. In D. Middleton & D. Edwards (Eds.), *Collective remembering.* (pp. 120–137). London: Sage.

Searle, J. (1984). *Minds, brains, and science.* Cambridge, MA: Harvard University Press.

Stich, S. (1983). *From folk psychology to cognitive science: The case against belief.* Cambridge, MA: MIT Press.

Taylor, C. (1985). *Human agency and language: Philosophical papers I.* Cambridge, England: Cambridge University Press.

Tolman, C. (1991). Introduction. In C. W. Tolman & W. Maiers (Eds.), *Critical psychology: Contributions to a historical science of the subject.* (pp. 1–13). New York: Cambridge University Press.

Vygotsky, L. (1962). *Thought and language*. Cambridge, MA: MIT Press.

Wegner, D. M., Erber, R., & Raymond, P. (1991). Transactive memory in close relationships. *Journal of Personality and Social Psychology, 61,* 923–929.

Wertsch, J. V. (1985). *Vygotsky and the social formation of mind*. Cambridge, MA: Harvard University Press.

Wexler, P. (1983). *Critical social psychology*. Boston: Routledge & Kegan Paul.

Wittgenstein, L. (1958). *Philosophical investigations* (G. Anscombe, Trans.). New York: Macmillan.

Author Index

Subject Index

257